THE UNIVERSITY NEXT DOOR

THE UNIVERSITY NEXT DOOR

What Is a Comprehensive University, Who Does It Educate, and Can It Survive?

Edited by

Mark Schneider
KC Deane

Teachers College, Columbia University
New York and London

Published by Teachers College Press, 1234 Amsterdam Avenue, New York, NY 10027

Library of Congress Cataloging-in-Publication Data

The university next door : what is a comprehensive university, who does it educate, and can it survive? / edited by Mark Schneider, KC Deane.
  pages cm
Includes bibliographical references and index.
ISBN 978-0-8077-5603-4 (hardcover : alk. paper)
ISBN 978-0-8077-5602-7 (pbk. : alk. paper)
ISBN 978-0-8077-7342-0 (ebook)
  1. Universities and colleges—Philosophy. 2. Universities and colleges—United States. 3. Education, Higher—Philosophy. 4. Education, Higher—Aims and objectives—United States. I. Schneider, Mark, 1946- editor of compilation. II. Deane, KC
LB2328.2.U555   2015
378.001—dc23   2014029846

ISBN 978-0-8077-5602-7 (paper)
ISBN 978-0-8077-5603-4 (hardcover)
ISBN 978-0-8077-7342-0 (ebook)

Printed on acid-free paper
Manufactured in the United States of America

21 20 19 18 17 16 15   8 7 6 5 4 3 2 1

Contents

Acknowledgments

Americans are calling on higher education to do more than ever before. Our colleges and universities are expected to deliver hundreds of thousands more skilled graduates who can meet the demands of an ever-evolving labor market. Students, for their part, are torn between the theoretical value of a college degree and the steep—and ever-rising—cost of tuition. Is an adulthood of indebtedness worth the degree? For students who drop out or who attend programs that fail to deliver, the answer is too frequently, "no."

In the past, America's public institutions of higher education have survived with public support, both through enrollments and state appropriations. And for institutions that boast impressive student outcomes, typically state flagship and research universities, this trend will likely continue. Academically qualified students will continue to fall in love with the bargain deal of attending selective public institutions, and state and federal dollars will continue to follow the call for research, even if at lower levels than in the past.

Comprehensive universities face a severely different fate. This motley group of institutions lacks the reputational prestige that accompanies selectivity and research. Even though tuition is lower than at many of the more selective public universities, low graduation rates mean students who take out debt may never reap the monetary benefits of a 4-year degree. And worse, those who graduate may not have the skills they need to succeed in the labor market.

When this project began, our primary goal was to push a set of institutions into a conversation that has largely ignored their presence and potential value. What we found was a far more puzzling narrative. Comprehensive universities fly under the radar because whenever expectations change, so too do they. In other words, they are one step behind history. While in the past this has served them well, the toll it has taken on their missions and on their student outcomes is beginning to show. Which left us with a challenging question: What comes next for the comprehensive university?

To this end, the editors asked contributors to present first drafts of their chapters at a research convening in Washington, DC. Present at this meeting were comprehensive university professors and presidents as well as state commissioners of higher education, all of whom raised concerns when they felt the research lacked context of the unique experiences faced by those at comprehensive universities. Authors then incorporated this feedback into their revised chapters. We are indebted to these participants' earnest engagement and frank criticism.

We also are indebted to the steadfast support provided by the American Enterprise Institute (AEI) and its president, Arthur Brooks. The Lumina Foundation generously provided financial support for this project, and we are deeply grateful for their involvement and encouragement throughout the process. We'd also like to thank the terrific staff at AEI, in particular Andrew P. Kelly, who helped shepherd the project forward, and Elizabeth Bell, whose sharp mind and knack for organization ensured that the volume became a volume. Our gratitude extends to AEI Education team members Sarah DuPre, Max Eden, Taryn Hochleitner, and Daniel Lautzenheiser. Finally, we express our gratitude to the Teachers College Press team, particularly our editor Brian Ellerbeck, who offered skillful and timely guidance throughout the course of this project.

Introduction

Mark Schneider and KC Deane

For decades, the multibillion-dollar federal financial aid system sought to induce colleges and universities to enroll more students from historically underserved populations. With the weight of these billions of federal dollars and a consensus on the importance of higher education, the resulting "access agenda" was remarkably successful, opening up the doors of postsecondary education to more and more students. But in the past few years, the nation came to realize that access without success is not success.

The resulting shift in policy—from access to completion—happened almost overnight. The thrust of policy that once called on colleges to improve opportunities for underserved populations expanded to include a focus on completion. But just as the completion agenda was taking hold, a new concern for the postcompletion success of students, especially their success in the labor market, emerged. If access without success was no longer sufficient, graduation without a good job became the next pressing concern. While this expanded focus is most evident in the attention given to the "gainful employment" of students enrolled in proprietary schools, the concern is growing beyond that sector. The federal government, for example, has proposed including information on employment and wages in its college scorecard and in its Postsecondary Institution Ratings System (PIRS). Many state governments are far ahead of the federal government and several, often through partnerships with College Measures, have been working to measure the labor market success of graduates and make that data more easily accessible to the public (College Measures, 2014).

As this "success agenda" continues to gain traction, institutions of higher education are now being asked not only about whom they let in, but also about who gets out and what happens to them after they leave.

This new policy emphasis inevitably will lead to more attention being paid to the hundreds of "comprehensive universities" that educate the bulk of America's postsecondary students. Name-brand private universities (such as Harvard, Princeton, Yale) and state flagships (Berkeley, Madison, Chapel Hill) boast high graduation rates, and their graduates benefit from cache in the labor market and high placement rates into graduate and professional programs. But most students enroll in and graduate from non-marquee schools (the Cal States and the SUNY colleges rather than the UCs or Stony Brooks). These campuses often have graduation rates less than half the rates of their more famous brethren, and they cannot take the labor market success of their graduates for granted.

Despite the critical role of the non-marquee 4-year comprehensive universities, we lavish far more attention on the extremes of our higher education system: the open-access, 2-year community colleges and the highly selective 4-year colleges and universities.

Community colleges, whose origins trace back to early 1900s job training, are once again en vogue—even Vice President Joe Biden's wife teaches at one! Moving quickly from the orphan also-rans of higher education (dismissed as "junior colleges" or "night school"), we now view community colleges as inexpensive and efficient pathways into the workforce. Students also are voting with their feet: The sub-baccalaureate credentials (associate's degrees and certificates) granted annually now outnumber bachelor's degrees. Moreover, the growth of these credentials is faster than bachelor's degree growth. On the labor market side, many with these credentials, especially those in technical areas such as advanced manufacturing or health care, often earn higher salaries than bachelor's graduates in the same fields (Schneider, 2013). Further, community colleges increasingly are viewed as an inexpensive path into 4-year colleges. Large numbers of students will spend their first 2 years in community colleges fulfilling their general education requirements at a low price and then transfer to a 4-year college—most often a comprehensive—to complete. While we often acknowledge that community colleges suffer from low completion rates, we respect them for the challenges they face and their seemingly tireless effort to educate the nontraditional student.

At the other extreme, we are fixated on the small number of highly selective 4-year institutions that provide a high-quality education at a high cost to small numbers of students. The names of these schools roll off our tongues and incite envy when we hear that a neighbor's kid got accepted to one of these prestigious universities, while we wonder where our own parenting went wrong. After all, our beloved 18-year-old is pondering offer letters from some no-name, local state university.

It is easy to be blinded by the allure and quality of elite colleges and universities. They boast impressive retention and graduation rates, and their students do well in the labor market. Of course, if they admit only valedictorians with perfect SAT scores, graduating over 90% of the incoming class may not be such a tough task. With that pedigree, even their graduates with poetry degrees can find good jobs. So, these marquee schools will continue to garner accolades (and increasing numbers of applications from high school seniors) for being the crown jewels of America's education system. They will remain center stage as the nation embarks on yet another new concern sweeping higher education: the problem of "undermatch."

Researchers, the media, and commentators now assert that many of the problems low-income minority students face in higher education can be addressed by helping high-achieving, low-income students find their way to elite institutions. After all, since the Obamas (and Bill Clinton and George W. Bush and so on) clearly benefited from attending Ivy League schools for their undergraduate education, why not others?

To be fair, some researchers have broadened the discussion of undermatch to include a wider range of schools and students (see Chapter 2 by Awilda Rodriguez), but focusing on undermatch at elite universities is still common.

Elite colleges and universities keep tight control over their admissions—in fact, their status as elites *requires* them to constrain the number of students they admit. Encouraging these elite schools to serve greater numbers of low-income and minority students will work only if they actively increase the number of students they enroll. Improving their recruitment efforts focused on high-achieving, low-income students allows them to find the best of those students and bolster their incoming class profile, while applauding themselves for nominal efforts at increased diversity. But, unless they substantially increase either the size of each incoming class or the number of low-income students who are admitted, the recruitment efforts will do little overall. The battle for selectivity and prestige will always limit the extent to which these schools will expand access to their degrees.

Sure, the relatively few students that are lucky enough to be tapped by elite schools will benefit greatly, but this ignores the larger need to improve completion and student success at the University of Texas (UT)–Brownsville or Bowie State University or any of the other comprehensive universities that educate the bulk of America's 4-year students. Perhaps this is best illustrated by example. If UT–Brownsville increased its overall graduation rate by 15% (from 53% to just over 60%), this would equate to an additional 109 Hispanic bachelor's graduates each year. On the other hand, if Harvard increased the number of Hispanic graduates it produces each year by 15%, this would yield only an additional 24.[1]

Clearly, any national discussion about access, completion, and student success has to go past selective schools to include the schools that educate the bulk of our nation's students. And the focus has to expand from the highest performing low-income students, who could attend more prestigious universities. Rather, increasing student success nationally requires increasing success rates among college-ready students at every level of college selectivity, not just those who gain access to the most selective colleges.

WHAT ARE COMPREHENSIVE UNIVERSITIES?

With the focus on community colleges and elite institutions, researchers and policymakers tend to pass over the colleges in the middle: America's comprehensive universities. But these 400 or so broad-access, "comprehensive" public 4-year colleges and universities are the workhorses of American postsecondary education. They enroll nearly 70% of all undergraduate 4-year students at public institutions. By the numbers alone, if the nation is to increase student success, this is the set of institutions that will be central to the effort.

Yet we know little about how they are responding to the new demands of the nation's changing policy agenda and the nation's changing economy. What have these institutions done to adapt to the needs of their students, who increasingly differ from the traditional 18- to 22-year-old, full-time student of previous generations? Are there new models of curriculum, delivery, and organization that can help them meet these challenges? Are they as cost effective as they can be? Are their graduation rates as high as they could be? How well do they prepare graduates for the labor market?

To focus on these and other related questions, this volume examines a set of institutions that historically has received little attention. One professor of a comprehensive university described the institutions as "more akin to a herd than to a single beast, for, while we share many characteristics, we have a great many differences as well" (Dalbey, 1995). And throughout this volume you will see these differences in how each author defines the herd, with some schools falling into and out of the core depending on the criteria used. We begin with a brief history of comprehensive universities, and then turn to our definition of "comprehensive university" and its inherent limitations.

The Origin Story of the Underdog

What about the evolution of comprehensive universities led to their position as an amorphous mass of schools? If necessity is the mother of invention, why, in this case, did it yield a product that is best known for being unknown? The comprehensive university, like the tail of a snake, follows along tirelessly. If the head of the snake decides to improve institutional quality—whether through research or the academic profile of the incoming class—the rest of the snake goes with it.

Historian Christine Ogren (2005) argues that this trait of higher education led to comprehensive universities' second-tier status: In their rush to catch up with the rest of the snake these institutions tend to ignore their histories. The elusive promise of future quality erases an institution's varied past. Education historians, for their part, do little to help matters. "Interested only in the head of the snake, historians of higher education have simply omitted [these institutions]. Their silence has further encouraged society and the schools themselves to measure their worth only according to the great snake" (p. 3).

Consider the evolution of normal schools, which collectively constitute almost 50% of modern-day comprehensive universities. Opening in the mid-1800s in response to the national need for more teachers, these 2-year schools did what existing institutions were unwilling to do. But few in the public eye held normal schools in high regard. "They were bare-bones institutions, most of whose students were barely educated beyond the elementary level" (Ogren, 2005, p. 4). Ultimately, harsh criticism pressured normal schools to abandon their role as teacher training schools in favor of slightly more prestigious teachers colleges.

Changing demographics all but ensured a second wave of evolution, this time from teachers colleges to state universities. After World War II and the passage of the GI Bill, college enrollment swelled. Existing universities absorbed much of this first enrollment increase. Then,

> as the state colleges continued to broaden their offerings into the 1960s and 1980s, the growing number of lower- and middle-class baby boomers wanted and expected access to higher education. The elite universities could take some students by growing, but the numbers were too great even for the research-oriented mega-universities to accommodate them (Henderson, 2009).

What in the decades before had been a slow convergence with the traditional collegiate model was no longer fast enough. Comprehensive universities had to adapt more quickly.

The remaining comprehensive universities that did not begin as normal schools are a mix of branch campuses, 2-year colleges, or even private schools turned public. Branch campuses, in close contact with their better endowed flagship universities, used the shared resources to expedite their own evolution. Especially in the southern United States, a number of Historically Black comprehensive universities began as technical or agricultural schools sponsored by the second Morrill Act (1890). Comprehensive universities that began as private schools made the change when financial struggles became too much to bear (Henderson, 2009). In other words, no matter the origins of a particular comprehensive university, its evolution was marked by necessity.

These universities once again must respond, lest the passage of time make them complacent. (After all, the most recent period of drastic change is now more than 50 years in the past.) The 4-year degree is still a good investment, but its purchasing power is weakening. High-debt burdens after graduation, coupled with the wrong skills for an increasingly technological labor market, are holding back the American economy. Students, for their part, are beginning to experience buyer's remorse. A recent Wells Fargo study, which examined the impact of student loan debt on 1,400 millennials (ages 22–32), asked students to comment on their decision to enroll in college. About one in three millennials felt that "they would have been better off working, instead of going to college and paying tuition" (Touryalai, 2013).

Defining "Comprehensive"

The question sounds simple enough: What is a comprehensive university? Initially, our answer was glib, waving our hands and calling them the compass schools. Northwest University East, for instance. Then, we added in a few identifiers: public nonresearch 4-year universities. This took us a good deal further but, if that is what they are, why give them their own name?

Our explanation was clearly insufficient; the glazed-over eyes of otherwise knowledgeable higher education experts said as much. So, what started as an amusing quirk became integral to the project's mission. First, to define them so that the reader knows what we mean, then to explain them so that the reader understands what they are.

So, we turned to the data: Is there an easy data-driven way to create a widely accepted and temporally stable group of comprehensive universities? The short answer, no: There is no natural break along which to conclusively identify "comprehensives." We considered degree offerings, patterns of student enrollment, and proximity to population centers, to name a few, but quickly discovered that these institutions operate on a complex continuum—one that we believe contributes to the lack of formal dialogue in both academia and among policymakers about their role and value.

Supporters of the U.S. higher education system often remark that its diversity—in size, purpose, and offerings—is one of its greatest strengths. Our institutions are granted the freedom to evolve from their original purpose and mission, and the comprehensive university embodies this freedom to change. However, this makes it difficult to develop definitions that encompass a stable set of institutions over time, especially among a class of schools that, as contributor Alisa Hicklin Fryar suggests in Chapter 1, often are known more for what they are not than for what they are.

For these reasons, any language we use to define the "comprehensive university" will appear incomplete or generic. But, in the interests of providing readers with a touchstone as they grapple with the varied landscape of the comprehensive university, we offer one here. The American Association of State Colleges and Universities (AASCU, 2014b), which historically is known for representing comprehensive universities, defines their membership as follows: "public colleges, universities and systems whose members share a learning- and teaching-centered culture, a historic commitment to underserved populations and a dedication to research and creativity that advances their regions' economic progress and cultural development." While the categorization of comprehensive universities varies across the chapters in this volume, the spirit always echoes this formal definition.

IDENTIFYING KEY CHALLENGES

There is great diversity across these schools. Some educate fewer than 1,000 undergraduates, others more than 40,000. Some are in urban environments, while others are in rural or suburban areas. Some offer doctoral degrees, but most do not. As a group, not only do they enroll around 70% of all undergraduate students at public 4-year institutions, but they also enroll almost 60% of graduate students at public institutions. Of all African American and Hispanic undergraduate students enrolled at public 4-year institutions, 85% and 74%, respectively, are enrolled at comprehensive universities. But, despite these differences, in one area there is incredible consistency: All of these institutions face similar challenges as higher education enters an era of upheaval—their finances, their accountability, their instructional methodologies, and their students' labor market success undoubtedly will come under greater scrutiny. We turn to these challenges next.

The Financial Challenge

Due to small endowments, the operating budgets of comprehensives are challenged by their reliance on tuition revenue and shrinking state appropriations. "Unrelenting enrollment demand in higher education [is] outpacing the ability of the states to finance this enrollment growth even with reasonable increases in productivity in higher education," said Paul

Lingenfelter, former president of the State Higher Education Executive Officers Association (SHEEO), when describing the implications of the 2009 recession on state appropriations for higher education (Stripling, 2010).

Cuts to higher education spending had begun long before the recession kicked in, but they became more systemic in the years during the recession. Between the start of the Great Recession in 2009 and its timid conclusion in 2012, 47 states cut higher education spending per full-time equivalent (FTE) students (Kelly & Deane, 2013). The implications for public colleges and universities were severe. When the share of their budget supported by state appropriations declines, these institutions pass along the costs to consumers. In 1987, 23.3% of educational revenue was supported by tuition revenue. By 2012, that number had reached 47% (State Higher Education Executive Officers Association, 2013).

Students, for their part, are in an equally tenuous position. Public institutions' increased reliance on tuition revenue translates into an increase in tuition (an average annual increase of 4.2% between 2003 and 2013) (College Board, 2014b). And federal aid dollars no longer have the same purchasing power. In 2003–2004, an eligible student could cover 87% of the average tuition and fees at a public 4-year institution with the maximum Federal Pell Grant. Ten years later, in 2013–2014, that same figure had fallen to only 63% (College Board, 2014c). Equally troubling, the net tuition and fees paid by full-time students enrolled at public institutions increased from $1,920 in 2003–2004 to over $3,000 in 2012–2013 (College Board, 2014a).

Remaining affordable, to both students and taxpayers, is crucial to the future of comprehensive universities. The effort to curb tuition hikes has begun in some states, led by Texas Governor Rick Perry. He challenged state universities to offer a bachelor's degree for no more than $10,000. Unfortunately, many of the universities that rose to the challenge did so through combinations of scholarships and the use of high school credits (Hamilton & Gibbs, 2013). Others within higher education criticize Perry's plan as vulnerable to cuts in quality, which does little to address the skills gap between what colleges offer and labor markets need. Still, this is proof of the opportunity to use comprehensive universities as a vehicle to lower the cost of a 4-year degree.

But the reality is that these schools are having to do more with less. How are they facing that challenge?

The Data Challenge

"Greater transparency and accountability in higher education can be achieved without threatening privacy," said David Shi (2006), then-president of Furman University, about early calls for a federal student unit record system. "It is ironic that we are considering such an assault on Americans' privacy and security in the shadow of the Fourth of July," echoed David L. Warren, who, at the time, presided over the National Association of Independent Colleges and Universities (NAICU, 2006). These seemingly hyperbolic cautionary tales were meant as a defense mechanism for an industry that wanted little to do with an expansion of federal accountability. Ultimately, institutional spokesmen's efforts to undermine the calls for transparency were successful, as the 2008 HEA reauthorization included a ban on the creation of any federal system.

At least at NAICU, little has changed about their opposition to a federal system that would track students across institutions and states, and across their postgraduation careers. NAICU represents the majority of private not-for-profit institutions, which have the most to lose from the system. "While public institutions spend much of their lobbying efforts trying to secure state funding, private institutions focus on federal funding" (McCann & Laitinen, 2014). Colleges and universities have grown accustomed to the hands-off approach to accountability. They receive support from students' federal financial aid dollars and, as long as they remain accredited, it's business as usual. Exposing themselves to the scrutiny that inevitably would befall the industry is the last thing that they want. The data they are required to report to the National Center for Education Statistics are enough, thank you very much.

Unfortunately, without such a system, efforts to better understand whether institutions adequately educate their students are hamstrung. Right now, the Integrated Postsecondary Education Data System (IPEDS) tracks metrics like graduation rate using only first-time, full-time students. But almost 40% of students do not meet these qualifications (McCann & Laitinen, 2014). At some institutions, especially comprehensive universities, the proportion of part-time students meets or exceeds the proportion of first-time, full-time students. Basing accountability efforts on these incomplete outcome metrics skews the sanctions and rewards. Schools that do not successfully educate their nontraditional students will escape punishment, while those who are successful will miss out on the recognition. Furthermore, the outcomes we focus on are not enough. Graduation rates matter—we do not want to set students up for indebted failure—but being able to pay off that debt after graduation matters too. Do students with a bachelor's degree in sociology from State University earn enough after graduation to make timely payments on their student debt? Or is tuition too high and quality too low?

Many comprehensive universities would benefit from a more exhaustive national accountability effort that both builds on the data used for key metrics and accounts for more than just the first-time, full-time student. And they are supportive of these efforts. Take a press release from AASCU (2014a) on President Obama's proposed ratings system: "AASCU supports federal efforts at better gatekeeping, improved accountability, and greater transparency for colleges and universities," as long as these efforts respect "the heterogeneity of institutional missions." The voice of the dissenters is loud (and powerful), but comprehensive universities are right to support a change that benefits students and enables previously overshadowed institutions to receive more attention. Transparency is a trade-off: Some comprehensive universities will struggle to defend their value, while others will gain respect and attention.

The Instructional Challenge

We know little about how much students learn while in college. Despite some efforts, especially through the Collegiate Learning Assessment (CLA), this most crucial task of colleges remains a black hole. We also do not know how instruction is delivered. We sense that many faculty do not ask a lot of their students—student hours devoted to homework on campuses have declined while grades have gone up. And we believe that the majority of faculty are anchored in the traditional method of lectures with little emphasis on active learning. But we really have no idea about the extent to which this traditional approach has changed in recent years. Nonetheless, we do know that there are two big movements afoot that can challenge the traditional instructional model of higher education.

While much is still unclear about how advances in technology will alter student learning, motivated students can now obtain skills outside of traditional colleges. These ever-developing technologies present pathways to a degree or career-specific credentials for students, providing nontraditional students an avenue to get what they need from higher education with less hassle. Online learning has grown exponentially in recent years, spearheaded by the sudden rise of massive open online courses (MOOCs). Interested students can enroll in a MOOC offered by a number of providers—Coursera, Udacity, edX—and earn a certificate of completion (if they complete). While these emerging innovations have a ways to go before they truly "disrupt" higher education, they are serious challengers to the existing model of classroom instruction, and comprehensives must consider how they will adapt to online courses offered by far more famous faculty than most campuses employ.

Competency-based learning is another approach that comprehensives need to monitor and ultimately adapt to. Western Governors University (WGU), a competency-based learning university founded by governors in 19 states, has been in operation since 1997 and now has state-affiliated universities in additional states, including Indiana, Washington, and Texas. Under WGU's competency-based learning model, students (typically adults without a degree) earn credits by proving what they have learned, rather than receiving credit for the amount of time they spend in class. Southern New Hampshire University launched its competency-based College for America program in January 2013, and in the same month the University of Wisconsin announced a similar program. In March 2013, the U.S. Department of Education gave a big nod of approval to competency-based learning programs with a "Dear Colleague" letter encouraging institutions interested in developing direct assessment programs to reach out to the DOE for guidance. All of these efforts still reside within the traditional university framework, which ensures that the college degree—and the gatekeepers of the degree, colleges and universities—will remain an integral part of the system of higher education. But the times are a-changing.

The Labor Market Challenge

American higher education and the U.S. labor market are misaligned. Researchers at Georgetown University have estimated that by 2020 the United States will fall 5 million degrees short of the necessary number of college-educated workers (Carnevale, Smith, & Strohl, 2010b). President Obama, who began his first term in the grips of a crumbling economy and high unemployment, set out to change this, promising, "By 2020, this nation will once again have the highest proportion of college graduates in the world" (White House, Office of the Press Secretary, 2009). Achieving this ambitious goal will require increasing the 2010 national attainment rate by over 20 percentage points (from 39% to 60%) (U.S. Department of Education, 2012).

But, graduating more students from college is not the only challenge facing campuses. Employers are increasingly dissatisfied with the training graduates receive while in college; in a recent survey, more than half of employers said it was difficult to find and hire qualified applicants (Fischer, 2014). In other words, even among degree holders, colleges are not training students for today's labor market.

In two Georgetown Center on Education and the Workforce reports, *Help Wanted: Projections of Jobs and Education Requirements Through 2018* (2010a), by Anthony Carnevale, Nicole Smith, and Jeff Strohl, and its 2013 update, *Recovery: Job Growth and Education Requirements Through 2020* (2010b), the authors use labor market data to show that demand for workers increasingly is tied to specific occupations and skills. With evidence that skill mismatch is responsible for about 30% of the change in the unemployment rate during the Great Recession, it is clear that simply granting more degrees is not enough. In *Hard Times: College Majors, Unemployment and Earnings*, Carnevale et al. (2012) use labor market data to show that, while college is still worth it, some majors fare better than others. Majors that are aligned more closely with particular occupations and industries tend to experience lower unemployment rates (e.g., health care and education). A 2013 report by College Measures showed a significant wage premium for graduates with technical degrees—and documented that students with technical associate's degrees and certificates can earn more than graduates with bachelor's degrees (Schneider, 2013).

As the evidence mounts in favor of college credentials tied to career training, the question becomes what to do about it. In *Working Learners: Educating Our Entire Workforce for Success in the 21st Century*, Louis Soares (2009) attempts to break down the bifurcated system of higher education, which separates traditional students from students seeking new skills, by retooling the delivery of skills-based education. Community colleges across the country have begun to refocus their efforts on preparing students for career-readiness. Three recent reports from Jobs for the Future—*The Best of Two Worlds: Lessons from a Community College–Community Organization Collaboration to Increase Student Success* (2012), *Aligning Community Colleges to Their Labor Markets: The Emerging Role of Online Job Ads for Providing Real-Time Intelligence About Occupations and Skills in Demand* (2011), and *Expanding the Mission: Community Colleges and the Functions of Workforce Intermediaries* (2010)—highlight how community colleges can develop partnerships, retool program and course offerings, and utilize labor market data to maximize student success postgraduation. The demonstration programs profiled are concrete examples of how community colleges can play an invaluable role in increasing postsecondary attainment.

Clearly there are many challenges to our nation's system of higher education—and most of these challenges will likely affect the comprehensives and their students more than they will affect the nation's most prestigious colleges and universities. Identifying these challenges—and the emerging and future responses—among public comprehensive universities is the task before us.

THE VOLUME AHEAD

Many edited volumes are a collection of essays, each of which relates to the central question in its own way. One might call this the "hub and spoke" model. In most instances, this is sufficient. The central question follows a certain theme, and from it there are a number of relatively obvious sub-questions, each of which can be tackled in under 8,000 words. Here, we are trying something different: From each chapter stems the question that forms the next. For a topic with so little clarity around it, this seems only natural. So, in this volume, we tell the story of the Comprehensive University.

We start with its history and its students. The first two chapters introduce the reader to the topic, developing a profile of the comprehensive university and its students. In Chapter 1, Alisa Hicklin Fryar, professor at the University of Oklahoma and herself a graduate of a comprehensive university, uses these institutions' collective history as a foundation for defining what is meant by "Comprehensive University." She develops two definitions: a historical definition, which considers a university's relationship to the state's flagship campuses, and a contemporary definition that relies on the more common Carnegie classification. Then she considers how the schools in each category differ. What does the student body look like, and how do graduation rates compare with other 4-year institutions? For those schools that are included in the historical definition but not the contemporary, what changed?

In Chapter 2, Awilda Rodriguez, professor at the University of Michigan, examines undermatch at comprehensive universities, a question typically reserved for the relationship between high-achieving, low-income students and highly selective institutions. Rodriguez isolates patterns in decision making for students choosing between open-access institutions, such as comprehensive universities, community colleges, and for-profit universities. What would drive middle-ability students to choose a public 2-year community college when they instead could attend a comprehensive university with a higher graduation rate and a higher likelihood of success after graduation?

Next, we continue the story of the comprehensive with an inward-looking investigation of how well these universities are serving their students. Chapter 3 is a qualitative analysis of recent efforts to increase student success by building stronger pathways between community colleges and comprehensive universities. Because this pathway is becoming even more common, the inefficiencies in how these two types of institutions interact with each other can have devastating effects on students. Alison Kadlec of Public Agenda and Mario Martinez of University of Nevada–Las Vegas survey the challenges associated with building intercollege partnerships, focusing on the need for clear credit transfer.[2] They conclude that while it is possible to create successful transfer pathways, doing so requires an articulated vision and willing institutions.

In Chapter 4, William Doyle, professor at Vanderbilt University, examines the productivity of comprehensive universities: Are these institutions maximizing their degree completion rates? Doyle argues that, given their existing resources and policy limitations, many of these institutions are working at the boundaries of what is possible. This suggests that large-scale improvements will likely require more than just tinkering on the edges of current funding and policies.

Chapter 5, authored by AIR researcher Michelle Lu Yin, explores risk-adjusted institutional retention and graduation rates, which take into account student characteristics across comprehensive universities. Yin calls into question the existing practice of using observed retention and graduation rates as a signal of institutional quality. These metrics are based on self-reported data that lacks any context for the students that attend an institution. Unless efforts to gauge quality across institutions include controlling for the profile of the student body, the resultant metrics will lend too much weight to highly selective schools and discount less-selective schools that still manage to improve graduation rates across time.

The story concludes with an exploration of the future of the comprehensive university. In Chapter 6, John Dorrer, a program director at Jobs for the Future, encourages comprehensive universities to incorporate real-time labor market information into their decisions about program and curriculum development. With this data, career services offices can provide better career counseling to graduating students and help solve one of the most vexing problems facing higher education: how to increase the probabilities that graduates will find well-paying jobs.

In Chapter 7, Jeffrey Selingo, editor-at-large for *The Chronicle of Higher Education* and professor of practice at Arizona State University, looks at several comprehensive universities that are using new technologies to improve the on-campus student experience, whether through improved academic counseling or more effective student services. Are these cases outliers or do they serve as guideposts to the future?

Finally, in Chapter 8, Michael B. Horn and Michelle R. Weise of the Clayton Christensen Institute, and Lloyd Armstrong, professor at the University of Southern California, ask whether disruptive innovation will lead to the collapse of the comprehensive university. They argue that unless comprehensive universities respond to new technologies by incorporating them into their delivery model, these institutions risk losing students to lower cost options that are more in tune with the evolving labor market.

Together these chapters, we hope, will alert the reader to the central role these 400 or more universities play in our nation's system of higher education. And we hope this volume will inspire others to look more closely at these schools, identifying the challenges facing them and evaluating the ways they can successfully negotiate the changing world of higher education.

NOTES

1. Based on NCES IPEDS. UT–Brownsville has a full-time graduation rate of 53%, and 89% of its student body identifies as Hispanic. There are a total of 12,547 undergraduates, 49% of whom (6,148) are full-time; 5,471 of those students identify as Hispanic. This is roughly 1,367 in each graduating class. At a graduation rate of 53%, this yields 724 graduates each year. Increasing the graduation rate by 15% to 60.95% would yield 833 graduates, or an increase of 109 per year. Harvard has a full-time graduation rate of 97%, and 9% of its undergraduate student body identifies as Hispanic. There are a total of 10,564 undergraduates, 68% of whom (7,183) are full-time; 646 of those students are Hispanic. This is roughly 161 in each graduating class. At a graduation rate of 97%, Harvard graduates 156 Hispanic students each year. If Harvard were to increase the number of Hispanic students in each class by 15%, this would lead to an additional 24 students, for a total of 185. Of those, 179 would graduate, producing an additional 23 Hispanic graduates per year.

2. For more on the importance of transfer of credit policies, see http://www.aera.net/Newsroom/RecentAERAResearch/TheCommunityCollegeRoutetothe-BachelorsDegree/tabid/15414/Default.aspx

REFERENCES

Altstadt, D. (2011). *Aligning community colleges to their local labor markets: The emerging role of online job ads for providing real-time intelligence about occupations and skills in demand.* Jobs for the Future. Available at www.joycefdn.org/assets/1/7/AligningCommunityColleges_LaborMarkets.pdf

American Association of State Colleges and Universities. (2014a). *AASCU's position on the Obama administration's proposed postsecondary institutions rating system (PIRS).* Available at http://www.aascu.org/policy/federal-policy/outreach/ratingsposition01162014.pdf

American Association of State Colleges and Universities. (2014b). *Strategic plan: Governing ideas.* Available at www.aascu.org/strategic-plan/governing-ideas/

Carnevale, A. P., Smith, N., & Strohl, J. (2010a). *Help wanted: Projections of jobs and education requirements through 2018.* Center on Education and the Workforce, Georgetown University. Available at https://cew.georgetown.edu/jobs2018

Carnevale, A. P., Smith, N., & Strohl, J. (2010b). *Recovery: Job growth and education requirements through 2020.* Center on Education and the Workforce, Georgetown University. Available at https://cew.georgetown.edu/recovery2020

Carnevale, A. P., Smith, N., & Strohl, J. (2012). *Hard times: College Majors, Unemployment and Earnings.* Center on Education and the Workforce, Georgetown University. Available at www9.georgetown.edu/grad/gppi/hpi/cew/pdfs/unemployment.final.update1.pdf

College Board. (2014a). *Average net price for full-time students over time—public institutions.* Available at trends.collegeboard.org/college-pricing/figures-tables/average-net-price-full-time-students-over-time--public-institutions

College Board. (2014b). *Average rates of growth of published charges by decade.* Available at trends.collegeboard.org/college-pricing/figures-tables/average-rates-growth-tuition-and-fees-over-time

College Board. (2014c). *Maximum Pell grant as percentage of tuition and fees and total charges over time.* Available at trends.collegeboard.org/college-pricing/figures-tables/average-rates-growth-tuition-and-fees-over-time

College Measures. (2014). *Economic success metrics (ESM) program.* American Institutes for Research & Matrix Knowledge Group. Available at www.collegemeasures.org/esm/

Dalbey, M. A. (1995). What is a comprehensive university, and do I want to work there? *ADE Bulletin, Modern Language Association.* Available at www.mla.org/bulletin_111014

Fischer, K. (2014). A college degree sorts job applicants, but employers wish it meant more. *The Chronicle of Higher Education.* Available at chronicle.com/article/The-Employment-Mismatch/137625/#id=overview

Hamilton, R., & Gibbs, R. (2013). A guide to getting one of Texas' $10,000 degrees. *The Texas Tribune.* Available at www.texastribune.org/2013/01/30/guide-getting-one-texas-new-10000-degrees/

Henderson, B. B. (2009). The work of the People's University. *Teacher-Scholar: The Journal of the State Comprehensive University, 1*(1). Available at www.fhsu.edu/teacher-scholar/resources/Previous-Issues/Volume-1/Introduction.pdf

Hoops, J., & Wilson, R. (2010). *Expanding the mission: Community colleges and the functions of workforce intermediaries.* Jobs for the Future. Available at www.jff.org/sites/default/files/publications/ExpandingtheMission_080910.pdf

Jobs for the Future, The Youth Development Institute. (2012). *The best of two worlds: Lessons from a community college–community organization collaboration to increase student success.* Available at www.jff.org/sites/default/files/publications/BestOfTwoWorlds_032112.pdf

Kelly, A. P., & Deane, KC (2013). Is there a conservative conspiracy to destroy college? *Center for the American University, Manhattan Institute.* Available at http://www.mindingthecampus.com/2013/03/is_there_a_conservative_conspi/

McCann, C., & Laitinen, A. (2014). *College blackout: How the higher education lobby fought to keep students in the dark*. Education Policy Program, New America Foundation. Available at education.newamerica.net/sites/newamerica.net/files/policydocs/CollegeBlackoutFINAL.pdf

National Association of Independent Colleges and Universities. (2006). *American public gives low marks to proposed federal database of college students*. Available at www.naicu.edu/printVersion/print_news.asp?newsID=249

Ogren, C. A. (2005). *The American state normal school: "An instrument of great good"*. New York, NY: Palgrave Macmillan.

Schneider, M. (2013). *Higher education pays: But a lot more for some graduates than for others*. College Measures, American Institutes for Research & Matrix Knowledge Group. Available at www.air.org/sites/default/files/Higher_Education_Pays_Sep_13.pdf

Shi, D. (2006). Don't invade student privacy. *USA Today*. Available at usatoday30.usatoday.com/news/opinion/editorials/2006-10-17-opinion-three_x.htm

Soares, L. (2009). Working Learners: Educating our entire workforce for success in the 21st century. *Center for American Progress*. Available at http://cdn.americanprogress.org/wp-content/uploads/issues/2009/06/pdf/working_learners.pdf

State Higher Education Executive Officers Association. (2013). State higher education finance FY 2012 [Press release]. Available at www.sheeo.org/sites/default/files/publications/SHEF_12_Press_Release.pdf

Stripling, J. (2010). Fading stimulus saved colleges. *Inside Higher Ed*. Available at www.insidehighered.com/news/2010/02/11/sheeo

Touryalai, H. (2013). Student loan problems: One third of millennials regret going to college. *Forbes*. Available at www.forbes.com/sites/halahtouryalai/2013/05/22/student-loan-problems-one-third-of-millennials-regret-going-to-college/?partner=yahootix

U.S. Department of Education. (2012, July 12). *New state-by-state college attainment numbers show progress toward 2020 goal*. Available at www.ed.gov/news/press-releases/new-state-state-college-attainment-numbers-show-progress-toward-2020-goal

U.S. Department of Education, Institute of Education Sciences, National Center for Education Statistics. (2013). *Integrated postsecondary education data system (IPEDS)*. Available at nces.ed.gov/ipeds/datacenter/Default.aspx

White House, Office of the Press Secretary. (2009, July 14). *Excerpts of the President's remarks in Warren, Michigan*. Available at www.whitehouse.gov/the_press_office/Excerpts-of-the-Presidents-remarks-in-Warren-Michigan-and-fact-sheet-on-the-American-Graduation-Initiative

CHAPTER 1

The Comprehensive University
How It Came to Be and What It Is Now

Alisa Hicklin Fryar

In 1880, the state of Wisconsin established Milwaukee State Normal School, an institution dedicated to training local teachers.[1] After its first class was admitted in 1885, the institution's popularity grew quickly, which soon led many local residents to call for an expansion of the institution's degree offerings. New programs in liberal arts and pre-medicine were added in 1911 and proved controversial. A number of individuals expressed serious concerns over the perception that the institution was abandoning its central mission as a teacher training college, and the ensuing battle over the curriculum reached from the campus to the state capitol, resulting in the forced resignation of the school's president in 1922. This fight even attracted national attention, with the Carnegie Foundation for the Advancement of Teachers commenting that "the Normal School that is true to itself finds it impossible to be a college." Although the school moved forward with the new programs, the decision was later made to rename the school Wisconsin Teachers College, as a sign of its commitment to training teachers. The College soon became recognized for its strong programs and selective admissions (Cassell, Klotsche, & Olson, 1992).

By the end of World War II, with the influx of GI-funded veterans and more middle-class families wanting their children to get a college education, Milwaukee once again faced a college enrollment crisis. These developments necessitated increased access and resulted in lower admissions standards, increased class sizes, more night classes for adult students, and another name change, to Wisconsin State College–Milwaukee. As national demand for graduate programs also increased, Wisconsin State College once again struggled to match student demand to institutional supply. This inspired the University of Wisconsin–Madison to begin investing in its Milwaukee extension campus. Facing competition from other Milwaukee-area schools, the faculty at the University of Wisconsin–Madison struggled to adapt existing programs for students taking only night classes. After a long political battle over how to best adapt, the UW extension center eventually merged with Wisconsin State College–Milwaukee to create the University of Wisconsin–Milwaukee in 1956. This new institution began the journey of becoming a large urban university, a journey punctuated by recurring tension over its identity in the state (Cassell et al., 1992).

Today, the University of Wisconsin at Milwaukee is home to almost 30,000 students, with roughly 5,000 graduate students populating its 53 master's programs and 32 doctoral programs (University of Wisconsin–Milwaukee, 2013). What began as a small teaching college dedicated solely to undergraduate education has now become a large, broad-access public university with a diversity of undergraduate and graduate programs. To understand the history and development of UW–Milwaukee, along with the conflict and tension over its mission and identity, is to understand the complexity and diversity of the American comprehensive university. These institutions make up the vast majority of public, 4-year universities in the United States and often are called upon to respond to an ever-changing environment.

Among undergraduate students enrolled in public 4-year universities, a massive 69% are enrolled in comprehensive universities. These institutions are truly the workhorses of higher education—the "hidden gems" of communities, making important contributions to educating their state's workforce, while rarely receiving the prestige and support enjoyed by their big research/flagship university peers. While state flagship universities benefit from selective admissions, more funding, prestigious research programs, and nationally recognized athletic programs, comprehensive universities can feel forgotten, consigned to divide up the leftovers of support and funding among themselves while working to educate a large percentage of a state's undergraduate students.

Yet, if there was ever a time to pay more attention to these institutions, it would be now. Public higher education is entering a new era, especially in the political arena, as more state legislators are expressing concerns over the rising cost of tuition and fees, the need to better serve nontraditional students, the gap between degree production and workforce needs, and the occasional tension about whether to focus on undergraduates or graduate students and research. Many comprehensive universities are focused on providing a low-cost, accessible undergraduate education that is aimed at meeting workforce needs, and yet we know relatively little about these universities' histories, missions, and ever-changing student demographics.

This chapter explores the origin, development, and current status of the comprehensive university in American public higher education and, in doing so, seeks to answer the most basic question: What is a comprehensive university? The idea of a strict definition for what "counts" as a comprehensive is difficult because of the incredible diversity across institutions and over time. Most people familiar with Wisconsin higher education would likely consider UW–Milwaukee to have more in common with UW–Madison than with UW–Eau Claire or UW–Green Bay, and recent data would support that claim. But there are differences that remain, many of which can be traced to Milwaukee's origins.

THE HISTORY AND DEVELOPMENT
OF THE COMPREHENSIVES

Given the sheer number of and diversity among comprehensive universities, it is surprising to see the similarities among most of their institutional histories. Most comprehensives began as either normal schools, branch campuses of larger universities, community colleges, or—much like UW–Milwaukee—some combination of the three. The normal schools often served as a starting point for the group that we now call the comprehensives for two reasons: (1) They were the largest set of institutions focused primarily on undergraduate education in the early part of the 20th century, and (2) they were the group that founded the American Association of State Colleges and Universities (AASCU), the organization that most often is identified as representing the interests of the comprehensive universities.

The establishment of normal schools began in the United States in the mid-1800s and expanded rapidly through the early 1900s, with most schools offering 2-year teacher training programs. Ogren (2005), who chronicles the creation and development of public normal schools, cites Massachusetts in 1839 as the beginning of the movement. By 1870, there were 39 schools; 4 decades later, the total reached 180, with the vast majority of states establishing at least one public normal school. In the early 20th century, 1920–1930, normal schools—and the teaching profession at large—were not held in high regard. However, compulsory attendance laws and an expansion of the American high school contributed to an explosion in school enrollments and, inevitably, an increased need for more teachers (Tyack & Cuban, 1997). Additionally, the increase in high school enrollment resulted in a call for increased training requirements for high school teachers: a high school diploma and, when possible, a college degree (Ogren, 2005). As demand for teachers with a bachelor's degree increased, many institutions adopted 4-year degree programs and changed their identity from a normal school to a more prestigious teachers college.

In retrospect, the shift to teachers colleges seems more like a brief stop on the path from normal school to comprehensive, rather than a major period in American higher education (Henderson, 2009). Indeed, the end of World War II and the introduction of the GI Bill are almost universally considered two significant developments in higher education, overshadowing the subtle transition of normal schools to teachers colleges. Post–World War II, more middle- and lower-income individuals and women were both financially able and culturally encouraged to pursue college degrees. The effect of this increase in college-going rates once again impacted the environment at teachers colleges. State flagship research universities struggled to meet increased demand, and more students, including the rapidly increasing female student population, wanted to pursue careers outside of teaching, while still attending college at these smaller institutions. Once again, the institutions that we now call the comprehensives did what they often do best: They adapted.

Henderson (2007) estimated the median time spent as a teachers college (between the institution's time as a normal school and its move to a state college) at only 24 years. Many institutions changed their name multiple times in the middle of the 20th century, as they continued to search for their "place" in the rapidly changing higher education landscape, a phenomenon that is most evident when comparing the history of comprehensives and their research/flagship counterparts. One example of these differences can be seen in the state of Oklahoma.

In 1890, two institutions of higher education were established in the Oklahoma territory, 17 years before statehood. One of these institutions was the University of Oklahoma, a research university whose mission and branding have been mostly stable over its nearly 125 years. The other institution was the Territorial Normal School, which, by comparison, has experienced tremendous change and re-orientation within the state. While the University of Oklahoma continued on with little revision, Territorial Normal School was renamed Central State Normal School in 1904, Central State Teachers College in 1919, Central State College in 1939, and Central State University in 1971; in 1990, it became the University of Central Oklahoma (University of Central Oklahoma, 2013).

As the history of comprehensive universities chronicles, the creation of new 4-year institutions—either as entirely new colleges or expanded 2-year schools—was largely a response to changing demographics, culture, and educational needs. However, it still does not fully explain why so many of these predominantly undergraduate institutions consistently have expanded their graduate degree offerings. Critics of comprehensive universities argue that these institutions are abandoning their core mission of undergraduate education and engaging in "mission drift" or "mission creep," as they invest more heavily in graduate programs. The creation and expansion of graduate programs has blurred the lines between research universities and comprehensives, so that any comparison between comprehensives and all other institutions must begin with an exploration of how we best identify the comprehensive university.

WHICH UNIVERSITIES ARE COMPREHENSIVES?

Compass schools, branch campuses, regional universities—these are all terms used interchangeably when referring to comprehensive universities. But most often these institutions are defined as what they are not: Comprehensive universities are not community colleges. Comprehensive universities are not research universities. Comprehensive universities are not flagship institutions. This method of description is both shortsighted and inaccurate, as many universities would consider themselves both comprehensive universities and, at times, community colleges, research universities, or flagship institutions.

Throughout this volume, there will likely be some inconsistencies in how we draw the boundaries around the comprehensives. Accordingly, this chapter does not seek to offer a single definition, but instead looks at how inclusion in this group of institutions varies depending on the decision rules used. For example, a definition of comprehensives that includes only those institutions that were established as normal schools would result in a list of 50–60 schools, some of which have closed and others that would hardly fit even the most liberal definition of a comprehensive university (such as UCLA). Others look to AASCU, the association that seeks to represent the interests of the comprehensive universities in the United States. AASCU's membership includes roughly 383 individual universities, yet not all institutions that would likely "count" as comprehensives are members of AASCU, and a small number of systems that represent research/flagship universities are members as well, including the Georgia Board of Regents, the University of Arkansas system, and the University of Massachusetts system (American Association of State Colleges and Universities, 2013).

The best way to understand the comprehensives is to consider how our decisions about "who's in" and "who's out" affect the characteristics of the group. In this chapter, I draw on three common ways of differentiating between the comprehensives and their counterparts—Carnegie classification, the awarding of graduate degrees, and flagship status—to construct two definitions of which institutions "count" as comprehensives. For the purpose of this exploration, and the need to set minimum boundaries, this discussion includes only those institutions in the 50 states that are public, degree-granting postsecondary institutions that currently award a bachelor's degree. All of the data in this chapter comes from the U.S. Department of Education's Integrated Postsecondary Education Data System for 2010, unless otherwise noted (U.S. Department of Education, National Center for Education Statistics, 2013).

Carnegie Classification

Across the 50 states, there are almost 700 public, postsecondary institutions that award bachelor's degrees. These institutions often are identified by their Carnegie classification, which is based on the types of degrees awarded and the size of the graduate programs. The breakdown by Carnegie classification for the 697 bachelor's–degree–granting institutions (as of 2010) reveals a wide range of institutions that award bachelor's degrees, roughly 10% of which include institutions most often identified as community colleges but that have the ability to award bachelor's degrees. Just under 20% of public universities are categorized as baccalaureate colleges, while over 35% fall into one of the "Master's Colleges and Universities" group, and almost 25% include research institutions. The 268 universities classified as Master's Universities, on average, awarded 1,390 bachelor's degrees, which constituted 75% of all of their degrees awarded. For the 73 "Very High Research Universities," the average number of bachelor's degrees awarded is 5,046, a much larger number than their Master's Universities counterparts, but bachelor's degrees constitute, on average, 68% of their total degrees awarded. These differences reflect variations in institutional size.

If we were to define comprehensives by Carnegie classification alone, we would likely have two options: (1) exclude institutions that fall into either of the Research Universities categories or (2) exclude only the "Very High Research Universities." Each option is problematic. Option one categorizes 173 universities as research universities (and therefore not comprehensives) despite the fact that many of these universities are widely considered to be comprehensive universities. Option two would result in a larger group of comprehensives, but it requires that we group a number of state flagship research universities as comprehensive institutions, despite their having a long history and identity as the state's research campus.

The real differences among these groups of universities can be seen by examining two categories: associate's degrees and doctoral degrees. Although most associate's degrees are awarded at 2-year institutions, 298 of the 697 institutions in this group awarded at least one associate's degree in 2010. Of the 298, we see a strong clustering of associate's degrees awarded at the institutions categorized by Carnegie as "Baccalaureate" (where associate's degrees constitute an average of 22% of degrees awarded). The clustering is most prominent among those institutions categorized as "Baccalaureate/Associates" (with an average of 65% of degrees at the associate's level) and an absence of associate's degrees awarded at research universities. In short, these differences suggest one clear observation that is true for almost any classification of comprehensives: A 4-year university's decision to offer associate's degrees—in almost any number—is unique to the comprehensive institutions.

Undergraduate Versus Graduate Degree Offerings

In policy circles, stereotypes often drive rhetoric, with many people describing the powerhouse research universities as institutions that spend the majority of their time and energy on research and graduate education, and treat bachelor's–degree–seeking students as a necessary afterthought. Others characterize the comprehensive universities as almost exclusively undergraduate-focused institutions, either positively constructed as a protected environment in which every faculty and staff member is dedicated solely to undergraduate teaching, or negatively constructed as a large, unwashed mass of less-prepared high school graduates and older students in night classes. Yet, the stark differences in stereotypes do not reflect the strong similarities seen in the data.

Four-year universities across all groups award the majority of their degrees at the bachelor's level. From "Baccalaureate Institutions" to "Very High Research Universities," the percentage of degrees awarded at the bachelor's level falls between 68% and 76%, which is a fairly tight margin, given the expected dissimilarity. Although some may see this data as unremarkable (and, admittedly, the fact that universities award bachelor's degrees is not groundbreaking), the similarity runs counter to the expectations commonly voiced in policy rhetoric. Furthermore, these similarities extend to the awarding of master's degrees. Among the 441 universities that are included in the "Master's" and "Research" Carnegie classifications, the percentage of degrees awarded at the master's level ranges from 21% to 24% of all degrees awarded.

The differences, then, become more obvious in the awarding of doctoral degrees, with research universities awarding the majority of doctoral degrees.[2] The highest classification for research universities is "Research Institution: Very High Research Universities (VHR)," a designation that is highly sought after by many universities working to increase their prestige and national reputation. Unsurprisingly, this group of 73 institutions awards the highest percentage of degrees at the doctoral level *and* the highest number of total doctoral degrees. As a group, the "Very High Research Universities" awarded 49,517 doctoral degrees in 2010. The next highest group, the "High Research" universities, awarded a total of 14,895 doctoral degrees in the same time period. All other universities, not including medical schools, awarded only 5,217 doctoral degrees, equal to 8% of those awarded by "Very High Research" and "High Research" universities combined.

If we were to construct a classification purely on the basis of undergraduate versus graduate emphasis, one might consider trying to find a natural break in the data, either on the number of doctoral degrees awarded or the percentage of degrees awarded at the doctoral level. Yet, arraying these institutions along the spectra of total degrees or percent doctoral degrees shows that, in both cases, there is no natural break, outside of possibly the top 10 universities. So many institutions have built multiple, sizeable graduate programs that graduate education, alone, is no longer an easy way to distinguish among groups of universities.

Research/Flagship Universities

Many higher education scholars would likely find it comical to hear someone argue in favor of using flagship status as a method to clearly identify comprehensive universities. Flagship status can be equally murky and controversial, depending on the state. In smaller states and states with strong, centralized structures, the flagships are usually easier to identify. Think of flagships like the University of North Carolina–Chapel Hill, the University of Wisconsin–Madison, and the University of Arkansas. In other states, the presence of multiple strong research universities (such as the UCs in California) or of multiple systems (like the University of Texas and Texas A&M systems) leads to the identification of multiple flagships. Equally daunting is the ability of smaller university systems to designate one of their campuses as a flagship campus (again, Texas complicates the designation with Texas Tech, the University of Houston, and the University of North Texas). Additionally, if the purpose of designating flagships is to identify which institutions will not be included with the comprehensives, excluding the land-grant universities like Pennsylvania State University and Virginia Tech from flagship status would leave these universities in an odd position, as few would consider it appropriate to include them with what traditionally are considered the comprehensives.

However, there are some advantages to focusing on flagship status, or some roughly equivalent designation that includes the institutions that were established with or soon adopted a largely research-focused mission. Using a decision rule that captures the idea of a longstanding research mission allows for a discussion of the change in the nature and function of comprehensive universities. If our focus is on institutional mission in a specific time frame, other decision rules may be more appropriate, but if the interest is to understand how comprehensive universities have changed, grown, and developed *over time*, a fixed categorization is necessary.

Conversely, many of the important questions regarding comprehensive institutions focus on issues related to contemporary challenges faced by broad-access institutions. Instead of centering on conversations about changing missions, these questions seek to understand how institutions in this diverse group operate, perform, and work to best serve their students and communities. These questions require a contemporary definition that will better distinguish between institutions that, despite their history as comprehensive universities, have become more selective, more focused on research, and more involved in graduate (particularly doctoral) education.

In the section that follows, I use institutional data to explore the ways in which the following two definitions (or decision rules) for comprehensive universities result in different "pictures" of the nature and functions of comprehensive universities. The *historical definition* categorizes comprehensive universities as bachelor's–degree–granting, public, 4-year universities that do not fall into any of the following categories: primary research university in the state; land-grant universities with long histories of research and graduate education; or institutions that, when founded, were created or elevated expressly to serve as a research institution, such as the institutions in the University of California system.[3] The final tally under the historical definition is 473 institutions. The *contemporary definition* uses the basic Carnegie classification to distinguish between comprehensive and research/flagship universities, for a total of 384 universities.

MEET THE COMPREHENSIVES

With the two definitions of "comprehensive university" identified, we now return to the central questions. What do we know about the comprehensives? Where are they located? What kinds of students attend comprehensive universities? How different is the financial profile of comprehensives, compared with research universities? What kinds of graduate offerings are housed in comprehensives? How are the institutions unique?

Institutional Diversity and Geographic Reach

Geographically, the comprehensives are spread throughout the United States, with at least one comprehensive in every state except Wyoming.

They serve students in the most densely populated areas and many of the most remote regions of the United States. Comprehensive institutions, broadly defined, are so widely spread across the country that at least one comprehensive is located in the jurisdiction of 408 of our 535 house and senate districts. In fact, over 75% of congressional members represent comprehensive universities in some capacity.

Using the historical definition, the comprehensives enroll on average 10,132 students, ranging from 711 (at Penn State, Wilkes-Barre) to 56,236 (at the University of Central Florida). Despite their reputation for being commuter schools, many institutions have a substantial percentage of students living on campus, with 191 universities housing between 25% and 50% of their students on campus, and 48 institutions housing over 50% in campus-owned or affiliated housing.

The numbers using the contemporary definition are similar, but the differences tell a story about how decades of transformation have affected institutions. Under the contemporary classification, institutions enroll an average of just under 9,000 students. Although some of these institutions are still quite large (up to 43,000), they do not reach the 55,000+ under the historical definition, which is likely due to the ability of larger institutions to build more programs and move further into graduate education. Moving to the narrower contemporary definition also *decreases* the percentage of comprehensive institutions that often are classified as "commuter schools." Although the common expectation is that the commuter school phenomenon is found primarily at less selective regional schools, the majority of these new research institutions—ones that began as comprehensives and moved into research activity and graduate education—are primarily nonresidential universities, with many located in urban areas (e.g., Colorado–Denver, San Diego State).

Students at Comprehensives

In the fall of 2011, 69%, over two-thirds, of all undergraduate students attending public, 4-year universities were enrolled in historically comprehensive institutions. Despite the fact that state flagship universities receive more attention and are often much larger than their comprehensive counterparts, the research universities are educating *less than one-third* of the undergraduate student population at public 4-year institutions.

Our comprehensive universities are truly the backbone of the American higher education system. This centrality is even more pronounced for students from under-represented racial/ethnic groups, who enroll at comprehensives at a higher rate. Using the historical classification, comprehensives enroll 85% of African American undergraduates, 74% of Hispanic/

Latino undergraduates, and 70% of American Indian undergraduates. These trends continue for graduate students at public universities, with 58% of all graduate students, 78% of African Americans, 68% of Latinos, and 56% of American Indians enrolled in graduate programs at comprehensive universities. This enrollment of historically under-represented groups is evident in both predominantly White institutions (PWIs) and minority-serving institutions. Although students from under-represented groups continue to be the minority at four-year institutions, their representation is much higher at comprehensive universities (see Table 1.1). Among the 473 institutions in this group of comprehensives, 38 are Historically Black Colleges and Universities and 48 are Hispanic-serving institutions.

However, if we move to the contemporary classification, we see important differences in the data. Moving the 89 institutions that make up these "new research universities" out of the comprehensives group and into the research/flagship category demonstrates the importance of this group of universities. Even though these 89 institutions make up only 16% of the universities in this analysis, they educate 23.4% of undergraduate students and 29.6% of graduate students at public 4-year institutions.

Table 1.1: Average Percentage of Student Population, by Level and Race, Fall 2011

	COMPREHENSIVES		RESEARCH/FLAGSHIP	
	Historical	Contemporary	Historical	Contemporary
Undergraduate				
White	61.0%	62.2%	66.1%	60.8%
Black	16.3%	15.4%	5.3%	12.8%
Hispanic	9.5%	9.2%	8.6%	9.6%
Asian	3.6%	3.3%	5.4%	6.9%
American Indian	1.0%	1.1%	0.8%	0.7%
Multiracial	2.0%	2.1%	1.5%	2.2%
Age: 25 +	23.8%	24.2%	11.0%	16.7%
Graduate				
White	63.9%	58.4%	60.1%	65.8%
Black	13.0%	9.5%	4.2%	12.6%
Hispanic	6.4%	5.8%	4.8%	6.3%
Asian	3.1%	4.6%	5.4%	2.8%
American Indian	0.8%	1.1%	0.7%	0.9%
Multiracial	1.1%	1.1%	1.5%	1.3%
Number of Institutions	473	384	84	173

Source: IPEDS, 2013.

Comprehensive universities also lead the field in the education of nontraditional students. Efforts to reach out to older students often have been a fundamental part of the mission of comprehensive universities, and they continue to succeed in doing so. Under the historical definition, comprehensive universities enroll 83% of all public university undergraduates over the age of 25. Although these numbers drop to 58% with the contemporary classification, there is still a clear trend. On average, these students constitute approximately 24% of the student population at comprehensive universities (historical definition), compared with only 11% at the research/flagship institutions (with an increase to 17% using the contemporary definition).

The trends are even more striking when we compare comprehensive universities with private universities, in addition to research/flagship institutions. In discussions about higher education, the private sector often is regarded as large, innovative, and leading efforts to expand access for a broader base of undergraduate students. With many for-profit institutions offering nationwide access through online programs, and not-for-profit institutions outnumbering comprehensives 2-to-1, some may be surprised to see that the comprehensives, using the historical definition, are leading the nation in undergraduate student access and degree production *by a substantial margin.* Nearly 43% of all undergraduates (including those at private institutions) attend comprehensive universities, more than those in the private for-profit and not-for-profit sectors *combined.* Similarly, over 41% of all bachelor's degrees awarded by 4-year institutions in the United States were awarded at comprehensive universities, which—again—is more than the for-profit and not-for-profit sectors *combined.* The true leaders in student access are the organizations that originally were designed for that purpose: the comprehensives.

Substantive Areas of Graduate Offerings

Many individuals have expressed concern over the decision by comprehensive universities to build and grow their graduate degree offerings. These critics are concerned that efforts to increase graduate offerings are a function of chasing prestige and aspirations of joining the ranks of the research/flagship institutions. However, the leaders of many comprehensive universities, along with state policymakers, identify graduate programs as an important part of the mission of comprehensive universities, particularly when those programs meet widely held goals.

In 2012, the Kentucky legislature passed a bill expanding the abilities of the state's comprehensive universities to offer doctoral programs, while retaining language that set clear boundaries on the nature and emphasis of those programs. The bill defined the mission of the state's comprehensive universities as delivering associate's and bachelor's degrees, along with master's degrees "in education, business, and the arts and sciences, specialist degrees, and programs beyond the master's level to meet the requirements for teachers, school leaders, and other certified personnel," along with a very limited number of "advanced practice" doctoral programs. The legislation clearly restricts comprehensive universities from offering PhDs, along with doctoral degrees in other specified areas, and even specifies that a comprehensive is prohibited from "describ[ing] itself in official publications or in marketing materials as a research university or research institution" (Kentucky State Legislature, 2012).

Not all states are as involved in setting parameters on program offerings. Comprehensive universities offer graduate programs in a wide range of academic fields, some more prevalent or faster growing than others. (Because we look to growth over time, only the historical definition is used here.) Education is the most popular area for graduate programs at the comprehensives; over 75% of comprehensives awarded graduate degrees in education. This is relatively expected, given that many of these schools have long histories of training school leaders. After education, business and health sciences programs are most common, consistent with mission-based expectations of many comprehensives. Graduate degrees in these three fields were awarded by over half the comprehensives in 2010.

Although education, business, and health sciences were the most common, they were not the fastest growing areas over the past 20 years. Between 1990 and 2010, more comprehensive universities added graduate programs in public administration; parks, recreation, and fitness; and computer science than in any other fields. Some might consider the identification of computer science as a high-growth area as unremarkable, given the state of computer-related technology in 1990, but it is important to note that more than 90% of the research/flagship institutions already awarded graduate degrees in computer science in 1990, while only 24% of comprehensives did so in the same year.

Degree offerings identify curricular development at these institutions, but not the differences in size among the graduate programs. In fact, comprehensive universities award more master's degrees than do research/flagship universities in 17 areas. A closer look at these areas may help us to identify the motivation and clientele targeted by comprehensive universities seeking to build larger graduate programs. These fields fall broadly into three categories: professional degrees needed in most metropolitan areas (MBA, MPA, health/nursing, police/fire, communication), advanced degrees that could be used for professional advancement in the K–12 system (MEd, psychology/counseling, traditional subject areas), and a third category defined by its lack of definition (liberal arts, interdisciplinary studies, multidisciplinary studies).

Research/flagship universities award more research-oriented doctoral degrees than do comprehensives in almost all areas, except for very small programs in first responder fields (homeland security/police/fire) and liberal arts. Comprehensives are more engaged than their research/flagship counterparts in the awarding of professional doctoral degrees. In business, education, psychology, and the visual/performing arts, the number of professional doctoral degrees awarded at comprehensives surpasses those awarded by research/flagship institutions. The comprehensives are also quite active in awarding professional doctoral degrees in the health sciences fields and in law.

Finances

The cost and financial profiles of comprehensives vary tremendously, as seen in the data on institutional finances available from the Department of Education (IPEDS). For historical comprehensive institutions, tuition and fees average $6,864 for an academic year, substantially lower than the average at research/flagship universities, which is approximately $8,532 for the 2010–2011 year. Interestingly, the averages remain very similar when moving to a more contemporary designation, with comprehensives at $6,679 and research institutions at $8,079. Taken together, it is clear that the comprehensives are continuing to offer a low-cost education, even as they are growing and adding graduate programs, but it is important to note that this average masks significant variation. Among the comprehensive institutions under the contemporary definition (the more narrow classification), 73 universities have tuition and fees above the average for research universities.

We also see substantial differences when looking at the revenue streams and expenditure breakdowns of the comprehensives. Using the historical classification, we can see that research/flagship universities are wealthier institutions across the board. In 2010, the median revenue per student at the comprehensives was $15,680, compared with $34,950 at the research/flagship universities, a difference that is even more pronounced under the contemporary classification ($14,449 and $27,348, respectively). Similarly, the median level of expenditures per student was much lower at comprehensive universities than at research/flagship institutions ($14,113 and $30,822 under the historical definition, $13,036 and $24,246 under the contemporary classification). The money generated by research grants, user services, athletics, extension services, and a host of other functions at the larger state universities is difficult to rival at many of these smaller, regional colleges. Thus, comprehensives rely more heavily on both state appropriations, which make up 32% of the revenue at comprehensives and only 24% at research/flagships, and tuition revenues (30% versus 25%).[4]

While research/flagship universities bring in more money in private gifts and generate more funds through endowment dividends, many comprehensive universities have begun to build substantial resources as well. Comprehensives generate an average of 3% of their revenue from private gifts, compared with 7% at research/flagships. The relative similarities of these percentages are misleading: Revenues at research/flagships often double those at comprehensives, which results in fairly wide discrepancies over time. These differences can be seen in the value of endowment holdings, which are, on average, $4,035 per full-time equivalent (FTE) student at historical comprehensive universities and $20,111 per FTE at state research/flagship universities.

One way to better understand the differences in financial profiles is to think of institutional finance much like we would think of personal finance. If we think of institutional revenue as earnings, institutional expenditures as spending, and endowment assets as what institutions have in a bank account, the data suggests very different "standards of living" among research/flagship institutions and comprehensive universities. The typical comprehensive, under the historical definition, "earns" roughly $14,000 per student, "spends" almost $13,000 per student, and has about $4,000 per student "in the bank" (endowment assets). Compare these numbers with the averages for research/flagship universities. These institutions "earn" around $30,000 per student, "spend" $27,000 per student, and have approximately $20,000 per student "in the bank" (endowment assets). These data, although admittedly oversimplified, demonstrate the advantages enjoyed by research/flagship universities. Administrators at comprehensives could reasonably view the financial "wiggle room," slack resources, and the ability to withstand fluctuations as a great luxury for their research/flagship university peers.

We also can see substantial differences in how institutions spend their money. As would be expected, comprehensives focus much of their spending on instructional and student-centered functions, with 45% of money spent on instruction, 11% on academic support, and 10% on student services. Although comprehensives spend comparatively more than research/flagship universities on instruction (45% versus 37%), the increase in the overall budget produces inequities in the total amount of instructional spending. To abuse the often-used metaphor of a pie as a budget, comprehensives give more of the "pie" to instruction, but because their pies are much smaller, research institutions still get the bigger slice, which, in this case contributes to faculty salaries. The average faculty salary for assistant professors at institutions that are classified as comprehensives under both the historical and the contemporary definition (378 universities) is $57,982, quite a bit lower than the average for universities that would be classified as research/flagship institutions under both definitions, which is $70,215. Interestingly, the group of institutions that have emerged as research universities have an average assistant professor salary of $64,611, which demonstrates that these institutions do seem to occupy some kind of middle ground, at least for certain indicators.

A similar pattern emerges in research expenditures. For research/flagship institutions, the average percentage of total expenditures devoted to research is around 25%. Among the historical comprehensives, spending on research is much lower, averaging 5%, with tremendous variation. More than 200 institutions spend less than 2% on research, and the remaining 70 dedicate 10% or more of their budgets to research spending. Again, the institutions that were founded as comprehensive universities but have moved to research institutions fall in the middle, with an average of 13% of their total expenditures dedicated to research.

Graduation Rates

For decades, the higher education community has focused on resource disparities as a measure of performance. In recent years, however, policymakers in many states have shifted their attention to student outcomes, most commonly student persistence and graduation rates. This focus on student outcomes can be quite controversial, particularly for the comprehensives whose aggregate numbers, when discussed without consideration of differences in student populations, are cause for concern.

Graduation rates, calculated by the U.S. Department of Education's National Center for Education Statistics and housed in the IPEDS dataset, are a cohort measure, calculated by taking the number of first-time, full-time freshmen in a given year and tracking their completion. The advantage of using this particular measure is that it is one of the only decent measures of graduation rates that is calculated and reported for multiple years across all institutions.

Despite its widespread use in policy discussions, the measure has a number of deficiencies that disproportionately affect comprehensive universities (more on this in Chapter 5). Two concerns are discussed here. Statistically, including only first-time, full-time freshmen means the exclusion of many of the comprehensives' core constituencies: part-time students and students that have "stopped out" (meaning they attended college for a year or two in the past and are returning to complete their degree). Neither of these groups appear in the graduation rate at all, and for comprehensives, these students made up an average of 43% of their student cohort in 2010.[5] Just to reiterate, this means that the most common metric of graduation rate—which informs both assessment and funding—excludes almost half of the students at many of these institutions.

The other concern is more of a normative issue. The measure calculates the percentage of students that complete the bachelor's degree in 4, 5, or 6 years, with the 6-year measure receiving the most attention. Presidents of comprehensives, especially those serving large disadvantaged populations, argue that this is a narrow view of student success. When speaking about degree attainment, the president of the University of Texas at El Paso, Diana Natalicio, often describes the difference between comprehensives and research/flagships as the differences between an express train and a local train. She argues that students at the selective, well-resourced universities have an experience much like riding an express train. They "get on" as freshmen and, with fewer distractions, the train goes to their destination (graduation). She describes the experience of many students at comprehensives much differently:[6]

> The experience of students at most public universities is often more analogous to a ride on a commuter (or local) train. At each semester break, the commuter train stops at a station, where some students get *on* (transferring in from other colleges and universities or returning to school after a hiatus), and others get *off*, to tend to personal, employment, military or other obligations, or to earn money to be able to return to school later. The 70% of UTEP graduates who are not counted in our graduation rate reveals just how seriously misaligned this metric is to the experience of students at "commuter train" institutions. (Natalicio, 2007, emphasis in original)

Indeed, the data suggests that students at comprehensives are less likely to complete a bachelor's degree in 6 or fewer years, and, for some of these institutions, graduation rates are alarmingly low (Schneider, 2008). For the incoming class of 2005, the average 6-year graduation rate at historical comprehensive universities was 43%, compared with 67% at research/flagship universities. For the group of universities that make up these new/emerging research institutions, the 6-year graduation rate is a bit better (48%). This increase is quite interesting, given the push/pull nature of moving to a research university. On one hand, the increases in resources may lead some to believe that graduation rates at these institutions should be much higher. On the other hand, many individuals concerned about mission drift cite the potential harm to undergraduate education. Given that these so-called "drifter institutions" do have slightly higher success rates for undergraduates, it certainly suggests the need for a better understanding of how institutional changes can affect student outcomes.

Most alarming are the institutions that populate the lower end of the distribution. Based on the dataset constructed for the study, at 123 of the 453 comprehensive universities, less than one-third of the first-time, full-time freshmen received a bachelor's degree in 6 years. Of those 123 institutions with 6-year graduation rates below 33%, 10 would be categorized below the 33% graduation rate are those that would be categorized as research universities under the contemporary classification, which raises many questions. This gap between comprehensives and research/flagships is even wider at the 5-year mark, with graduation rates at 37% and 62%, respectively. Although some of these numbers are troubling, the earlier discussions of institutional resources, student characteristics, and historical mission help us put them in context.

LEADING THE COMPREHENSIVES

Few individuals better understand the complexities, opportunities, and constraints faced by comprehensive universities than their own chief executives. This examination of administrative attitudes draws on an original survey of university presidents conducted in the summer and fall of 2012 (Fryar & Rabovsky, 2012). This mail survey was sent to presidents of public, 4-year universities whose Carnegie classifications fall between "Baccalaureate/Associates" and "Very High Research" institutions, and yielded a response rate of 23% after two waves, comparable to recent, similar surveys (Martin, 2013). The identification of comprehensives and flagship/research institutions followed the basic decision rules as described earlier in the chapter, yielding useable responses from 116 comprehensives and 22 research/flagship institutions.[7]

Demographically, the presidents are remarkably similar. Both groups have an average age of 61, women make up 23% of both sets of leaders, and the vast majority of presidents are White, with the exception of the Historically Black Colleges and Universities (HBCUs). There were also striking similarities in their professional backgrounds. For both groups, the presidents had served an average of 5–6 years in their current position, and approximately 33% of the institutional leaders had spent time at their current institution before assuming the presidency. For those internal hires, there was a significant difference in the amount of time spent at their current institution in other capacities, with presidents of comprehensives averaging 13 years prior to becoming president, and those at flagship/research institutions, 21 years.

Across the board, university leaders expressed some concerns over recent criticism about higher education and the new push for increasing performance. However, the attitudes of institutional leaders diverged in areas related to the political environment and the influence of external stakeholders. Overall, the presidents of research/flagship institutions did perceive their environment to be slightly better than their comprehensive university peers.[8] When asked to respond on a seven-point Likert scale to the statement, "When people think of our state, they often think of my university," leaders of the flagship/research universities averaged two points higher than leaders of the comprehensives, with most presidents of comprehensive universities rating on the "disagree" half of the scale and the flagship/regionals on the "agree" half of the scale. The reputational advantage is also evident in the extent to which administrators believed they had to be more proactive than their peers in recruiting students. Presidents of comprehensives averaged a full standard deviation higher than presidents of the state flagship/research universities when rating the extent to which they agreed with the statement, "In order to maintain enrollment and student quality, my institution must be more proactive than others to recruit new students."

Many of these dynamics also emerged in attitudes on economic fluctuations and revenue volatility. Presidents were asked about their perceptions of the volatility of four sources of revenue (state appropriations, tuition revenues, research/grant funding, and private donations/endowments). The majority of presidents, regardless of institutional category, considered state appropriations to be the most volatile, with no significant differences between comprehensives and research/flagship universities in the ranking or magnitude of their perceptions. Instead, the statistically significant differences emerged in the other three categories—tuition, research/grant funding, and donation/endowments—with presidents of comprehensive institutions rating their revenue streams to be more volatile in all three groups.

In addition to increased sensitivity to fluctuations in their environment, leaders of comprehensive universities perceive less autonomy than their flagship/research institutional peers. Presidents of research universities were significantly more likely to agree that "generally, state actors do not interfere with the day-to-day operations of my university." Given this difference, we might expect that presidents of comprehensives spend more time interacting with state political leaders, but the opposite is true. On average, presidents of research universities spend more time interacting with regents, the governor's office, and federal agencies, while presidents of comprehensive universities rated higher levels of external interactions with only local community leaders. Unfortunately for the comprehensives, this data supports many of the stereotypes suggesting that the big research universities are considerably more advantaged in financial resources, institutional autonomy, and access to political resources.

DRIFTING, CREEPING, EXPANDING, OR IMPROVING?

If there is one consistent thread throughout this chapter, it is that comprehensive universities are always in flux. The efforts of comprehensives to build and expand are well-documented, and few people would negate the fact that these institutions are changing. Instead, the controversy over the comprehensives often is centered on other issues. Discussions about the changes in comprehensives often invoke a number of assumptions about the motivations for pursuing graduate programs or increased selectivity. Others express concern that any move away from a fully focused undergraduate mission will lead to lower quality undergraduate education, often citing concerns over graduation rates and learning outcomes. Many of the concerns raised carry an implicit (and occasionally explicit) normative concern, arguing that the decision to invest in research and graduate education undermines the historical commitment to undergraduate education and workforce development.

The development and growth of graduate degree offering, research programs, and increased selectivity in admissions at the comprehensive universities often is called *mission creep* or *mission drift*. These terms often carry negative connotations, suggesting that mission drift is a process by which institutional leaders engage in empire building and, over time, begin neglecting their core mission. However, the history of the comprehensives suggests that this movement may be as much a function of external pressures from students, the state, and the community as it is a function of administration-led ambitions.

In his study of the decision to change an institution's name from "college" to "university," Morphew (2002) offers three possible explanations: building prestige/legitimacy, increasing revenue, and expanding access. These three dynamics are likely motivators for many of the behaviors and decisions we associate with mission drift or mission creep. Many critics accuse institutions of empire building if their presidents chase prestige for its own sake. It is quite likely that some of these changes are prestige-driven, but it is impossible to know whether this behavior is purely ego-driven or a reaction to the realities of the environment. Unfortunately, when the most sought-after prospective faculty members begin looking for their first job, few seek out appointments at less selective, regional, comprehensive universities. Similarly, it can be difficult to recruit and retain bright students who often are lured away to more prestigious institutions. If prestige attracts good people, it is not hard to see why some institutions want to pursue that path.

Additionally, there are some areas in which there are financial incentives to engage in what we may consider mission creep. Graduate programs can be quite lucrative for universities. In many states, these programs can bring in more revenue in state appropriations, given enrollment-based funding formulas that fund graduate students at a significantly higher level than undergraduate students. The difference in funding levels often is designed to compensate for the higher costs incurred in graduate education, as many programs have smaller class sizes and higher expectations of individual student mentoring. However, unlike the expensive doctoral programs and degrees in fields that require multimillion-dollar laboratories, practitioner degree programs can be much less expensive to deliver, and students in these programs rarely receive scholarship support at the same level as some of the undergraduates at the same institutions. Given these advantages, it is not surprising to see so many comprehensives offering more graduate degrees at an increasing rate.

Lastly, these increases in graduate programs may be more of a "pull" than a "creep" or a "drift." The history of the comprehensives and the fields in which we see most of the graduate programs suggest that many of these efforts could be seen as serving an underserved market. While we may all agree that West-Southwest State College (not a real school, thankfully) should not be in the business of awarding PhDs in neuroscience, it is difficult to know where to draw the line. Is it appropriate for a comprehensive university to offer a master's in business? What about philosophy? What if a comprehensive university, the only one in the region, has a long history of training engineers to work in the large number of refineries in the area and wants to start a part-time doctoral degree in engineering? Given our national interest in awarding more graduate degrees in STEM fields and most employees' inability to quit their jobs for 6–8 years, should we support that move?

If we look to quantitative data to help inform our decisions, we will likely find some useful information, but it is still incomplete. Given the low (measured) graduation rates at many comprehensives, we may encourage these institutions to spend their time and efforts solely on improving undergraduate education. On the other hand, in the aggregate, graduation rates correlate very strongly with increased graduate programs, increased selectivity, higher Carnegie classifications, and the resources that these institutional differences bring. Will building graduate programs indirectly improve undergraduate education, or are these efforts more of a zero-sum game?

Even with the best data and research, we are left with the normative debate. Should we have institutions that are dedicated solely to undergraduate education? If so, how do we best support these institutions in their efforts to recruit and retain faculty and students and best leverage resources that are often not available to comprehensive universities? Should state governments encourage or restrict the development and growth of graduate programs? If we decide that some institutions should be given more latitude than others in program building, how do we decide which institutions will enjoy those advantages? Does our commitment to broad-access education require a commitment to broad-access *graduate* education?

When reflecting on the history of the comprehensives, the opportunities they extend to many underserved populations, the identity crisis that many institutions face, and the controversy over policy and performance, the lack of research and attention dedicated to the comprehensives is surprising and a bit troubling. Many of our broad-access institutions are providing a valuable service to their communities and states. If we want to see social mobility in action, we only need to look at the campus of the comprehensive university.

NOTES

1. Much of the data collection and research for this chapter was funded through the generous support of the W.T. Grant Foundation.

2. The information used to assign Carnegie classifications relies heavily on graduate and especially doctoral degrees as a way of differentiating among the groups, and accordingly, the dissimilarity among the groups is largely by design.

3. Generally speaking, I looked for the largest and/or most research-focused institutions in the state and factored in land-grant status, graduate offerings over the past 40 years, and AASCU membership. Obviously, there are still gray areas in this approach. Institutions like Utah State and New Mexico State have a somewhat weaker research profile than some of their counterparts, and some universities have shorter histories as public research institutions, such as Stony Brook University and the University of Pittsburgh.

4. These figures are similar for both the historical and contemporary classifications.

5. Excluded students constitute an average of 30% of the student population at research/flagship institutions, which is still quite high but much smaller than at their comprehensive counterparts.

6. In response to these concerns, the U.S. Department of Education (2012) unveiled a plan to improve and expand the ways in which graduation rates are calculated.

7. For the purpose of the discussion in this section, all classifications represent the historical classification scheme.

8. All empirical findings discussed in this section are differences of means across the two groups and are statistically significant at a minimum of the $p < .10$ level, with most significant at the $p < .05$ level.

REFERENCES

American Association of State Colleges and Universities. (2013). Available at AASCU.org

Cassell, F. A., Klotsche, M. J., & Olson, F. (1992). *The University of Wisconsin–Milwaukee: A historical profile, 1885–1992.* Milwaukee, WI: The UWM Foundation, Inc. Available at digital.library.wisc.edu/1711.dl/UW.MilwaukeeHistorical

Fryar, A. H., & Rabovsky, T. (2012). *Survey of university presidents.* Information available upon request.

Henderson, B. B. (2007). *Teaching at People's University: An introduction to the state comprehensive university.* San Francisco, CA: Jossey Bass/Anker Series.

Henderson, B. B. (2009). The work of the People's University. *Teacher-Scholar: The Journal of the State Comprehensive University, 1*(1), 5–29.

Kentucky State Legislature. (2012). SB 131, an act related to advanced practice doctoral programs at comprehensive universities. KY 12 Regular Session.

Martin, A. (2013, January 10). Downturn still squeezes colleges and universities. *New York Times.* Available at http://www.nytimes.com/2013/01/11/business/colleges-expect-lower-enrollment.html?_r=0

Morphew, C. C. (2002). "A rose by any other name": Which colleges became universities. *The Review of Higher Education, 25*(2), 207–223.

Natalicio, D. (2007). *Convocation speech at the University of Texas at El Paso.* Available at www.utep.edu/aboututep/speeches/2007_Convocation_Remarks.doc

Ogren, C. A. (2005). *The American state normal school: "An instrument of great good".* New York, NY: Palgrave Macmillan.

Schneider, M. (2008). The cost of failure factories in American higher education. American Enterprise Institute. *Education Outlook, 6,* 1–9.

Tyack, D., & Cuban, L. (1997). *Tinkering towards utopia: A century of public school reform.* Cambridge, MA: Harvard University Press.

University of Central Oklahoma. (2013b). *History of the University of Central Oklahoma.* Available at www.uco.edu/about/history.asp

University of Wisconsin–Milwaukee. (2013). University of Wisconsin–Milwaukee academic programs website. Available at www4.uwm.edu/academics/programs.cfm

U.S. Department of Education. (2012, April 11). Education department releases action plan to improve measures of student success [Press release]. Available at http://www.ed.gov/news/press-releases/education-department-releases-action-plan-improve-measures-postsecondary-success

U.S. Department of Education, Institute of Sciences, National Center for Education Statistics. (2013). *Integrated postsecondary education data system*. Washington, DC: Author.

CHAPTER 2

On the Margins

Understanding the Patterns and Consequences of Undermatch at Comprehensive Universities

Awilda Rodriguez

The narrative of high-achieving students who forego their opportunities to attend the top colleges in the country has been a recent focus of many research studies, captured the attention of the media, and resulted in efforts to provide top students with more easily accessible information about their college options.[1] This focus on the college choices of those who have the most postsecondary options, and whether they pair themselves off with marquis-named colleges, has shed light on the problem of undermatch, or when students enroll at institutions that are less selective than their academic qualifications (Bowen et al., 2009; Roderick, Nagaoka, & Allensworth, 2006). While it is undoubtedly important to improve high-achieving students' equitable access to selective institutions, few students are able to enroll in the top colleges in the country. Approximately 6% of students in postsecondary education enroll in 172 institutions that are considered the most highly selective colleges in the country (or 2.5% of all postsecondary institutions).[2] This focus on high-achieving students and selective institutions has left the vast number of middle-ability students—and their postsecondary options—largely unexamined.

Research on undermatch reveals that there are potential consequences for high-achieving individuals who undershoot on college selectivity. These students are less likely to graduate from college (Bowen et al., 2009; Roderick et al., 2006) and therefore will miss out on a host of benefits that a college degree, and particularly a bachelor's degree, affords (Baum, Ma, & Payea, 2013; Carnevale & Strohl, 2013). Moreover, students potentially opt to enroll at colleges that have fewer resources and higher net prices (Hoxby & Avery, 2012).

But undermatch is problematic at all levels of academic preparedness (Roderick et al., 2008; Smith, Pender, & Howell, 2013). Many middle-ability students—the largest segment of the college-ready population—enroll at 2-year colleges or for-profits, or fail to enroll altogether. In other words, from the institutional perspective, comprehensive institutions—one of the primary destinations of middle-ability students—may be losing qualified students to colleges that have lower graduation rates (Wyner, Bridgeland, & Diiulio, 2009), have fewer resources (Hulburt & Kirshstein, 2012), and in some cases produce higher debt burdens (Deming, Goldin, & Katz, 2011).

Comprehensive institutions are a vital segment of the higher education landscape. In Chapter 1, Hicklin Fryar notes that under the historical definition, these institutions enroll 43% of undergraduates overall (69% of all students at public 4-year institutions), and produce 41% of bachelor's degrees. Thus, this group of institutions serves as a major developer of local and national human capital. The majority of these institutions, however, fall outside of the most selective categories (85% range from moderately selective to nonselective). Therefore, comprehensive institutions (and many of the middle-ability students they serve) frequently are excluded from the narrative of matching top students to top colleges.

As a group, middle-ability students with a desire for postsecondary education have all the trappings for success. However, the colleges they select matter, as not all postsecondary institutions produce the same outcomes (e.g., likelihood of completion, price, and indebtedness). A student at a public 2-year or for-profit institution (but with the qualifications to attend a comprehensive university) potentially could have a lower likelihood of completion or end up in greater debt.

While comprehensive universities play a crucial role in educating a large share of college students, we know very little about how or why students decide to enroll at or opt out of these institutions. Much of the literature on college choice examines the factors that influence students' choices between enrolling in college and opting out (Ellwood & Kane, 2000; Engberg & Wolniak, 2010); 2-year programs versus 4-year programs (Alexander, Holupka, & Palla, 1987; Engberg & Wolniak, 2010; Perna, 2000); for-profit sector versus not-for-profit sector (Oseguera & Malagon, 2011); or highly selective institutions versus all other institutions (Hoxby & Avery, 2012). However, the choices students face between comprehensive institutions and other postsecondary pathways have gone understudied.

Moreover, there are gaps in the academic literature on the benefits or consequences of enrolling in a particular postsecondary pathway. We know some of the benefits of enrolling at 4-year versus 2-year institutions, such as increased likelihood of completing, higher wages, and increased job satisfaction (Baum et al., 2013). Research also has shown the benefits accrued by attending selective institutions: The institutions have more resources (Carnevale & Strohl, 2013; Gansemer-Topf & Schuh, 2006) and the students tend to find higher paying jobs (Zhang, 2005). However, we do not know what the outcomes are for middle-ability students, given their options. As a result, the literature is less clear on the potential benefits of attending a 4-year comprehensive public institution over enrolling in a 4-year noncomprehensive private , 2-year public, or for-profit institution.

This chapter attempts to understand the various postsecondary pathways of middle-ability students, particularly as they relate to comprehensive universities. In addressing this gap in the college choice literature, we can advance a more holistic dialogue around the potential benefits of matching to a comprehensive university instead of other postsecondary options. Where do middle-ability students enroll, why do they choose that institution, and what are the outcomes of their decision? If middle-ability students tend to enroll in institutions that match their academic abilities, this would indicate that, at least at this level of selectivity, students are relatively successful at sorting themselves by ability. But, if undermatch is prevalent among students who historically enroll in higher education at the lowest rates, and who could benefit from comprehensive universities, then stakeholders of recent efforts to improve completion rates should pay attention not only to whether students are graduating, but also to how to more effectively match other students to the appropriate institution.

Only a third of degree-seeking, middle-ability students enroll at comprehensives, whereas over half enroll at either public 2-year or private for-profit institutions. Degree aspirations play a large role in where students end up. Very few students who sought bachelor's degrees enrolled at 2-year institutions or for-profits, perhaps challenging the notion that researchers should consider students who match on degree aspirations "undermatched." Students who enrolled in comprehensives were quite concerned with affordability and convenience—more so than their counterparts at other 4-year colleges, who were more likely to cite institutional prestige and programs as important considerations. And depending on the path students took, their outcomes differed. Those students who went to comprehensives were as likely as those who went to noncomprehensive 4-year universities to persist, but students in the latter category were more likely to earn a degree in 4 years (at a higher price and greater debt). In short, middle-ability students face many trade-offs.

WHAT DO WE KNOW ABOUT UNDERMATCH?

Many studies have used various approaches to examine undermatch rates exclusively for high-achieving students (Bowen et al., 2009; Hoxby & Avery, 2012; Roderick et al., 2009). As part of a series of studies, Roderick and her colleagues (2009) focused exclusively on students in the most rigorous academic tracks who graduated from Chicago Public Schools (CPS) between 2003 and 2006. The authors found that 63% of students with adequate test scores and GPAs to be competitive college applicants did not enroll in selective institutions. Many of these students ended up in less selective or nonselective 2-year colleges or no college at all. While it is disconcerting that students with the greatest amount of academic preparation were not matching, the students featured in their study represented only about 20% of students in the school district.

Bowen and his colleagues (2009) studied 1999 high school graduates who were eligible to attend the state flagship institutions in North Carolina (i.e., North Carolina State University or University of North Carolina–Chapel Hill) and found 40% of students who met the academic benchmarks to attend these schools chose to go elsewhere (30% to comprehensive institutions, 1% to HBCUs, and 3% to 2-year colleges). This study's sample was rather narrow in scope, as only about 10% of the students had requisite SAT scores and GPAs to gain admission to the state flagship institutions.

In a recent study focused on low-income students with SAT or ACT scores in the 90th percentile or above and at least an A- GPA, Hoxby and Avery (2012) show that 53% of these high-achievers did not apply to any selective colleges that matched their academic qualifications. However, the study's narrow focus includes only about 4% of high school seniors, even before considering income.

While many of these studies looked at the small number of top students, middle-ability students (those with SAT scores between 870 and 1180) constitute a large share of students enrolled in postsecondary institutions. Every year, droves of middle-ability students apply to and enroll in postsecondary institutions, yet we know very little about how the largest segment of students entering postsecondary education makes their decisions. This is because fewer studies have examined the undermatch rates of middle-ability students. Roderick, Coca, and Nagaoka's (2011) study examined the prevalence of undermatch in the entire range of academic abilities for 2005 CPS graduates and found that 57% of students who were eligible for less selective institutions and 68% of those eligible for nonselective institutions undermatched. Smith and his colleagues (2013) used a nationally representative sample of students to examine undermatch, categorizing institutions by modified Barron's categories, similar to Roderick et al. (2008). They found that 35% of students in their sample who were eligible for selective and somewhat selective institutions undermatched.

While the aforementioned studies provide some information on the college choices of middle-ability students, they do not exclusively consider comprehensive institutions. Both the Roderick et al. (2009) and Smith et al. (2013) studies used a modified version of Barron's competitiveness index, which masks the differences between institutional types, particularly at the less selective institutions. The studies can tell us whether students of mid-range ability match or undermatch, but not whether they are matching to comprehensive institutions. This is an important distinction, as comprehensive institutions are often the more affordable and accessible option for students who want a 4-year degree. We also do not know the extent to which comprehensive institutions are missing out on eligible students who choose other, more expensive postsecondary pathways.

Very little is known, in general, about the benefits of match or, conversely, the consequences of undermatch. Many of the touted benefits of match typically are couched in the benefits of attending selective institutions: higher per-pupil spending (Carnevale & Strohl, 2013; Hoxby & Avery, 2012), increased likelihood of completing (Bowen et al., 2009; Carnevale & Strohl, 2013), and increased likelihood of continuing on to graduate school (Carnevale & Strohl, 2013). However, these findings are comparisons of high-ability students attending selective institutions versus attending less selective institutions (Bowen et al., 2009). Consequently, there has been no attention paid to the potential benefits of or consequences observed in the options from which middle-ability students select.

UNDERMATCH AT COMPREHENSIVES

Comprehensive institutions play an essential role in producing an educated workforce, particularly for local markets. And as William Doyle notes in Chapter 4, they are incredibly efficient at doing so. In particular, students who attend comprehensive colleges are generally middle-ability students with relatively average SAT scores and high school grades that are in the B to A- range.[3] Given their stated degree goals, students' aims are high—four out of every five students who enroll at a comprehensive institution plan on getting a bachelor's degree. And compared with other 4-year degree pathways, comprehensives are teaching the bulk of students, which means many students already see them as a viable path to a degree.

Comprehensive institutions also are doing the heaviest lifting among all 4-year postsecondary pathways in educating students who are least familiar with college. They serve the largest share of low-income and first-generation college students of any group of 4-year colleges. No other 4-year degree pathway serves as a vehicle for mobility for so many students in the same way comprehensive institutions do.

Accordingly, opting out of a comprehensive pathway might have consequences for both comprehensives and middle-ability students. Comprehensive universities may be missing out on talent that they could develop for regional labor markets. And students might be missing out on an opportunity to get a 4-year degree and all of the benefits that come with it.

Who Are the Students, and How Is Undermatch Defined?

Do middle-ability students, as defined in this chapter, accurately match to institutions with similar academic profiles? To find out, I use a sample of 4,280 students and compare students' qualification levels to the first institution where they enroll.[4] As in other studies that examine undermatch (Roderick et al., 2008; Smith et al., 2013), I use Barron's 2004 Competitiveness Index as a starting point to categorize institutions.[5] Since the majority of comprehensive institutions (85%) are concentrated in the "Selective" to "Nonselective" categories, this study focuses on students who are academically eligible for institutions that are categorized as Barron's "Selective," "Less Selective," or "Nonselective" categories. I create four distinct college pathways, two of which are considered a "match" for a middle-ability student (comprehensive or noncomprehensive 4-year institutions), and two of which are considered an "undermatch" (public 2-year colleges or for-profit institutions).

Next, I identify the academic benchmarks of middle-ability students in the BPS sample. For this chapter, I define middle-ability students as those with SAT scores between 870 and 1180 (combined verbal and math scores for the 25th and 75th percentiles of SAT[6] test-takers in 2004) *and* GPAs between 2.5 and 4.0 (College Board, 2004). These students meet the academic requirements to gain acceptance to a comprehensive institution, whether or not they ultimately enroll at one. Students that overmatch— enroll at an institution that is of higher selectivity than their academic qualifications—will not be considered in this study.

Student Pathways by Academic and Demographic Characteristics

Of the sample of middle-ability students, half matched into either a comprehensive or noncomprehensive 4-year institution (33% and 17%, respectively). The other half of students undermatched into either a public 2-year college or a for-profit institution (41% and 9%, respectively). Descriptive statistics in Table 2.1 compare the academic and demographic composition of the four different pathways.[7]

The differences in the academic composition of the four groups, while statistically significant, are for the most part substantively small. Students

Table 2.1. Middle-Ability Student Characteristics by Postsecondary Pathway[a]

		MATCH		UNDERMATCH	
OUTCOME	N[b]	Comp.[c,d]	Noncomp.[d]	2-Year[e]	For-Profit[f]
Total	976,120	33%	17%	41%	9%
Academic					
GPA, 2003–2004***	976,120	6.2	6.3	6.0	6.0
SAT[g] scores***	976,120	1012	1027	979	960
Female*	976,120	60%	55%	57%	56%
Race*	**976,120**				
Asian		4%	4%	5%	3%
Black		8%	6%	5%	8%
Latino		7%	8%	13%	21%
Other		5%	4%	5%	11%
White		76%	78%	72%	56%
Income*	**976,120**				
$0 <= x < $25K		20%	17%	28%	51%
$25K <= x < $50K		23%	23%	28%	26%
$50K <= x < $75K		23%	20%	23%	11%
$75K <= x < $100K		19%	21%	11%	5%
> $100K		15%	19%	10%	7%
Parental Education*	**972,220**				
Bachelor's		51%	57%	38%	25%
Associate's		8%	8%	10%	7%
Some college, no degree		18%	17%	22%	23%
High school or less		23%	18%	31%	46%

Notes: ***$p < .001$, **$p < .01$, *$p < .05$; (a) Middle-ability students were defined as students with SAT scores between 870 and 1180 as well as GPAs between 2.5 and 4.0; (b) figures were weighted using NCES's WTB000 sample weight and rounded to the nearest 10; (c) comprehensive institutions are defined as non-flagship, 4-year public institutions, as defined in Chapter 1; (d) includes institutions that are Selective, Less Selective, and Nonselective as defined by Barron's 2004 Competitiveness Index and excludes research institutions; (e) includes public institutions only; (f) includes both 2-year and 4-year institutions; (g) includes ACT test-takers.

Sources: Analysis of BPS:04/09.

who matched into 4-year colleges have slightly stronger academic profiles: Their high school GPAs and SAT scores are higher than those of students who undermatched. In contrast, the differences in racial/ethnic composition across the four postsecondary pathways are quite large. For example, Latino students are overwhelmingly represented in the undermatched pathways (one-fifth of the for-profit pathway and 13% of the 2-year track), but are a much smaller share of the students in the matched tracks. The opposite is true for White students, who constitute over three quarters of students in the two matched pathways. Black students, on the other hand, are well represented in the comprehensive pathway. This may be due to their enrollments in public HBCUs, which should be further explored through future research.

There are also differences in representation by income and parental education. Compared with those who attended public 2-year colleges or for-profits, the students who matched are less likely to be poor (20% make less than $25,000 at comprehensives versus 51% of students at for-profits) and their parents are more likely to have a college degree (51% of students at comprehensives had at least one parent with a bachelor's versus 38% at public 2-year colleges). In particular, students who undermatched into for-profits are overwhelmingly poor and first-generation college goers: Seventy-seven percent of these students are from families that earn less than $50,000 and nearly half (46%) are the first in their family to go to college.

While many tout that more students from under-represented backgrounds are entering postsecondary education than ever before, there are still differences in where students enroll. The extent of stratification illustrated in Table 2.1—where students who are Black, Latino, low income, or first generation are found in the undermatched tracks—is consistent with the stratification by institution that other researchers have found (Carneval & Strohl, 2013; Gerald & Haycock, 2006; Roderick et al., 2006; Smith et al., 2013). Student pathways are very much linked with race and class. The differences in the types of students that constitute each pathway will certainly shape the subsequent findings. For example, low-income students are also more likely to have lower levels of academic achievement and preparation. Therefore, pathways that have higher concentrations of low-income students also might have higher numbers of students dropping out than those pathways that do not.

WHERE STUDENTS WANT TO GO AND WHAT HAPPENS TO THEM

By the very nature of their academic profile, the college choice process for most middle-ability students is limited because they likely do not possess the academic qualifications to gain admission to more selective institutions. For the most part, middle-ability students can choose to either match to 4-year institutions or undermatch to 2-year institutions or for-profits. Students match by enrolling at either a public comprehensive institution or a private institution that is moderately selective or open access. But how do students choose? What institutional characteristics do they consider? And does where they go make a difference? It is well-documented that these different groups have varying levels of resources available to them, particularly between the 2-year and 4-year pathways. However, we do not know how this would play out for similarly abled students.

Convenience, Pragmatism, and Prestige:
College Choices and Preferences by Pathway

Students' college destinations begin with the college search and application process: the number of schools to which they apply, the number of schools to which they are accepted, and their stated college preferences.[8] For many students, the undermatch process is determined largely by whether they actually apply to institutions that match their academic qualifications (Roderick et al., 2008).

First, let's take a look at the application behaviors of students who undermatched to 2-year public colleges or private for-profits. Overall, students in the undermatched pathways applied to fewer schools, received fewer acceptances, and were less likely to have consulted a list of published colleges than students who enrolled at comprehensives (Table 2.2, column 1 versus columns 3 and 4).

Taken together, students who attend comprehensives apply to more schools than their peers at 2-year or for-profit colleges, even if they do not get into their top choice at higher rates. One potential reason is that public 2-year institutions and for-profit institutions enroll greater shares of low-income and first-generation students than comprehensive universities. For a variety of reasons, students with this demographic background tend to take a more limited approach to the college search process (McDonough, 1997; Roderick et al., 2006). A comprehensive college may not even make the list for a student who submits only two applications (the average for students in this sample who undermatch).

To better understand what might lead students down one path rather than another, we turn to the preferences students indicated as important factors in selecting a college. While the applicant behaviors of those who undermatched were similar, they had vastly different college preferences. For example, middle-ability students who chose public 2-year colleges instead of comprehensive universities were similarly concerned with affordability and location (82% at public 2-year colleges versus 80%

Table 2.2: Applicant Behaviors and College Preferences for Middle-Ability Students by Postsecondary Pathway[a]

OUTCOME	N[b]	MATCH		UNDERMATCH	
		Comp.[c,d]	Non-comp.[d]	2-Year[e]	For-Profit[f]
Application Behaviors, 2003–2004					
Number of schools applied	4,280	2.8	3.4	2.0	2.0
Number of schools accepted	4,280	2.5	2.9	1.8	1.7
Consulted published list of colleges	4,280	34%	39%	18%	18%
Institutional Characteristics					
Price of first institution	3,910	$12,821	$20,576	$7,193	$17,800
Distance from first institution, 2003–2004	4,280	138.4	227.0	34.7	92.0
Preferences/Considerations, 2003–2004					
Attended first choice school, 2004	4,280	70%	73%	77%	75%
Graduation rate considered in school choice	4,280	47%	55%	27%	48%
Job placement rate considered in school choice	4,280	0.4%	0.0%	0.8%	19%
Reason Attended Their Chosen Institution[g]					
Program or coursework	4,280	56%	63%	37%	82%
Reputation	4,280	52%	65%	33%	48%
Affordable or financial	4,280	69%	43%	73%	31%
Location	4,280	80%	72%	82%	61%
Personal or family reasons	4,280	43%	43%	40%	31%

Notes: (a) middle-ability students were defined as students with SAT scores between 870 and 1180 as well as GPAs between 2.5 and 4.0; (b) figures were weighted using WTB000 and rounded to the nearest 10; (c) comprehensive institutions are defined as non-flagship, 4-year public institutions, as defined in Chapter 1; (d) includes institutions that are Selective, Less Selective, and Nonselective as defined by Barron's 2004 Competitiveness Index and excludes research institutions; (e) includes public institutions only; (f) includes both 2-year and 4-year institutions; (g) students were able to select multiple options from a list of reasons.

Source: Analysis of BPS:04/09; Barron's Competitiveness Index, 2004.

at comprehensive institutions listed location as a reason they chose their institution). However, those who went to community colleges seem to have put a premium on staying much closer to home and paying less—they went to institutions that were four times closer and cost about half the sticker price. A convenient postsecondary option, public 2-year institutions are the primary destination of middle-ability students. While comprehensives are designed to cultivate the regional talent pool, many students have to travel over 100 miles to attend one. Therefore comprehensives would do well to consider their marketing strategies if they are to expand their pool of eligible middle-ability talent.

A smaller share of students undermatched to for-profit colleges. These students have a unique set of preferences that lead them to opt out of comprehensive colleges. As a group, they are less concerned with affordability and location than students in any other postsecondary pathway. However, they expressed very targeted interests in the program or coursework institutions offer, and were more likely to be aware of job placement rates when considering their postsecondary options. In contrast, less than 1% of students in each of the other three pathways reported considering job placement rates. These preferences reflect a pragmatic approach to postsecondary education that is tied to outcomes (whether their hopes are realized we will examine in the next section). This may be due to the vocational nature and marketing of many for-profit programs that emphasize job placement. For what many of these students aim to do, comprehensive institutions may not seem a good programmatic match.

The last group of middle-ability students who have opted out of comprehensive institutions are students who enroll at private noncomprehensive 4-year institutions. They do so at a cost: Students who matched at private noncomprehensives traveled almost 50% further (138 miles versus 227 miles) than students who matched at comprehensive institutions. Furthermore, these students chose institutions with sticker prices that were nearly double the price of the comprehensives ($12,821 versus $20,576). These students also prioritized reputation more than students who selected any of the other pathways (65% versus 56% at comprehensives). This preference for prestige rather than price is consistent with group demographics; these students tend to be more affluent and have parents with college degrees. Interestingly, the institutions in the noncomprehensives group are as selective as comprehensives. Therefore many of the students who are opting out of comprehensives may have inaccurate perceptions about the prestige of comparable private options.

It is clear that there are diverging priorities that lead students down separate paths. While many of the students at 2-year institutions may indicate similar preferences as those in comprehensives, distance and price seem to be stronger factors in their enrollment decisions. For students at for-profits, their educational goals seem targeted and perhaps not necessarily aligned with what comprehensives offer. Students who selected private noncomprehensive institutions were much more willing to pay for what they perceived as prestige.

College-Going Outcomes by Pathway

Because not all postsecondary institutions are created equal, choosing one school over another could influence a student's degree attainment outcome. In this particular case, the question is whether middle-ability students who undermatch to public 2-year colleges or for-profit institutions are likely to experience significantly different outcomes than those who attend 4-year comprehensives. And, moreover, do students who attend comprehensive institutions have outcomes that differ from those of their peers at 4-year private noncomprehensive institutions? To find out, I compare students' intended degree paths to their persistence and degree attainment, indebtedness, satisfaction, and labor market outcomes.[9]

One could argue that different kinds of students enroll in the various pathways—with different academic records, demographic characteristics, degree goals, and so on, all of which could drive the observed differences in the outcomes shown in Table 2.3. I account for these compositional differences by controlling for students' academic and demographic characteristics in the regression analysis.[10] The table of results for this analysis is included in the Appendix at the end of this chapter.

In some ways, many students matched on degree plans. For example, four out of every five students who enrolled at public 2-year colleges planned on attaining an associate's degree. However, because students were asked about their degree plans after they enrolled in college, it is impossible to disentangle the directionality of their aspirations (i.e., whether students planned to get an associate's before or after they enrolled). An analysis of middle-ability high school seniors from 2004 (around the same time as the sample used for this chapter) shows that students' subsequent postsecondary enrollments were similarly aligned with their educational aspirations stated in their senior year (available upon request from the author). In other words, four out of every five high school graduates who said they wanted to attain at least a bachelor's degree during their senior year enrolled at a 4-year college, and two out of every three who said they wanted a 2-year degree enrolled at a community college. Therefore, many middle-ability students are matching their degree aspirations to the corresponding institutional sector before they enroll. This form of match has yet to be included in the current conversations that are very much about institutional selectivity, flagship status, or institutional SAT averages.

With many preferring proximity to home and lower tuition prices, middle-ability students in the sample went to public 2-year institutions in droves. Consequently, these students, on average, ended up spending and owing less than students who enrolled at comprehensives ($6,192 versus $10,364 in cumulative debt owed in 2009, respectively; see Table 2.3). In addition, students who enrolled at 2-year colleges were the least likely of all groups to factor in completion rates and program offerings to their decision-making process. Indeed, with only about half of students still in their degree track 2 years later, students who went into the 2-year public pathway were less likely to persist than students who had enrolled at comprehensives, even after controlling for student characteristics. This group was also half as likely as their peers in comprehensives to complete a degree after 4 years—about a quarter of students completed either a

Table 2.3: Outcomes for Middle-Ability Students by Postsecondary Pathway[a]

OUTCOME	N	MATCH		UNDERMATCH	
		Comp.[b]	Non-comp.	2-Year	For-Profit[c]
Degree Plans and Attainment					
Degree Plans, 2003–2004*	4,280				
Certificate		2%	1%	7%	41%
Associate's		9%	8%	81%	40%
Bachelor's		89%	91%	12%	19%
Type of First Persistence Track Exit, June 2006*	4,280				
Did not leave track, same school		63%	64%	31%	43%
Did not leave track, transferred		7%	10%	20%	2%
Immediate downward transferred		8%	6%	1%	1%
Stopped out		12%	12%	21%	21%
Left without return		11%	8%	26%	33%
Attainment or Level of Last Institution Enrolled Through 2008*	4,280				
Attained bachelor's degree		46%	56%	11%	8%
Attained associate's degree		3%	4%	15%	17%
Attained certificate		1%	1%	8%	21%
No degree, enrolled at 4-year		23%	14%	11%	5%
No degree, enrolled at less-than-4-year		4%	3%	11%	6%
No degree, not enrolled		23%	21%	43%	43%

**Table 2.3: Outcomes for Middle-Ability Students by
Postsecondary Pathway[a] (continued)**

		MATCH		UNDERMATCH	
OUTCOME	N	Comp.[b]	Non-comp.	2-Year	For-Profit[c]
Satisfaction with College Choice					
Satisfaction with quality of undergraduate education	4,280	89%	90%	90%	76%
Satisfaction with choice of major	3,780	85%	87%	87%	73%
Academic and Social					
Academic integration index 2004[e]	4,120	80	93	58	59
Social integration index, 2004[f]	4,120	51	72	20	13
Employment					
Employed, 2009	2,940	86%	87%	81%	84%
Job 2009 satisfaction: Overall	2,380	75%	78%	73%	77%
Unemployed 3 months or more since graduation, 2009	2,890	23%	24%	20%	31%
Annual income for current job, 2009	2,470	$30,949	$34,183	$31,309	$28,718

Notes: ***$p < .001$, **$p < .01$, *$p < .05$; (a) included in these analyses are students who have a high school diploma, are claimed as a dependent, recently graduated high school, did not delay enrollment into postsecondary, and the selectivity of their postsecondary enrollment was known; (b) comprehensive institutions are non-flagship public 4-year institutions, as defined in Chapter 1; (c) includes both 2-year and 4-year institutions; (d) the total net price after all grants for the 2003–2004 academic year; (e) this variable is derived from the average of the responses indicating how often they did the following: participated in study groups, had social contact with faculty, met with an academic advisor, or talked with faculty about academic matters outside of class; (f) this variable is derived based on the average of the responses indicating how often they had done the following: attended fine arts activities, participated in intramural or varsity sports, or participated in school clubs.

Source: Analysis of BPS:04/09; Barron's Competitiveness Index, 2004.

bachelor's or an associate's degree—again, even after controlling for the differences in student characteristics found in the two pathways. In other words, many degree- or certificate-seeking, middle-ability students (43%) who sought out the most affordable and proximal college pathway come up empty-handed after 4 years.

Students who chose the for-profit path had very particular preferences (they were more likely to care about specific programs and coursework, as well as job placement). However, once controlling for student characteristics, they fared no better or worse than their peers at comprehensive colleges in earnings, job satisfaction, and the likelihood of being unemployed since graduation.

Compared with those who attended comprehensive colleges, students who attended the for-profit postsecondary pathway were less likely to have earned a degree (bachelor's or associate's) than students who attended comprehensive institutions (25% versus 49%). When controlling for student characteristics (which included their degree aspirations), middle-ability students at for-profits and comprehensives were equally likely to get a bachelor's or associate's degree. Moreover, 41% of students who enrolled at for-profits were seeking a certificate. When including certificates earned, there are only small differences in the completion rates of students who enroll in comprehensive colleges versus for-profits (50% and 46%, respectively). Bachelor's degrees take much longer to earn than certificates; therefore, students who seek certificates are more likely to complete in 4 years than students who seek bachelor's degrees.

Despite the prevalence of shorter degree programs at for-profits, students who graduate from for-profits are paying more and, in turn, going into more debt than students who enroll at comprehensives ($14,827 versus $10,350, respectively, in net price). This is unsurprising, given that students in the for-profit pathway were also the least concerned with affordability, and for-profits on average have higher sticker prices. This is also disconcerting, since the for-profit pathway was made up almost entirely of low-income students, as shown in Table 2.1. When asked in 2009 whether they felt their cumulative loan debt (not including parent debt) was a worthwhile investment, over 80% of borrowers who enrolled in comprehensive institutions stated it was worthwhile, compared with 70% of students who enrolled in for-profits. Even after adjustments for student characteristics, students at for-profits were still less inclined (52% less likely) to believe their loan debt was a worthwhile investment. They were also less likely to report being satisfied with their major and undergraduate education, after accounting for student characteristics and degree aspirations (49% and 47% less likely, respectively). As many have argued before, for-profits meet a need not met by traditional higher education institutions. Therefore, some middle-ability students would be forced to "undermatch" in order to enroll in a desired degree program. However, these students paid less attention to affordability, and most ended up paying a lot more for a less satisfying education.

The final comparison group is students who matched to similarly selective private noncomprehensive institutions. Students who enrolled at these institutions were more likely to come from college-educated families with more money, and to have a greater preference for prestige. On average, they were willing to travel far and pay more to go to college. Did it pay off? Students who enrolled at noncomprehensives were as likely as their peers who enrolled at comprehensives to persist through their junior year, as Table 2.3 illustrates. Degree attainment through 2008 tells a different story, however. While they were not statistically different in GPA and SAT scores than students at comprehensive colleges, students who matched to private noncomprehensives had higher degree attainment rates than those of students who matched to comprehensive institutions (60% versus 49%). Once these same figures are adjusted to account for student characteristics, the difference between attainment rates between private noncomprehensive students and comprehensive students widen, as students who enrolled at noncomprehensives were even more likely (43% more likely) to attain an associate's or a bachelor's degree.

While these large differences in degree attainment may seem to incriminate comprehensive institutions, 27% of students who enrolled at a comprehensive were still enrolled in college (if not still at the same institution), but had not earned a degree. Therefore, it could be that students at comprehensives just take *longer* than students at noncomprehensives to earn a degree. Because this graduation data does not go beyond 2008, however, this hypothesis cannot be confirmed. The modest set of controls used in this study to account for differences across pathways is in no way exhaustive and does not account for many factors that delay on-time completion (such as hours worked or whether students have familial obligations). There could be a number of reasons why students in the comprehensive track take longer. Notwithstanding this blind spot, there are clear trade-offs in affordability and completion between these two pathways. To be as attractive as their private 4-year counterparts, comprehensives need to improve their on-time completion rates.

ENROLLMENT TRENDS AND THEIR CONSEQUENCES

The purpose of this chapter was not to assert that every student with average SAT scores and GPA should enroll in a comprehensive college, but to understand the choices and subsequent student outcomes that receive less attention in the undermatch literature. Students have selected a particular college for a variety of reasons, including familial obligations, personal preferences, choice of major, and so on, that can render their college enrollment decisions logical. Accordingly, this chapter did not set out to dissect individual decisions, but rather to identify trends in enrollments and potential consequences.

The findings suggest that the four postsecondary pathways examined here serve students with distinct degree goals and preferences. Most students are sorting themselves based on their desired level of educational attainment. In fact, a large share of bachelor's degree seekers in the sample found their way to a 4-year postsecondary pathway right after college. While many typically consider college match by the selectivity of the college, middle-ability students are generally not likely to gain admission at institutions with competitive admissions processes and may have limited options. Therefore, middle-ability students that select an institution offering the degree path they desire can effectively be considered a form of college match. One caveat to match by degree path, however, is that many students start at 2-year institutions with the intention of transferring to 4-year colleges. Indeed, 11% of middle-ability students who enrolled at community colleges had bachelor's degrees 4 years later. And an additional 11% did not have a degree but had transferred into 4-year colleges (see Table 2.3). Therefore, even this basic form of match has its limitations. Students in a state with strong articulation agreements and transfer culture (e.g., Florida) might appear to undermatch at higher rates. Nonetheless, these students ultimately would achieve their goal.

But matching by degree path should not be the only goal. After all, the rationale for mitigating undermatch for high-achieving students is that they will enroll at institutions that will increase their likelihood of completing, have more resources, and are more affordable. Should match for middle-ability students not be the same? The trade-off of these various pathways for middle-ability students is either time or money. If students opt out of comprehensives, they have four options: (1) a noncomprehensive that will cost more but might graduate them on-time, (2) a public 2-year institution that will be much cheaper and reduce their likelihood of completion, (3) a for-profit that will be more expensive and where they will be much more likely to be dissatisfied with their experience, or (4) opting out of a postsecondary education altogether. The tensions between price and completion are clear. And although the labor market outcomes seem remarkably similar, it is too soon to tell how student trajectories and their earning capacity will take shape later in life.

Acknowledging these tensions, the comprehensive institution is the more economical path for those who desire a bachelor's degree. Comprehensive colleges potentially are missing out on some students who enroll at community or other 4-year colleges instead. Among students who enrolled at public 2-year colleges, 12% said they wanted a bachelor's degree and were within the academic range of comprehensive institutions. On the other hand, comprehensives also are losing out to private noncomprehensive 4-year colleges. Students who attend these institutions are more likely to graduate on time, but will have to pay more (on average) to do so (in both net price and cumulative debt). There is also incongruence in the preference for noncomprehensives. These students were more likely to indicate that prestige was an important factor in their college choice process, but the private noncomprehensives used in the comparison were as selective as the comprehensives. This could be why students are willing to shell out more to enroll. Although comprehensive institutions are a viable option, they are being overlooked because of important differences that are both real (e.g., distance and price) and perceived (e.g., prestige). This can inform comprehensive universities' approach to marketing and recruitment.

More students than ever before desire a postsecondary degree. We need a better understanding of where the majority of students go and how they fare. As the conversations of match and undermatch take shape, a large number of students has been left out of the conversation. By showing that the notions of institutional selectivity are not very useful for categorizing middle-ability students, this chapter provides invaluable insight into the possible enrollment options and consequences for these students, without whom we cannot move the needle on college attainment goals.

Many of the differences in how middle-ability students approach the application process, their preferences in college characteristics, and their

APPENDIX

Differences in Outcomes for Middle-Ability Students by Postsecondary Pathway[a]

	MATCH		UNDERMATCH	
OUTCOME	Comp.[b]	Non-comp.	2-Year	For-Profit[c]
Persistence and Attainment				
Persistence through June 2006	ref.	as likely	−44%	−56%
Attained a bachelor's or an associate's degree through 2008	ref.	43%	−50%	as likely
Cost and Debt				
Net price[d]	ref.	$3,713	−$3,392	$5,730
Cumulative student loans owed, 2009	ref.	$5,028	−$2,023	$5433
Loan debt worthwhile investment, 2009	ref.	as likely	as likely	−52%

Differences in Outcomes for Middle-Ability Students by Postsecondary Pathway[a] (continued)

OUTCOME	MATCH		UNDERMATCH	
	Comp.[b]	Non-comp.	2-Year	For-Profit[c]
Satisfaction with College Choice				
Satisfaction with quality of undergraduate education	ref.	as likely	as likely	−49%
Satisfaction with choice of major	ref.	as likely	as likely	−47%
Academic				
Academic integration index 2004[e]	ref.	11.5	−11.5	−10.4
Employment				
Employed, 2009	ref.	as likely	as likely	as likely
Job 2009 satisfaction: overall	ref.	as likely	59%	as likely
Unemployed 3 months or more since graduation, 2009	ref.	as likely	as likely	as likely
Income	ref.	$2,871	as likely	as likely
Other				
Social integration index, 2004[f]	ref.	18.3	−18.2	−24.9

Notes: "Ref." denotes the reference group in logistic regression models. (a) Included in this analysis are students who have a high school diploma, are claimed as a dependent, recently graduated high school, did not delay enrollment into postsecondary, and the selectivity of their postsecondary enrollment was known (selectivity defined by Barron's Competitiveness Index, 2004); (b) comprehensive institutions are defined as non-flagship public 4-year institutions, as defined in Chapter 1 using the historical definition; (c) includes both 2-year and 4-year institutions; (d) the total net price after all grants for the 2003–2004 academic year; (e) this variable is derived from the average of the responses indicating how often they did the following: participated in study groups, had social contact with faculty, met with an academic advisor, or talked with faculty about academic matters outside of class; (f) this variable is derived based on the average of the responses indicating how often they had done the following: attended fine arts activities, participated in intramural or varsity sports, or participated in school clubs.

Sources: Analysis of BPS: 04/09; Barron's Competitiveness Index, 2004.

outcomes can best be characterized as trade-offs. No matter the quality of one sector over another, there are no guarantees of success. One comprehensive institution might outperform another noncomprehensive, depending on both the student and the school. But, generally, we know that comprehensive students pay less, graduate with less debt, and do relatively well in the labor market compared with their peers in other pathways, some of whom match and some of whom undermatch. If comprehensives generally can offer students—particularly those from under-represented populations—a successful outcome, it sounds like quite the accomplishment.

NOTES

1. For more on research studies, see Bowen, Chingos, McPherson, & Tobin, 2009; Carnevale & Strohl, 2013; Hoxby & Turner, 2013; Roderick, Nagaoka, Coca, & Moeller, 2009. For more on undermatch in the media, see Byng, 2013; Leonhardt, 2013a, 2013b; Otani, 2013; Pérez-Peña, 2013; Radford, 2013; Ryan, 2013.

2. Analysis of Integrated Postsecondary Education Data System (IPEDS) Enrollment Survey, 2004, and Barron's Competitiveness Index, 2004.

3. This is not to say that comprehensive institutions should not enroll high-achieving students, or that high-achieving students should enroll only in highly selective institutions.

4. As reported in the 2004/09 Beginning Postsecondary Students Longitudinal Study (BPS:04/09). The National Center for Education Statistics (NCES) collected demographic, academic, and employment data from a sample of almost 16,700 students that started their postsecondary education for the first time in the United States beginning in 2003–2004 (at the end of their first academic year). NCES followed up with students at the end of their third year (2005–2006) as well as in 2009 (6 years after their first enrollment). The resultant sample includes 4,280 students after I restricted the dataset to students who had data for all three waves of data collection, earned a high school diploma, were claimed as dependents, recently completed high school, and did not delay enrollment into college. The nature of the dataset presents its own limitations. For example, we do not observe any outcomes beyond 2009. Therefore, we do not know whether the observed differences in some of the outcomes are exacerbated, diminished, or stabilized over time. Moreover, the dataset includes only students who enrolled in college. Therefore, the sample is biased toward students who actually took the necessary steps to enroll in college and excludes many students who traditionally are underserved (Roderick et al., 2006). Another set of limitations involves measurement of variables. The high school GPA was self-reported and measured in bands (e.g., 3.5 to 4.0), therefore losing precision. Another variable with inherent limitations is the reasons given by students for selecting an institution. Location is a vague concept that does not indicate direction. In other words, some students may respond that location is important to them because the college is close (i.e., proximity), whereas other students may be responding to location as urbanicity or region of the country. BPS:04/09 also includes financial aid information and characteristics about the postsecondary institutions. Finally, I addressed the limitation of missing SAT and high school GPA data by using multiple imputation.

5. Barron's categorizes 4-year institutions into seven groups (Most Selective, Highly Selective, Very Selective, Selective, Less Selective, Nonselective, and Special). Institutions were placed into these categories by several characteristics: the SAT scores of the accepted students from the previous year, the GPA and class rank required for admission, and the percentage of applicants accepted from the

previous year (Schmitt, 2009). Students who attended institutions that were considered "Special" were excluded from the analyses (e.g., institutions such as art or music institutions, bible colleges, etc.) as well as those who attended institutions with unknown selectivity.

6. NCES converted ACT scores to SAT scores. Therefore these analyses include ACT test-takers.

7. I employed chi-square tests and ANOVA with multiple comparisons adjustments to determine differences in the distributions and means.

8. Most people enroll in colleges close to home (Mattern & Wyatt, 2009) and the local postsecondary landscape influences the type of college one enrolls in (Turley, 2009), I therefore examined the role of proximity in undermatch by including the distance (in miles) of the institution where students enrolled. I also included sticker price, given that the amount families expect to pay is also an important factor in the college choice process (Perna & Steele, 2011), which could dis/incent students from considering an institution (Pender et al., 2012). NCES also surveyed individuals on whether they considered graduation or job placement rates, as well as their particular reasons for attending the institution in which they enrolled. These measures are important in understanding students' choice processes and also were included in the analyses.

9. The timing of the data collection of BPS:04/09 allowed for outcomes from three different time points, since the first wave of data was collected after students made their college choice decision in 2003–2004, then again in 2005–2006 and in 2008–2009. I was able to examine interim outcomes from as early as end-of-freshman-year GPA in 2003–2004 to labor market outcomes 6 years later in 2009. I included data on their stated degree intentions from 2003 to compare with persistence in 2006 and degree attainment measures in 2009. I also included measures of cost and debt, satisfaction with their college choice, interim academic and social outcomes, and employment outcomes in 2009.

10. While in no way do the findings from this approach imply that the relationship between enrolling in a postsecondary pathway and the observed outcomes is causal, this approach acknowledges the potential relationships between student characteristics (as inputs) and the observed differences in outcomes (as outputs). Students' high school GPA, combined SAT scores, and highest math course were included in the model, as academic achievement and preparation are closely related to degree plans. For more information, see Berkner, Choy, and Hunt-White, 2008, Tables 2.2, 2.3, 2.4, and 2.5, as well as Lauff, Ingels, and Christopher, 2014, Table 1. As a reflection of the extent of students' college search process, I included the number of college applications students submitted. I also included race/ethnicity, which has been shown to have an association with degree plans (Berkner et al., 2008, Table 1.8), persistence (Berkner et al., 2008, Table 4.1), completion (U.S. Department of Education, National Center for Education Statistics, 2012, Tables 376 & 377), and the extent to which students socially integrate onto a campus

(Berkner et al., 2008, Table 3.9). Moreover, I used familial resources in the form of both income as well as parental education to adjust outcome measures, as research has shown they are associated with degree plans (Berkner et al., 2008, Tables 1.10 & 1.11), persistence (Berkner et al., 2008, Tables 12 & 4.1), completion (U.S. Department of Education, National Center for Education Statistics, 2012, Table 379), and the ability to garner grant aid (Berkner et al., 2008, Table 10.1). Finally, I adjusted for the degree path students reported during their freshman year, as their degree plans would have bearing on their degree attainment outcomes. Because their degree plans were collected by NCES at the same time as their academic and social integration variables, and end-of-freshman-year GPA were captured, I excluded the degree plan measure to adjust for these three outcomes for reasons of endogeneity, or inability to establish the direction of causality (e.g., poor first-semester grades could have influenced the degree path chosen).

REFERENCES

Alexander, K. L., Holupka, S., & Pallas, A. M. (1987). Social background and academic determinants of two-year versus four-year college attendance: Evidence from two cohorts a decade apart. *American Journal of Education 96*(1), 56–80.

Barron's Educational Series, Inc. (2004). *2005 Barron's Profiles of American Colleges* (26th ed.). New York, NY: Author.

Baum, S., Ma, J., & Payea, K. (2013). *Education pays: The benefits of higher education for individuals and society.* New York, NY: College Board.

Berkner, L., Choy, S., & Hunt-White, T. (2008, July). *Descriptive summary of 2003–04 beginning post-secondary students: Three years later.* National Center for Education Statistics, Institute of Education Sciences, U.S. Department of Education. Available at nces.ed.gov/pubs2008/2008174.pdf

Bowen, W. G., Chingos, M. M., McPherson, M. S., & Tobin, E. M. (2009). *Crossing the finish line: Completing college at America's public universities.* Princeton, NJ: Princeton University Press.

Byng, R. (2013). College diversity still an issue at America's top schools, study finds. *The Huffington Post.* Available at www.huffingtonpost.com/2013/07/31/college-diversity-issue-top-schools-study_n_3685145.html

Carnevale, A. P. & Strohl, J. (2013). *Separate & unequal: How higher education reinforces the intergenerational reproduction of white racial privilege.* Washington, DC: Georgetown University Center on Education and the Workforce.

College Board. (2004). *College bound seniors: A profile of SAT program test-takers.* Available at http://research.collegeboard.org/programs/sat/data/archived/cb-seniors-2004

Deming, D. J., Goldin, C., & Katz, L. E. (2011). *The for-profit postsecondary school sector: Nimble critters or agile predators?* (NBER Working Paper No. 17710). Cambridge, MA: National Bureau of Economic Research.

Ellwood, D. T., & Kane, T. J. (2000). Who is getting a college education? Family background and the growing gaps in enrollment. In S. Danziger & J. Waldfogel (Eds.), *Securing the future: Investing in children from birth to college* (pp. 283–324). New York, NY: Russell Sage Foundation.

Engberg, M. E., & Wolniak, G. C. (2010). Examining the effects of high school contexts on postsecondary enrollment. *Research in Higher Education 51*(2), 132–153.

Gansemer-Topf, A. M., & Schuh, J. H. (2006). Institutional selectivity and institutional expenditures: Examining organizational factors that contribute to retention and graduation. *Research in Higher Education 47*, 642.

Gerald, D., & Haycock, K. (2006). Engines of inequality: Diminishing equity in the nation's premier public universities. Washington, DC: Education Trust.

Hoxby, C. M., & Avery, C. (2012). *The missing "one-offs": The hidden supply of high-achieving, low income students* (NBER Working Paper No. 18586). Cambridge, MA: National Bureau of Economic Research. Available at www.nber.org/papers/w18586

Hoxby, C., & Turner, S. (2013). *Expanding college opportunities for high-achieving, low income students.* Stanford, CA: Stanford Institute for Economic Policy Research. Available at siepr.stanford.edu/publicationsprofile/2555

Hulburt, S., & Kirshstein, R. J. (2012). *Spending: Where does the money go?* Washington, DC: Delta Cost Project at American Institutes for Research. Available at http://www.deltacostproject.org/sites/default/files/products/Delta-Spending-Trends-Production.pdf

Lauff, E., Ingels, S. J., & Christopher, E. M. (2014). *Education longitudinal study of 2002 (ELS:2002): A first look at 2002 high school sophomores 10 years later.* National Center for Education Statistics, Institute of Education Sciences, U.S. Department of Education. Available at nces.ed.gov/pubs2014/2014363.pdf

Leonhardt, D. (2013a, March 16). Better colleges failing to lure talented poor. *The New York Times.* Available at www.nytimes.com/2013/03/17/education/scholarly-poor-often-overlook-better-colleges.html

Leonhardt, D. (2013b, September 25). A nudge to poorer students to aim high on colleges. Available at www.nytimes.com/2013/09/26/education/for-low-income-students-considering-college-a-nudge-to-aim-high.html

Mattern, K., & Wyatt, J. (2009). Student choice of college: How far do students go for an education? *Journal of College Admission, 203*, 18–29.

McDonough, P. M. (1997). *Choosing colleges: How social class and schools structure opportunity.* Albany, NY: State University of New York Press.

Oseguera, L., & Malagon, M. C. (2011). For-profit colleges and universities and the Latina/o students who enroll in them. *Journal of Hispanic Higher Education, 10*(1), 66–91.

Otani, A. (2013, November 19). Black UCLA students decry lack of diversity in video. *USA Today*. Available at www.usatoday.com/story/news/nation/2013/11/14/youtube-ucla-lack-diversity/3518373/

Pender, M., Smith, J., Hurwitz, M., & Howell, J. (2012, October). *College choice: Informing students' trade-offs between institutional price and college completion.* Washington, DC: The College Board Advocacy & Policy Center.

Pérez-Peña, R. (2013, May 30). Income-based diversity lags at some universities. *The New York Times*. Available at www.nytimes.com/2013/05/31/education/college-slots-for-poorer-students-still-limited.html

Perna, L. W. (2000). Differences in the decision to enroll in college among African Americans, Hispanics, and Whites. *Journal of Higher Education 71*, 117–141.

Perna, L. W., & Steele, P. (2011). The role of context in understanding the contributions of financial aid to college opportunity. *Teachers College Record, 113*(5), 895–933.

Radford, A. W. (2013). 'No point in applying': Why poor students are missing at top colleges. *The Atlantic Monthly*. Available at www.theatlantic.com/education/archive/2013/09/no-point-in-applying-why-poor-students-are-missing-at-top-colleges/279699/

Roderick, M., Coca, V., & Nagaoka, J. (2011). Potholes on the road to college: High school effects in shaping urban students' participation in college application, four-year college enrollment, and college match. *Sociology of Education, 84*, 178–211.

Roderick, M., Nagaoka, J., & Allensworth, E. (2006). *From high school to the future: A first look at Chicago public school graduates' college enrollment, college preparation, and graduation from four-year colleges*. Chicago, IL: Consortium on Chicago School Research.

Roderick, M., Nagaoka, J., & Coca, V. (2008). *From high school to the future: Potholes on the road to college*. Chicago, IL: Consortium on Chicago School Research.

Roderick, M., Nagaoka, J., Coca, V., & Moeller, E. (2009). *From high school to the future: Making hard work pay off: The road to college for students in CPS's academically advanced programs*. Chicago, IL: Consortium on Chicago School Research.

Ryan, J. (2013). It's oddly difficult to find good college advising online. *The Atlantic Monthly*. Available at www.theatlantic.com/education/archive/2013/12/its-oddly-difficult-to-find-good-college-advising-online/282186/

Schmitt, C. M. (2009). Documentation for the restricted-use NCES-Barron's Admissions Competitiveness Index data files: 1972, 1982, 1992, 2004 and 2008 (NCES 2010-330). Washington, DC: National Center for Education Statistics, U.S. Department of Education.

Smith, J., Pender, M., & Howell, J. (2013). The full extent of student-college academic undermatch. *Economics of Education Review, 32*, 247–261.

Turley, R.N.L. (2009). College proximity: Mapping access to opportunity. *Sociology of Education, 82*(2), 126–146.

U.S. Department of Education, National Center for Education Statistics. (2004). *IPEDS 2004 Enrollment Survey* [Data File]. Available from http://nces.ed.gov/ipeds/datacenter/InstitutionByName.aspx

U.S. Department of Education, National Center for Education Statistics. (2012). *Digest of education statistics*. Available at nces.ed.gov/programs/digest/d12/tables/dt12_376.asp

Winston, G. C., & Zimmerman, D. J. (2004). Peer effects in higher education. In C. M. Hoxby (Ed.), *College choices: The economics of where to go, when to go, and how to pay for it* (pp. 395–424). Chicago, IL: University of Chicago Press.

Wyner, J. S., Bridgeland, J. M., & Diiulio, J. J., Jr. (2009). Achievement trap: How America is failing millions of high-achieving students from lower-income families. Lansdowne, VA: Jack Kent Cooke Foundation.

Zhang, L. (2005). Do measures of college quality matter? The effect of college quality on graduate earnings. *The Review of Higher Education, 28*(4), 571–596.

CHAPTER 3

Putting It All Together
Strengthening Pathways Between Comprehensive Universities and Community Colleges

Alison Kadlec and Mario Martinez

"How many of you have lost time or money because of college classes not transferring?" Seven of the 10 students around the table raise their hands. That might not seem like many, but this is one of more than 40 focus groups with students from bachelor's–degree–granting colleges and nearby community colleges that Public Agenda, an opinion research and stakeholder engagement organization, has conducted within 3 months. In nearly every group a majority of hands go up. At this point during the 90-minute conversations, we go around the table and the students share their stories, all of them remarkably similar from group to group. Frequently, students at community colleges are advised to take courses that end up not being accepted by the local 4-year campus. Or when courses transfer, many are accepted only as electives and do not count toward the students' majors. In other instances, students unwittingly take courses out of sequence and have to wait another semester or year to enroll in bachelor's programs. For the unconfident learner or the student who lacks goal clarity, the stakes of these challenges seem particularly high: Most of the students we spoke with had stopped out at some point along their path.[1]

Embedded within the individual stories students told are a number of recurring themes: well-meaning but overwrought and underprepared general advisors at community colleges; faculty advisors who are critically important but dangerously siloed; diffuse and scattered resources on transfer that students have difficulty accessing or effectively navigating; a choice architecture that exacerbates swirl instead of empowering students to make good decisions; dysfunctional channels of communication between faculty and staff within and across 2-year and 4-year institutions, fueled by institutions' cultural histories of suspicion and competition; and quality gaps—both perceived and real—that prevent 4-year institutions from accepting credits accumulated at community colleges.

The eminently sensible idea that baccalaureate-seeking students could save a great deal of money by starting at a community college and finishing the last 2 years at the local 4-year college is belied by the endless stories students tell of time and money wasted on classes that end up not transferring toward their degree (Hyman & Jacobs, 2009). The roadblocks students face as they seek to flow between community colleges and regional 4-year institutions have serious impacts on student persistence and completion, particularly for those students who arrive at college unconfident and underprepared.

Accumulation of excess credits has been identified by states and systems as a leading challenge to timely completion. The failure of regional universities and community colleges to respond effectively to the needs of the "new traditional" student—two-thirds of whom take credits at multiple institutions—may be a chief contributor to the accumulation of excess credits that cost students, families, taxpayers, and the nation. According to research by the National Center for Higher Education Management Systems (NCHEMS), even a 10% decrease in the number of excess credits accumulated by students on their way to a degree could bring substantial savings to institutions and states (Lumina Foundation, 2010).[2] By and large, institutions seem ill-equipped to navigate the new realities of student flow. Students should be able to take classes from multiple institutions and even change majors without accumulating excess credits or losing time and money, but the realities of the higher education landscape do not seem to allow institutions to shape their practices to meet the needs of 21st-century students.

Policies that allocate a portion of funding according to outcomes instead of enrollment, or that mandate meaningful transfer agreements between institutions, might encourage colleges to pay more attention to student success. Unfortunately, too many policies focused on institutions and systems lack attention to incentives and accountability. Students are given little help directly, and many of the challenges they face are the result of failures of regional universities and community colleges to hold up their end of the bargain by creating clear pathways.

While Public Agenda's conversations with transfer students focus on wasted time, effort, and money, what we have come to find most distressing is the apparent loss of hope and dissipation of determination that students suffer from as they hit roadblocks on an already daunting path. One especially memorable first-generation student brought this into focus when she said:

I'm getting tired of school. I had a plan and thought I was doing everything right, and everyone I talked to [at the school] seemed so sure they were giving me the right information, so I never questioned it because I had no idea what I was doing. But here I am and I've probably lost two whole semesters taking classes I didn't need or that ended up not transferring or counting toward my major. I don't even want to think about the money I lost because I couldn't afford to lose it. . . . At this point, honestly, I don't know if I'm ever going to finish. I'm just getting tired.

Instead of expressing outrage and recrimination, most students—like this one—sound deflated and defeated. In so many of these conversations it is as though students blame themselves for the roadblocks they hit—even for those problems that, from the outside, appear to result from the clear failures of institutions and systems to collaborate effectively. This is perplexing.

Underneath all of their comments one can sense a churning doubt, and the idea that maybe they should have known all along that they were not "college material" (Flaga, 2006). And herein lies the moral imperative of efforts aimed at providing smooth and seamless pathways for students seeking to flow between community colleges and comprehensive institutions. The students who come to college with the greatest challenges lose more than time and money when they hit roadblocks on their path toward a degree: They lose hope in their ability to make a better life through education.

For the majority of Americans who struggle to make ends meet without a credential, college feels like a stretch to begin with. Their aspirations are often in danger of being overwhelmed not only by the challenges that come with reliance on unstable, low-wage jobs, but also by their self-doubt. Students who lack clear goals and "grit" are far more likely to swirl and end up in debt without a credential, but even those like the young woman above are in danger of having their hope for a better life through education snuffed out by systems that feel—and often are—impossible to navigate efficiently.

Regional 4-year colleges often are overlooked in the higher education landscape, but they have the potential and obligation to become engines of postsecondary attainment at a time when the country is in desperate need of a more educated population. Together, regional 4-year colleges and community colleges serve a significant majority of students. These institutions must find better ways of doing business if they are to fulfill their potential, and their very survival may depend on their ability to do so (Kelly, 2012). Working more effectively with community colleges to create clear, seamless pathways for students is both good business and the right thing to do.

While barriers to effective collaboration between regional 4-year insti-tutions and community colleges seem to proliferate in every direction, a number of institutions, systems, and states across the country are stepping up to the challenge. In these cases, concerted efforts are being made at a number of levels to adopt policies and practices aimed at encouraging col-laboration, mitigating competition, and improving channels of communi-cation within and between institutions.

OUR CASES, OUR PROPOSITIONS

While we are interested in the state story around transfer issues, our pri-mary lens is on collaboration at the institutional level on behalf of seamless student flow. In the absence of a solid research base on these issues, we are most interested in what can be learned from looking at especially creative partnerships between specific regional 4-year colleges and community col-leges. We looked at three such partnerships: Northern Arizona University (NAU) and its partnership with Yavapai College; the University of Texas at El Paso (UTEP) and El Paso Community College (EPCC); and Indiana Uni-versity East (IUE) and Ivy Tech Community College–Whitewater.

In each we interviewed institutional leaders, senior administrators, and faculty.[3] Because of the fortuitous timing of a related project, we were able to draw on dozens of focus groups with transfer students flowing between comprehensives and community colleges in other areas to com-plement our interviews. Our selection of these three cases allows us to consider a range of geographical contexts, governance structures, and stu-dent population sizes in which robust and creative cross-sector collabora-tions have been developed.

We augmented the focus on institutional collaboration with litera-ture scans in organizational collaboration, transfer, and higher education policy, and through interviews with national experts in higher education research and policy. Given the exploratory and qualitative nature of this project, we are not in a position to make detailed and definitive claims about the conditions for robust collaborations, but our case studies pro-vide promising hypotheses for further exploration. In all three of our cas-es, four themes are particularly central:

- Meaningful state and institutional policy sensitive to actual conditions on the ground
- Enlightened institutional leadership exercised from the top and middle

- Formal and informal collaboration among and between faculty and staff at many levels
- Creative use of systems and data to track and understand student flow and progression

In some cases, state policy led the way and institutional leaders responded. In other cases, leaders of community colleges and 4-year institutions pushed for state policy to enable more seamless pathways. But in all of the cases, success came about only because leaders inspired cultures that supported collaboration throughout the institutions and because of faculty ownership of these efforts. Interestingly, in all of these cases, geographical circumstance and proximity were also background considerations that leaders skillfully used to their advantage.

NORTHERN ARIZONA UNIVERSITY AND YAVAPAI COMMUNITY COLLEGE

The story of the partnership between Northern Arizona and its community college partners illustrates a blending of leadership, creation of policies, powerful change in systems, and collaboration at multiple levels. With only three 4-year institutions, centrally coordinated by a board of regents, and 12 independent community college districts that operate without a centralized governance structure, Arizona is a somewhat simpler landscape in which to explore issues around institutional collaboration. The fact that NAU, with a student population of over 25,000, is significantly larger than its partners Yavapai College and Coconino Community College (which have approximately 8,000 and 4,000 students, respectively) is significant to understanding the dynamics of that partnership. NAU is also the only comprehensive university in our study that has a primarily residential undergraduate population. The tuition differential in this case is the most significant, with NAU's in-state tuition around $9,000 per year and Yavapai and Coconino both under $2,000 for full-time enrollment.

Leadership

Academic leaders in these institutions started forming partnerships over 25 years ago. The partnership between Northern Arizona and Yavapai Community College dates back to the 1980s, although the more recent partnership between Northern Arizona and Coconino Community

College is no less robust and represents one of the earliest examples of a 2+2 program in which students are dual enrolled and guaranteed transfer with junior standing upon completion of the first 2 years at the community college. There are now variations of 2+2 programs in nearly every state because they have the potential to graduate three times the number of students for the same amount of funding as one undergraduate student in a 4-year program. As one of the first comprehensives to craft regional agreements about pathways with its local community colleges, Northern Arizona University became a model for the state of Arizona.

More than a decade ago, Northern Arizona's longstanding partnership with Yavapai College (along with the established partnerships between the larger 4-years and their urban community college districts) drew attention to the fact that the four most rural community colleges in Arizona were operating without strong transfer pathways to any 4-year institution. As former statewide transfer facilitator Gretchen Schmidt described, "Before the legislation, the rural colleges were left out and their kids were stuck. There was no real mobility for them because their classes weren't accepted anywhere."

Policy

Flexing the collective muscle developed through close relationships with local legislators, leadership of the rural community colleges agitated for a statewide transfer agreement. More than 10 years before it became a national trend, Arizona passed legislation that called for system-wide transfer agreements, the infrastructure of which would be jointly funded by the institutions and the state, with the work being overseen by the Trustees and Regents. "It wasn't prescriptive," said Schmidt, "but it was prescriptive enough to bring everyone to the table."

With a wide-open charter, the Academic Program Articulation Steering Committee (APASC) was composed of senior administrators from the universities and a selection of community colleges, along with a committee of front-line practitioners. The group began by building particularly sophisticated General Education blocks in three main program areas (arts, business, and science). Instead of stopping there—which is where many similar efforts often end—APASC then dug into the program areas and convened faculty early on to get to the core issues around applicability of credits toward degrees. Schmidt commented:

> In retrospect, their foresight was amazing. They understood that it's not enough for a community college course to be accepted by a comprehensive; it has to mean something. The conversation about the difference between merely accepting credits and actually applying

those credits toward degrees is starting to take hold, and Arizona was having that conversation 12 years ago.

Systems

As part of this process, APASC created an electronic system and infrastructure for a course equivalency process so that when a community college introduces a new course, it goes through a process at all three universities whereby the course gains equivalency *and* applicability. In other words, through this electronic process, students learn not only whether a community college course will be accepted by the 4-year but also where it will be applied in their program.

Every year, faculty in 20 disciplines come together to talk about the courses and pathways for students in the major, changes in admission requirements, and anything students would need to know to transfer more effectively from the community colleges to the universities. The results of these conversations are then fed back into the electronic system, which serves as a "centralized, updated, dynamic repository of information." With a solid electronic infrastructure now in place, there are more than 13,000 courses in the course equivalency guide. Students can now learn quickly not only what the course represents at their own institution but whether and how it will apply toward their major at the receiving institution.

So far we have described an excellent example of the interplay between leadership, policy, and systems. Enlightened leadership worked together to create the conditions for meaningful change, which led in turn to policy and systems to support seamless pathways for students. But the real work, as we will see, came through collaboration at multiple levels.

Collaboration

Based on this groundwork—and with the inclusion of faculty from the outset—the changes moved beyond initial high-level conversations and dug down past the Gen Ed core into the programs. With that foundation, 4-year institutions in Arizona have expanded transfer practice by doing things like creating a bachelor's of applied science degree that opens the door for the associate's of applied science (AAS) to be more than a terminal degree. At least three regional institutions have built "upside down degrees" in which students with an AAS are able to transfer that degree as a block to the comprehensive, arriving with junior standing, and then stack the bachelor's on top. This means that a student who got an AAS in fire science, but who found midway that she needed a bachelor's degree to advance to captain within the profession of firefighting, would not have to start that degree from scratch.

In other words, success rests on the climate and culture of particular institutions like NAU where especially strong partnerships with community colleges have been cultivated over the years. NAU forged uncommonly creative partnerships with Yavapai Community College and Coconino Community College where practitioners from both the comprehensives and community colleges work side by side. While these partnerships have been fueled and bolstered in part by economic necessity, as fewer state dollars flow to colleges, it is the intentionality of these partnerships and the shared focus on student success that sustain commitment.

In 2010, NAU and Yavapai College launched a new program with the aim of providing seamless transition from the community college to NAU in the Prescott Valley 90 miles south of Flagstaff. In place of athletic facilities, residence halls, and full-service dining, this unique partnership between the institutions offers a fully integrated 2+2 program with tailored, focused, and collaborative advising to Yavapai students that puts them on the right track for an NAU bachelor's degree. Benefits to students include automatic admission to NAU with a waived application fee, collaborative advising, access to NAU programs and events, and a host of support services. Yavapai and NAU share facilities, services, and resources, which fosters deep collaboration because both institutions have "skin in the game." The institutions work closely together—both within and outside of the APASC-led transfer and articulation process—to help students complete their degree, in part because funding constraints necessitate such collaboration.

The "new traditional" student does not start at one institution and finish at another, but instead swirls between the institutions based on schedule, cost, and convenience. Critical to these students' success are robust and creative partnerships between regional 4-year institutions and community colleges. Rather than viewing this swirl as a negative that ought to be discouraged, NAU embraces the realities of student flow and works closely with Yavapai and Coconino to accommodate it. As a senior administrator from Northern Arizona described it, "NAU says, 'Go ahead and take what you need from Yavapai and then come here and take what you need, or take classes from both institutions at the same time, whatever. Just be thoughtful and make sure you're getting advised early and often and by both institutions.'"

This case makes it clear that state-level activity creates the formal structures for senior administrators, faculty, and staff to work together in a number of informal ways. Yet, it is also clear that the relative simplicity of the Arizona higher education landscape and the specific efforts at co-location are contributing factors. Fred Hurst, senior vice president of Northern Arizona and dean of the extended campus, summed up this confluence of elements when he said:

Arizona is the Wild West and we're independent, pretty entrepreneurial. That's our culture. And it's easier to be that here because we're only 12 community college districts and three 4-year institutions. Every time you add a new player, if you're trying to do something collaborative, it adds to the complexity.

While it is clear that state-level activity is a powerful driver of more effective collaboration, NAU, and Arizona more generally, is a story about the commitment of leadership at a variety of levels, the power of external financial pressures to do more with less, and the importance of deep inclusion of faculty.

INDIANA UNIVERSITY EAST AND
IVY TECH–WHITEWATER

Indiana University East is an example of a single, and comparatively small, comprehensive rural institution that has emerged as an innovator within a loose confederation of IU regional campuses (Indiana Commission for Higher Education, 2008). While IUE is one of seven relatively autonomous IU regionals, it is co-located with the Ivy Tech–Whitewater campus, a member of the centralized and remarkably young statewide community college system. Each institution has roughly 3,000 students, and in-state tuition at Ivy Tech is about half the price of IUE. When Ivy Tech became a comprehensive community college system in 2005, regional agreements with IU were created to support collaboration (Ivy Tech Community College, n.d.). Among the regionals, IUE and Ivy Tech have developed the most creative partnerships thus far, with IUE being the first of the regional 4-year institutions to voluntarily stop providing remediation and to focus instead on its role as a site for baccalaureate degree completion. While financial pressures influence all of our cases, in IUE these pressures are acute and have played a central role.

Policy

As with any major change, the partnership between IUE and Ivy Tech–Whitewater is the product of multiple, interacting factors, including financial crisis, innovative leadership, and close proximity. State policy and developments at the state level also played a role in creating and facilitating the partnership. While IUE is one of seven loosely coordinated Indiana University comprehensives, Ivy Tech–Whitewater is one member of a highly centralized statewide community college system (the youngest in the country). Through a community donation of land, the two campuses have been co-located since the early 1970s. And, the transformation of Ivy Tech from a technical college into a comprehensive community college presented a host of challenges (and opportunities).

In 2008, following a period of declining enrollment at IUE and financial hardship that called into question the future of the institution, IUE and Ivy Tech launched a partnership that required IUE to discontinue its developmental education and associate's degree program offerings. Under this agreement, students in need of remediation, along with students seeking a 2-year degree, enrolled at Ivy Tech. Although it was no doubt a difficult decision to voluntarily deviate from their mission, the efforts were significantly eased by proximity. As a senior administrator at Ivy Tech–Whitewater said, "It's easy to get things done together when you share a parking lot."

Without belittling the contributions of institutional leadership (which we discuss below), broader policy efforts played a critical role in creating the conditions for collaboration. As former Indiana higher education commission executive Jeff Stanley explained:

> As statewide articulation came together and Ivy Tech evolved [into a comprehensive community college], we also created regional campus agreements that provided a "no harm" guarantee for the regionals, meaning they would be held harmless if they lost enrollment to Ivy Tech. This provided the cover for regionals to phase out the 2-year degrees and participate in the regional campus agreements in earnest.

In addition to these discrete policy victories, the state's sustained focus on productivity priorities is clearly a stimulus to institutional collaboration. While Indiana does not have the history of data generation and sharing that Arizona and Texas have, the Indiana Commission for Higher Education recently has been instrumental in creating strategic planning documents that outline state-level goals and metrics, generated with the support of policymakers. In addition to system policy, state policy efforts around outcomes-based funding, transfer, and core curriculum create incentives and space for collaboration and innovation on behalf of improved pathways.

Leadership

While state policy activities create conditions for creative partnerships between comprehensives and community colleges, the story of IUE and Ivy Tech–Whitewater is also one of bold leadership during times of financial crisis. President Nassar Paydar has been cited as a driving force behind the creation of the innovative partnership between IUE and Ivy Tech. IUE, for example, was the first regional to drop all of its 2-year degrees and remedial offerings and, as interim chancellor Larry Richards described the decision, "We did it on our own, and we chose to do it because we felt like we needed to." In describing Paydar's leadership, Stanley said, "It does take real leadership for someone to come in and say, 'We are no longer doing remediation, we are restructuring, we are cutting cabinet positions, we are doing a marketing campaign for traditional students.' Those are bold moves."

In conversations with us, Paydar described how the decisions he made created anxiety for staff and faculty at IUE. He focused on restructuring rather than eliminating positions and made his office and presence more visible on campus, a sign of leadership commitment. From his new, visible position he set about making difficult decisions aimed at providing real mission differentiation between IUE and Ivy Tech, and true pathways for students.

Although the state supported the changes, it was the leadership of both institutions that drove the transformation. IUE became a more traditional 4-year institution, while Ivy Tech's own evolution made it into a comprehensive community college. A shared focus on student success has made collaboration between the institutions nonthreatening and even desirable—especially considering their close proximity. The early results of this partnership are promising. A 2011 independent evaluation of the partnership found that Ivy Tech–Whitewater experienced a 71% increase in enrollment over the first 3 years of the partnership and a 54% increase in the number of graduates. During the same period, IUE's enrollment grew by 48% and its graduation rates by 23%.

Systems

Since 2008, the two institutions have put in place a number of processes and structures that allow students to flow between Ivy Tech and IUE in an efficient, nearly seamless way. Counselors and advisors work in close coordination across the institutions and participate in various formal and informal activities with one another. A joint advisor—who splits time between the institutions and maintains a highly visible position—serves as a point person to ensure students are directed to the right information. Additionally, this advisor flags transfer and articulation problems for the articulation committees to address.

Collaboration

The two institutions also have put into place a number of innovative collaborations that make the pathway to transfer seamless. IUE hosts a special orientation for transfer students that is attended by Ivy Tech advisors, provides additional financial aid for transfer students who enter with an associate's degree, and has created a "Take a Course on Us" trial offer for Ivy Tech students. Through the creation of its online BA completion programs, IUE became *the* leader within the IU system around online course offerings (offering more courses than even the flagship in Bloomington). Students receive support to help them choose a program concentration early, which puts them on a clear pathway to a degree. Similarly, the institution engages in efforts to limit the number of degree offerings and ensure that transfer students arrive with junior standing in their major.

In 2010, we spoke with transfer students who told us that before the agreement was in place, they felt uncomfortable leaving Ivy Tech for IUE. One young woman described her experience this way:

> I was intimidated walking in the door over here, even though it's just across the parking lot, because of how things used to be here. But now when I walk in [at IUE] everyone is so friendly and welcoming. . . . And there's always someone right there ready to answer my question or send me to the right person.

THE UNIVERSITY OF TEXAS EL PASO AND EL PASO COMMUNITY COLLEGE

We included UTEP because of its longevity and depth, and for the role that leadership plays in responding to El Paso's location on the border between the United States and Mexico. With between 20,000 and 30,000 students at each institution, UTEP and EPCC represent a case of creative collaboration between large urban institutions of roughly equal size. UTEP is somewhat unique because it is one of Texas' emerging research institutions, and like NAU, its geographic isolation lends itself to high levels of research. With in-state tuition under $2,000 per year, EPCC is roughly 70% cheaper than UTEP at its $7,000 annual in-state tuition rate.

Along with Ciudad Juarez in Mexico, El Paso is the second largest binational metropolitan area on the U.S.–Mexican border, with a combined population of over 2 million. Both UTEP and EPCC have enrollments over 20,000, with between 80% and 90% of those students identifying as Hispanic. With no other public higher education institutions in the area, UTEP and EPCC are each other's "only game in town." As one senior administrator from EPCC said, "Being out here in the middle of the desert means we're all necessarily connected. If we improve in one area, it affects others, and really we just have to work together."

Leadership

The story of UTEP and EPCC is one about the power of enlightened leadership to serve as a catalyst for change. By all accounts, UTEP and EPCC
did not always have a strong working relationship, and neither institution
actively owned the process of student transitions. As a senior administrator at UTEP said,

> I think it's easy for people to attribute our successes to our geographic
> conditions because it gives them a way out. They can say, "Oh, well,
> we're not isolated like El Paso and so we can't do it because we're
> different." I don't buy that. We don't have these partnerships and
> collaborations at multiple levels because of our geography; we have
> them because we choose to have them and we work to have them.
> Those kinds of agreements don't happen because of geography; they
> come from a true shared commitment to the students of this region.

Two extraordinary leaders—UTEP president Diana Natalicio and
then EPCC president Richard Rhodes—shared a mutual passion to
serve the surrounding community and to support greater student success among the Latino population. As a senior administrator at EPCC
described, "When Dr. Rhodes starting meeting with Dr. Natalicio, the
message went out that the relationships should be as collaborative as
possible, and that message filtered down in several ways and became the
way we do things here."

When we asked why Diana Natalicio and Richard Rhodes have been
such successful leaders, we heard things like, "Some presidents are 60%
focused on students, 20% focused on board management, and 20% on fund
raising, but [here] there is 100% focus on student success." UTEP Provost
Junius Gonzales described it this way: "Effective leadership is about a
shared commitment that allows each to transcend the usual institution-
specific needs of enrollment and to focus instead on a higher level commitment to raising the education level of the people of the region." For
mid-level administrators and front-line staff, the message is this: "I don't
think of this work we do as belonging to UTEP or belonging to EPCC. I
think of this as our work. We own it together, and we share in the suc-
cesses and the failures."

In cross-sector higher education partnerships, effective leaders were
described as those who articulate a lofty vision and set clear priorities
while straightforwardly acknowledging the difficulties, hard choices,
tensions, or practical constraints. They express their expectations clearly,

consistently, and in ways that resonate both with the institutional mission and the values/identity of faculty and staff. They treat institutional practitioners at all levels—whether rank-and-file faculty or front-line staff—with respect and in ways that recognize their value as committed experts. Lastly, they listen as much as they talk. As a former senior administrator from EPCC explained, "Dr. Rhodes listens so loud it's amazing."

Policy

Policy achievements of the UTEP/EPCC partnership include one of the earliest examples of a joint admissions agreement and an automatic reverse transfer agreement, which recognizes students' achievements with an associate's degree after they have transferred to a 4-year school and have accumulated the credits needed to fulfill the 2-year degree program requirements. Reverse transfer agreements also recognize the degree completion for the community college, which is significant as performance funding takes hold across the nation. This agreement has served as a model both within and beyond Texas.

Additionally, a robust Early College High School program has led to steadily increasing numbers of students who graduate from high school with their associate's degrees and with junior standing at UTEP (and who receive stop-gap aid until they become eligible for federal financial aid). Other elements contributing to the partnership's success include shared advisors who are jointly funded by both institutions; the hard-fought creation of transfer guides for a number of programs; department-level transfer and articulation workgroups that allow the institutions to hammer out agreements to ease student flow; and a number of robust formal and informal collaborations between K–12 superintendents and higher education leadership.

Systems

Employees without postsecondary credentials are most vulnerable during times of economic downturn, and having an associate's degree can make the difference between keeping and losing a job. This makes the reverse transfer process all the more valuable. Up to 2013, UTEP has awarded over 3,000 associate's degrees through its automatic reverse transfer initiative. That's 3,000 individuals in the workforce who now enjoy formal recognition of the degree they earned—but were never awarded because of failures of institutional collaboration. By the end of spring 2013 alone, UTEP expected to grant another 1,200 degrees. In addition, nearly 500 students currently are enrolled in the Early College High School (ECHS) program, and over $240,000 in stop-gap scholarships were provided to ECHS students during the 2012–2013 school year. These scholarships make it possible for students to earn an associate's degree while in high school and stay on track for a bachelor's degree even in the absence of federal financial aid eligibility.

Collaboration

This partnership exemplifies the role that top-level commitment to partnership plays in proliferating formal and informal collaborations at all levels across the two institutions. UTEP and EPCC have pooled resources to address advising needs to smooth transfer. Staff members from both institutions interact regularly in both formal and informal ways on each other's campuses, and have worked on various projects and initiatives to create seamless articulation and transfer between the institutions. While top-level leadership's commitment to working together appears to drive efforts, a hard-fought culture of collaboration appears to be part of the fabric of both institutions.

In our conversations, UTEP associate provost Donna Ekal stressed the distinction between the "nuts and bolts" aspects of the partnership (e.g., reverse transfer) and what she calls the broader "philosophical commitment" that fuels and sustains the partnership. In describing this philosophical commitment, she identified six elements, the first of which is a student-centered focus oriented by mission-driven leadership. The other elements are:

- Top-to-bottom cooperation ("You have to start with high-level commitment but then you start working wherever you are and then move out in every direction.")
- Side-to-side cooperation ("It's not enough to have one advisor represented; all of the advisors at UTEP and EPCC meet twice a year.")
- Overlapping collaboration ("I don't serve on one committee; I serve on four or five committees, and being connected to others in those different, overlapping ways helps us avoid reinventing the wheel.")
- Long-term commitment ("What we're trying to do isn't going to be accomplished in a year or two; success will take decades of commitment.")
- The inclusion of multiple perspectives ("Different populations of students, faculty, staff, administration, all these people have a perspective on a shared challenge that needs to be included for sustainable progress.")

Strong and capable leadership, emanating from the top but exercised at multiple levels, is critical for the creation and maintenance of meaningful collaborations. This is especially true when considering the countervailing incentives created by traditional funding mechanisms that are tied to enrollment rather than outcomes. Moreover, transfer policies that lack the supporting incentives and accountability are unlikely to achieve the intended aims.[4]

LESSONS

When we look across the cases, a core group of themes emerge that strike us as especially instructive for leaders interested in developing improved collaboration between regional 4-year colleges and community colleges: (1) the power and limits of policy, (2) the importance of micro-practices of collaboration, (3) the specifics of what constitutes effective leadership, and (4) the challenges around data generation and use.

Pursue Strong, Meaningful, and Realistic Policy

When improving cross-sector collaboration, state policy and system policy are critical levers. However, over-reliance on the power of policy to *make* lasting change is bound to disappoint. Policy is essential for setting priorities around things like mission differentiation and focusing attention on student success and completion; creating the infrastructure for collaboration through convening state-level committees; aligning policy with practice in ways that attend to the incentives for collaboration across sectors; and collecting data and sharing information.

But policy is unlikely to achieve its intended results unless it also is designed with implementation in mind. As Jobs for the Future executive Michael Collins said, "You really have to make sure that incentives and accountability are working together at all the different levels." When considering improved transfer pathways, he goes on to say, "it's important to distinguish between transfer policies that are intentional and have incentives, versus those that are just 'there.'" Although policy is essential to the creation of structures for formal collaboration, it is also clear from our research and experience that even the most intentional policies cannot themselves guarantee the creation of strong and efficient pathways for students. It is through alignment of policy and the specific practices of collaboration that the real work of creating strong pathways does or does not happen.

Cultivate Strong Leadership at All Levels

Strong and capable leadership of a particular kind, emanating from the top but exercised at multiple levels, is critical for the creation and maintenance of meaningful collaborations. In the monograph *Good to Great and the Social Sectors*, Jim Collins (2005) adapts his now-classic *Good to Great* argument to speak to the special challenges facing leaders in public institutions. "Level 5 leadership," the highest form of leadership in his hierarchy, is about getting things done in a diffuse and complex power structure. Level 5 leaders "build enduring greatness through a paradoxical blend of personal humility and professional will" (p. 39). But Collins is clear that Level 5 leadership is about making the right decisions "—no matter how difficult or painful—for the long-term greatness of the institution and the achievement of its mission" (p. 39).

In all of our cases, we see examples of Level 5 leadership. These leaders balance lofty vision with an honest acknowledgment of the challenges; are skillful in their approach to data; connect the dots between discrete initiatives and the core mission of the institution; articulate clear expectations in ways that resonate with the identities/values of those they depend on for implementation of innovations; and listen as much as they talk. Effective leaders keep everyone's eyes on the prize, and they do so in a way that recognizes and values the insight and expertise of institutional practitioners at all levels. They do not necessarily make popular decisions, but their decisions are transparent, thoughtful, and respectful of front-line faculty and staff. A faculty member at UTEP once said to me, "I don't agree with everything that Dr. Natalicio does, but she listens to us and she is honest about what is hard about the decisions she's making." This approach makes tough decisions conscionable, and encourages mutual respect (Kanter, 1994).

Attend to the Real, Day-to-Day Practices of Collaboration

While formal collaborations create a framework for the pursuit of shared goals, it is through informal collaborations that trust, commitment, and sense of shared purpose and efficacy around the creation of strong pathways for students are incubated. Deep, sustainable collaboration does not automatically follow from either the creation of formal structures or the adoption of policy; it is ultimately the result of changes in micro-practices (day-to-day habits, dispositions, and activities) of critical practitioners at and across every level of the institutions.

Attending to the health of the actual practices of communication and collaboration (i.e., the climate and culture of the organization) is indispensable for making and sustaining real progress in the creation of efficient pathways that save students time and money. Authentic engagement of a range of stakeholders, including students, faculty, staff, and employers, is essential for maintaining focus on the ultimate goals of improved collaboration. The most successful formal and informal leaders are those who are committed to, and skillful in, both creating a culture of inquiry around data translation/usage and practicing the principles of "early and often" when it comes to engaging critical stakeholders.

Get Serious About Data Collection, Translation, and Use

Nearly everyone we spoke with stressed that strong data systems and effective information sharing are essential for robust and scalable cross-sector collaboration on behalf of seamless pathways. Yet nearly everyone also explained that challenges abound when it comes to the ability of leaders and institutional actors at various levels to generate, access, translate, and use data and information to understand student outcomes. But being able to do so is critical, because, as Davis Jenkins at the Community College Research Center explained,

> Data showing how students actually flow through can be very powerful for changing mindsets. Even when the incentives aren't aligned, if you're able to show what's happening to students it's a powerful motivator to act because faculty and leaders care about students.

Unfortunately, in each of our cases we learned that even when a commitment to collecting good data exists, there is a general dearth of institutional and system capacity for operationalizing this commitment. And where there's will and capacity, information bottlenecks are persistent challenges for even the most sophisticated and committed proponents of evidence-informed decision making. Robust data systems within institutions, states, and systems are difficult to establish and maintain, and few incentives exist for data sharing across institutions. As one senior administrator in Texas said, "Just because data is being collected or information is being shared doesn't mean that it's getting into the right hands."

Beyond the challenges of generating and accessing good data, there are the arguably more difficult challenges around translation and actual use of data to inform decision making. Complex as it may be, data generation is largely a technical issue. But data translation and use are not primarily technical challenges; they are what Heifetz (1994) calls "adaptive" problems. While some problems have a clear fix that can be implemented by an expert, adaptive problems cannot be solved by an expert alone. These problems require changes in the way people think, work, and relate to one another. Too many naively assume, or at least act as though they believe, that clear answers will flow effortlessly from data without skillful interpretation, translation, and commitment to authentic deliberation and collaborative problem solving. But there is a high probability that data will be misunderstood, misinterpreted, or misused when databases are complex, analytic capacity is low, and presentations/conversations around data are weak.

CONCLUSION

Regional 4-year colleges may be, as Jeffrey Selingo has said, the "undistinguished middle child" of higher education, but they also have the potential and responsibility to become engines of postsecondary attainment for the majority of Americans who are not well-served by flagships and elite universities. And their very survival may depend on their ability to do so. Through our conversations with current, former, and prospective students of these institutions, it has become clear that failures of cross-sector collaboration—fueled by policy that incentivizes competition instead of mission differentiation and poor channels of communication within and across institutions—conspire to become the Bermuda Triangle of college aspirations for far too many students. If this country is to make good on its social contract in which educational attainment is the primary path to a better future, regardless of accidents of birth and fortune, identifying and systematically dismantling the obstacles to the creation of clear pathways for the "new traditional student" must become a national priority.

At present there are far more questions than answers, in part because innovation in higher education too often occurs in silos. Yet there is a great deal to be learned from the places and cases where 4-year institutions and community colleges are breaking down barriers and smoothing pathways on behalf of student success and completion. To be clear, there is no silver bullet and no simple technical fix for the multilevel challenges facing these institutions in the contemporary higher education landscape. Although we are deprived of easy answers, we have on our side three critical assets: tremendous opportunity to learn from those on the leading edge, a clear moral imperative to do so, and unprecedented cross-partisan support for the (re)imagining of a higher education system befitting the 21st century.

NOTES

1. Previous research that informed this chapter includes: Alfonso (2006); Anderson, Sun, & Alfonso (2006); Bettinger & Long (2005); Burke (2005); Burns (2010); Gross, Goldhaber, DeBurgomaster (2008); Gross & Goldhaber (2009a); Gross & Goldhaber (2009b); Hagedorn, Moon, Cypers, Maxwell, & Lester (2006); Hagedorn, Cypers, & Lester (2008); Kelly & Carey (2012); Kezar (2003, 2006); Kotter (2008); Laanan (2007); Long & Kurlaender (2009); Martinez & Smith (2012); Miller & Skinner (2012); Moore, Shulock, & Jensen (2009); Richardson, Bracco, Callan, & Finney (1998); Richardson & Martinez (2009); Roksa (2009); Roksa & Calcagno (2010); Schneider & Yin (2012); Tinto (2006); Townsend & Wilson (2006); Ullman (2011); Wellman (2002).

2. According to the NCHEMS calculations, such a reduction could bring savings equivalent to nearly 25% of the additional investment needed to help a significant majority of Americans achieve postsecondary credentials by 2025.

3. Interview subjects are listed in alphabetical order: Irma Camacho, director, Student Success, El Paso Community College; Michael Collins, associate vice president, Post-secondary State Policy, Jobs for the Future, formerly at the Texas Higher Education Coordinating Board; Patty Crawford, career/experiential learning coordinator, Indiana University East; Donna Ekal, associate provost, University of Texas at El Paso; Shirley Gilbert, special assistant, President's Office, Austin Community College; Greg Gillespie, vice president Academic and Student Affairs, Yavapai; Junius Gonzalez, provost & vice president Academic Affairs, University of Texas at El Paso; Stephanie Hawley, associate vice president, College Access Programs, Austin Community College; Fred Hurst, senior vice president, Northern Arizona University—Extended Campuses; Davis Jenkins, senior research fellow, Community College Research Center; Susan Johnstad, assistant vice president, Northern Arizona University; Karen Nicodemus, principal, KA Nicodemus Consulting Services (Arizona); Laurence "Larry" Richards, interim chancellor, Indiana University East; Gretchen Schmidt, Jobs for the Future; Chris Seger, admissions director, Ivy Tech–Whitewater; Steve Smith, vice president of instruction, El Paso Community College; Carol Spencer, executive director, Academic Program Articulation Steering Committee (APASC) in Arizona; Jeff Stanley, State Advisor—HCM Strategists and former Associate Commissioner for Policy and Planning at Indiana Commission for Higher Education; Steve Tincher, chancellor, Ivy Tech–Whitewater.

4. In Florida, community college students are incentivized to complete an associate's degree before transferring by being guaranteed junior standing at the 4-years. As a result, the number of students who transfer with an associate's degree is nearly three times the national average (Garcia Falconetti, 2009). In Texas, current transfer policy lacks the built-in incentives and accountability necessary for scalable success.

REFERENCES

Alfonso, M. (2006). The impact of community college attendance on baccalaureate attainment. *Research in Higher Education, 47*(8), 873–903.

Anderson, G., Sun, J. C., & Alfonso, M. (2006). Effectiveness of statewide articulation agreements on the probability of transfer: A preliminary policy analysis. *The Review of Higher Education, 29*(3), 261–291.

Bettinger, E. P., & Long, B. T. (2005). Remediation at the community college: Student participation and outcomes. *New Directions for Community Colleges, 129*, 17–26.

Burke, J. C. (2005). The many faces of accountability. In J. C. Burke & Associates (Eds.), *Achieving accountability in higher education: Balancing public, academic, and market demands* (pp. 1–24). San Francisco, CA: Jossey-Bass.

Burns, J. M. (2010). *Leadership.* New York, NY: HarperPerennial Modern Classics.

Collins, J. (2005). *Good to great and the social sectors.* New York, NY: HarperCollins.

Flaga, C. T. (2006). The process of transition for community college transfer students. *Community College Journal of Research and Practice, 30*(1), 3–19.

Garcia Falconetti, A. M. (2009). 2+2 statewide articulation policy, student persistence, and success in Florida universities. *Community College Journal of Research and Practice, 33*(3–4), 238–255.

Goldhaber, D., Gross, B., & DeBurgomaster, S. (2008). Community colleges and higher education: How do state transfer and articulation policies impact student pathways? CRPE Working Paper No. 2008-4. Available at www.crpe. org/sites/default/files/wp_crpe4_cc_may08_0.pdf

Gross, B., & Goldhaber, D. (2009a). Can transfer and articulation policies propel community college students to a bachelor's degree—and Is This the Only Goal? Available at www.crpe.org/sites/default/files/crpe_brief_lumina_cc_jun09_0.pdf

Gross, B., & Goldhaber, D. (2009b). Community college transfer and articulation policies: Looking beneath the surface. CRPE Working Paper No. 2009-1. Available at files.eric.ed.gov/fulltext/ED504665.pdf

Hagedorn, L. S., Cypers, S., & Lester, J. (2008). Looking in the review mirror: Factors affecting transfer for urban community college students. *Community College Journal of Research and Practice, 32*(9), 643–664.

Hagedorn, L. S., Moon, H. S., Cypers, S., Maxwell, W. E., & Lester, J. (2006). Transfer between community colleges and 4-year colleges: The all-American game. *Community College Journal of Research and Practice, 30*(3), 223–242.

Heifetz, R. A. (1994). *Leadership without easy answers.* Cambridge, MA: The Bellkap Press of Harvard University Press.

Hyman, J. S., & Jacobs, L. F. (September 16, 2009). 10 tips for transferring from community college. *US News and World Report.* Available at: http://www.usnews.com/education/blogs/professors-guide/2009/09/16/10-tips-for-transferring-from-community-college.

Indiana Commission for Higher Education. (2008). *Reaching higher with IvyTech Community College of Indiana: Focusing on the role of community colleges.* Available at www.in.gov/che/files/Community_College-7-10.pdf

IvyTech Community College. (n.d.). *Transfer and articulation in Indiana: The community college perspective.* Available at www.in.gov/che/files/Transfer_of_Credit.ppt

Kanter, R. M. (1994). Collaborative advantage: The art of alliances. *Harvard Business Review, 72*(4), 96–108.

Kelly, A. (2012). *Can our public universities still compete with rich private ones?* Available at www.aei.org/article/education/higher-education/can-our-public-universities-still-compete-w-rich-private-ones/

Kelly, A., & Carey, K. (2012). *Stretching the higher education dollar: How innovation can improve access, equity and affordability.* Cambridge, MA: Harvard Education Press.

Kezar, A. (2003). Enhancing innovative partnerships: Creating a change model for academic and student affairs collaboration. *Innovative Higher Education, 28*(2), 137–156.

Kezar, A. J. (2006). Redesigning for collaboration in learning initiatives: An examination of four highly collaborative campuses. *The Journal of Higher Education, 77*(5), 804–838.

Kotter, J. P. (2008). *Force for change: How leadership differs from management.* New York, NY: Free Press.

Laanan, F. S. (2007). Studying transfer students: Part II. Dimensions of transfer students' adjustment. *Community College Journal of Research and Practice, 31*(1), 37–59.

Long, B. T., & Kurlaender, M. (2009). Do community colleges provide a viable pathway to a baccalaureate degree? *Educational Evaluation and Policy Analysis, 31*(1), 30–53.

Lumina Foundation. (2010). *Navigating the new normal.* Available at www.luminafoundation.org/publications/Navigating_the_new_normal.pdf

Martinez, M., & Smith, B. (2012). Systems, ecosystems, and change in state public higher education. In J. E. Lane & B. D. Johnstone (Eds.), *Harnessing systemness* (pp. 169–192). Albany, NY: State University of New York Press.

Miller, E. R., & Skinner, R. A. (April 6, 2012). Presidents and boards as change agents: Essay on next generation of public comprehensive university presidents. *Inside Higher Education.* Available at: http://www.insidehighered.com/advice/2012/04/06/essay-next-generation-public-comprehensive-university-presidents.

Moore, C., Shulock, N., & Jensen, C. (2009). *Crafting a student-centered transfer process in California: Lessons from other states.* Sacramento, CA: California State University, Institute for Higher Education Leadership & Policy.

Richardson, R. C., Jr., Bracco, K. R., Callan, P. M., & Finney, J. E. (1998). *Designing state higher education systems for a new century*. Phoenix, AZ: Oryx Press.

Richardson, R. C., Jr., & Martinez, M. (2009). *Policy and performance in American higher education: An examination of cases across state systems*. Baltimore, MD: Johns Hopkins University Press.

Roksa, J. (2009). Building bridges for student success: Are higher education articulation policies effective? *Teachers College Record, 111*(10), 2444–2478.

Roksa, J., & Calcagno, J. C. (2010). Catching up in community colleges: Academic preparation and transfer to four-year institutions. *Teachers College Record, 112*(1), pp. 260–288.

Schneider, M., & Yin, L. M. (2012). Completion matters: The high cost of low community college graduation rates. Available at: www.aei.org/outlook/education/higher-education/community-colleges/completion-matters-the-high-cost-of-community-college-graduation-rates/

Tinto, V. (2006). Research and practice of student retention: What next? *Journal of College Student Retention: Research, Theory and Practice, 8*(1), 1–19.

Townsend, B. K., & Wilson, K. (2006). "A hand hold for a little bit": Factors facilitating the success of community college transfer students to a large research university. *Journal of College Student Development, 47*(4), 439–456.

Ullman, E. (2011). Higher calling. *Community College Journal, 81*(5), 38–40.

Wellman, J. V. (2002). *State policy and community college-baccalaureate transfer*. San Jose, CA: National Center for Public Policy and Higher Education.

CHAPTER 4

Efficiency in Degree Production Among Public Comprehensive Universities

William Doyle

The past few years have been difficult ones for public institutions of higher education. According to the State Higher Education Executive Officers' 2012 State Higher Education Finance report, these colleges and universities have had their state funding steadily cut since the beginning of the most recent recession. Institutions have been forced to make difficult choices regarding their overall levels of costs, labor force, enrollments, and student services.

The problem has been particularly difficult for institutions commonly known as "comprehensives"—those institutions that are mostly or entirely open access and award primarily bachelor's degrees. These institutions depend heavily on tuition and state funding, without access to either research funding or (typically) large private donations. Nationally, they award one-fourth of all bachelor's degrees in the United States, yet typically are not on the radar of the popular media or the general public. Many argue that these institutions have had to make the most difficult choices in the face of state budget cuts, since they have few options for survival except increasing tuition, cutting faculty, or cutting enrollment (Fischer, 2011).

There are two views regarding what has happened to broad-access public 4-year institutions.[1] The more common view is that public colleges and universities are being strained to the breaking point by these changes. Many argue that there is no more "fat" to trim from public college and university budgets, and that these institutions currently are operating as efficiently as they possibly can—and some have been cut so deeply that they are no longer capable of accomplishing their stated goals (Kelderman, 2011a, 2011b).

The less common view (but one that has received attention) is that public colleges and universities are operating on bloated budgets—that these institutions have long been working inefficiently, and that the budget cuts have resulted in organizations that are leaner and more efficient than they have been in the past. Advocates of this position suggest that many institutions could continue to accomplish their missions even in the face of lower levels of funding (Vedder, 2004).

At its heart, this is a debate about productivity—how much of a given good can be produced for a given level of inputs. Advocates from the first camp suggest that institutions of higher education are as productive as they can be, and that further cuts will only reduce outputs. Advocates from the second camp state that institutions of higher education could be even more productive, and that cuts in funding will not necessarily result in reduced outputs, as long as institutions stop performing unnecessary functions and inefficient practices (Kelly, 2009; Kelly & Jones, 2005).

In many enterprises, productivity is easy to define, as both outputs and inputs are relatively clear. The output for a car maker is cars, and the inputs are the component materials, the capital, and the labor required to manufacture the cars. For colleges and universities, neither the outputs nor the inputs are clear. The outputs of higher education could include degrees produced, research created, service to the community, and other, less tangible concepts. The inputs are somewhat more clear, since we need students, faculty, and money to run an institution of higher education, but reasonable people can and do disagree over the proper list of inputs into higher education. Despite these disagreements, there is currently a widespread push for greater productivity, defined loosely as doing more with less.

The contribution of this chapter is to identify what is known about the productivity of a well-defined segment of the higher education market—those public institutions whose primary role is to create bachelor's degrees for the state. I begin by discussing the key theories of higher education productivity. I then turn to challenges in measuring productivity, explaining why many commonly used measures of institutional productivity are imperfect and why productive efficiency is the right way to analyze bachelor's degree completions at these institutions. Next, I place comprehensive institutions in the context of other sectors of higher education, showing how their production of bachelor's degrees compares with the other major types of institutions in the United States. Using the concept of productive efficiency, I estimate the returns that comprehensive colleges have realized on their major inputs—students, faculty, and money. Last, I discuss some of the possible ways in which comprehensive institutions may become dramatically more productive in increasing educational attainment.

THEORIES ON HIGHER EDUCATION PRODUCTIVITY

The productivity of higher education has been a topic of debate and research for many decades. Over time, the literature has separated into three distinct camps, each theorizing on the relationship between costs and productivity in higher education. First, Baumol and Bowen's theory of "cost disease" posits that labor-intensive industries are doomed to become more expensive over time as increases in productivity in other sectors increase wages for all workers. The second theory, Howard Bowen's revenue theory of costs, states that in the absence of clear definitions of the "product" for higher education, institutions of higher education will raise all the money they can and spend all they raise. And, finally, the "arms race" theory of higher education costs, popularized by Gordon Winston, suggests that the competitive race for prestige drives higher education costs in an ever-increasing cycle.

Baumol and Bowen: Cost Disease

According to Baumol and Bowen (1965), the economy can be thought of as having two parts: a part where productivity increases and a part where productivity does not increase. In the "productivity increasing" part of the economy, the number of outputs produced for a given level of inputs increases every year. This results in both reduced unit costs and higher wages for workers. In the other part of the economy, the amount of output produced for a given level of inputs remains the same year after year. However, since individuals in the non–productivity–increasing part of the economy seek wages that are on par with those in the productivity-increasing side of the economy, wages increase for workers on this side as well. This implies that unit costs in the side without increased productivity must go up.

The implications for higher education are straightforward: Under this model, higher education cannot become more productive, since any changes to the inputs (students, faculty, and expenditures) by definition would change the product. Further, as faculty demand salaries that are on par with those they would earn in other parts of the economy, costs must go up. This theory has been termed "cost disease" since it implies that in industries such as higher education, there is no cure for increasing unit costs (Archibald & Feldman, 2010).

Bowen's Revenue Theory of Cost

Another theory of the costs of higher education comes from Howard Bowen (1980). Bowen states that for most institutions, the required cost of providing an education is however much money the institution happens to have at a given time. For an institution that is well funded, costs are higher; for an institution with little funding, costs are lower. He points to the fact that there are very large differences between institutions in the amount spent on a per-student basis, yet institutions manage somehow to provide an education for their students. For example, in the dataset I use in this chapter, the median value of expenditures per full-time equivalent (FTE) student is about $14,000, while the smallest amount is $6,500 and the largest is $32,000. Yet, the latter two institutions are functionally quite similar—public, nonselective 4-year institutions.

The revenue theory of costs is simple, but has profound implications for policy. It implies that if policymakers wish to reduce the cost of providing higher education, they must reduce the amount of revenues available to higher education.

The Arms Race in Higher Education

The final theory of increasing costs and productivity in higher education comes from Gordon Winston, among others. Winston suggests that institutions of higher education are engaged in an activity with no clear markers of quality beyond the types of inputs. Institutions are engaged in a competition with other institutions to garner better qualified students and more prestige. One insidious feature of this competition is that it is based on rankings, not on any measures of adequacy. Institutional leaders have every incentive to attempt to bring in more and better inputs—higher expenditures, more faculty, better buildings—in order to garner more prestige and recruit more highly qualified students (Winston, 2000).

Since this competition is positional, there is no logical stopping point. Proponents of this theory insist that institutions will continue to increase their costs in order to move up in the rankings—and that their competitors will do the same as well. Institutional competition takes on the same aspects as an arms race: Institutions increase their inputs (costs) simply in order to have more than their competitors, much as countries engaged in an arms race increase the size of their militaries simply because their enemies are increasing the size of their militaries.

The extent to which any of these theories applies to public 4-year, open-access institutions is unclear. Cost disease certainly could play a role in the productivity of these institutions—without ongoing changes in the underlying process of education, these institutions will produce fewer bachelor's degrees per dollar as faculty salaries and the costs of other inputs increase. The revenue theory of costs may be relevant, in that institutional education and general spending differ on a per-student basis from institution to institution, even in a sector where institutions are quite

similar. Finally, while comprehensive universities generally are not perceived to be in pursuit of prestige, a quick visit to many of the web pages
reveals that these institutions prominently place their rankings from various sources on their home pages. I would contend that the pursuit of prestige extends very far in higher education and includes these institutions as
well as their more selective peers.

Which One Is It?

The analysis in this chapter cannot resolve which of these theories is most
likely to explain the rising costs of higher education. What the analysis
will do is reveal how the basic inputs to comprehensive institutions—expenditures, faculty, students—translate to bachelor's degrees produced.
In addition, I will show how these relationships may have changed over
time, revealing whether institutions have become more or less efficient in
their use of inputs. Last, this analysis will demonstrate which key variables may increase or decrease the efficiency of public 4-year, open-access
institutions in turning their inputs into bachelor's degrees.

EFFICIENCY

All of the theories above describe why higher education may be less efficient than it could be. But when they talk about efficiency, what do they
mean? Cost per student, cost per graduate, adjusted cost per graduate, and
graduation rates—these are all common measures of efficiency that have
been used in the literature (and which I explore below). They are insufficient
when attempting to measure productive efficiency, defined as the amount
of inputs required to produce an output whereby a maximally productive
unit uses the least amount of inputs to produce a certain output amount.

One possible measure of the efficiency of institutions is *cost per student*,
which consists of all spending related to educational activities (educational and general spending) divided by the number of students in the institution. This measure has the virtue of being clear and easy to understand.
However, it has one obvious flaw: It does not reference the outcome of
higher education. Some institutions with very low costs may never graduate a single student, while others with much higher costs may graduate
a large number. While useful as the basis for an input measure, cost per
student is not a useful measure of the efficiency of institutions.

One response to the problems identified above is to measure the level of *cost per graduate produced*. This measure, like cost per student, is also
very simple. However, measuring efficiency this way also would miss

important aspects of the efficiency of institutions of higher education. The easiest way for institutions to lower the cost per graduate would be to enroll fewer students and focus on graduating those students who are most likely to succeed. For example, an institution could choose to accept only those students who transfer in with more than 100 credit hours. On a cost per graduate basis, such an institution would look quite efficient, but we would miss the overall picture of enrollment and degree production.

Another possible measure of efficiency is the *adjusted cost per graduate*. In this approach, the analyst adjusts the cost per graduate based on the characteristics of the institution. For instance, an institution that employs more full-time faculty may be more expensive, which the adjusted calculation would incorporate. This approach relies on defining a set of relationships between inputs and outputs that we assume are fixed and not subject to institutional policy. Such an approach does not allow for the possibility of improvements in efficiency, but instead assumes that current policy is the best that could possibly be achieved.

Another possible measure of the efficiency of comprehensive institutions is *graduation rates*. A basic definition of graduation rate is the percent of students who graduate within a certain amount of time. Hidden within this rather simple definition are two particularly tricky methodological issues. First, how to decide which students are included? First-time students only? Full-time students only? Second, what is an appropriate length of time? Some analysts suggest 4 years, some 6, some 8. The current federal definition of this measure is the percent of full-time, first-time students who graduate from the same institution within 6 years. For many comprehensive institutions, this definition leaves out a majority of their students, meaning that they will not count for or against the graduation rate. For instance, many students will transfer into comprehensive institutions from a community college; they will not be included in the calculation. Nor will part-time students. For this sector, such a measure leaves much to be desired.

The above definitions of productivity have, for the reasons described, obvious shortfalls. Most important, a measure of efficiency for higher education should answer the question: For a given level of inputs—expenditures, faculty, and students—what outcomes are produced? And how does this level of production compare with the best possible level of production?

To combat these shortcomings, I define the central role of comprehensive institutions as the production of bachelor's degree holders. The production process for these institutions transforms inputs—money, students, and faculty—into bachelor's degrees. A school's production process may have higher or lower degrees of efficiency. Efficiency is defined as how many bachelor's degrees are produced for a given level of inputs, relative to how many could be produced based on the performance of other institutions. This definition has many virtues when compared with the definitions above. In particular, it takes into account the multiple inputs in producing bachelor's degrees and does not assume an overall level of productivity but instead uses the data to estimate what can be done currently.

One final note about efficiency: When estimating a production function, an analyst at the same time can determine whether firms in a given sample have increasing, decreasing, or constant returns to scale. The issue of returns to scale is separate from the estimation of efficiency. If a firm has increasing returns to scale, then a proportional increase in inputs will result in a proportionally larger increase in outputs. For example, for colleges and universities in our sample, if increasing returns to scale hold, then a 1% increase in expenditures will lead to a more than 1% increase in the number of bachelor's degrees produced. Under decreasing returns to scale, a 1% increase in expenditures will lead to a less than 1% increase in bachelor's degrees produced.[2]

In this analysis I examine productivity at one type of institution: public comprehensive universities. The data is defined in this way in order to minimize one of the key problems in designing efficiency studies in higher education: joint production. In a research university, there are multiple outputs, including research, service, and teaching. Within the teaching component, outputs could include PhDs, professional degrees, master's degrees, and bachelor's degrees. Similarly for community colleges, their output could include community service, transfers, certificates, and associate's degrees (Breneman, 2001). Estimating the production process with multiple outputs can be quite difficult. In this case, the production process produces only one relevant output: bachelor's degrees.

The key inputs are defined as the total amount of education and general expenditures, the total number of full- and part-time faculty, and the total number of students. I also include variables that provide important context at the state and institutional level (the student–faculty ratio, the proportion of students attending full-time, and the share of students who are first-time students at the institutional level; and the governing board structure in the state, the proportion of students in community colleges, the total amount of state grant aid, and the level of unemployment in the state at the state level). These contextual variables have been found to play a role in the production of bachelor's degrees in other studies, and so are included here in order to accurately model the production process.

BUILDING CONTEXT: PRODUCTION OF BACHELOR'S DEGREES ACROSS SECTORS

In 1987, comprehensives accounted for 11% of institutions, while in 2009 they accounted for 12% of institutions. The biggest change in the overall number of institutions during this period comes from the decline in private not-for-profits (from 71% of all 4-year institutions to 60%, while private for-profits increased their share from 9% to 18%). Despite accounting for the largest proportion of institutions, private 4-year colleges account for only about 35% of enrollment. Comprehensive institutions consistently have accounted for about 23% of all enrollments during the time of this study, while all other public institutions account for the final 40% of enrollments. Furthermore, comprehensive institutions accounted for a steadily declining share of overall instructional expenditures, from 17% in 1987 to 14% in 2009.

Finally, comprehensive institutions consistently awarded about 24% of all bachelor's degrees during this period. Looking only at the constant proportion of degrees masks the overall increase in this number, since all other institutions were awarding more degrees as well. (This chapter's Appendix includes summary statistics for all variables in the analysis over time.) In short, although comprehensive institutions are only 11% of institutions and account for only 14% of all expenditures, they award almost a quarter of all bachelor's degrees annually. Solely in terms of their contribution to the number of bachelor's degrees, these institutions would appear to be more efficient than other institutions in their use of resources.

One question to ask before getting into the results is whether there is an easily observable deterministic relationship between spending and the number of bachelor's degrees produced. There is a modest positive relationship between spending and bachelor's degrees produced. However, there is tremendous variation in output at any given level of spending.

PRODUCTIVITY AT COMPREHENSIVE UNIVERSITIES

The comprehensive universities described in this study have one primary function: producing bachelor's degrees.[3,4] These are by definition not research universities, but they are 4-year institutions. While the dataset does include institutions that grant master's degrees, the primary focus of these institutions is (or ought to be) awarding the bachelor's degree, which limits the severity of the joint production problem.

This chapter does not take on the question of variation in quality of bachelor's degrees. Not only is this not possible given the current state of knowledge about the quality of higher education, but it also would not be worthwhile to include such measures. With the exception of a very limited subset of institutions, there is little to no knowledge about the variation in quality of degrees (to the extent that it exists) among institutions of higher education. For instance, most experts in higher education would be hard-pressed to say even in a qualitative sense what the difference is in bachelor's degrees awarded by California State University Fresno, Valdosta State University in Georgia, and Western Illinois University. It is safe to assume that most employers would know even less and would treat bachelor's degrees from these institutions as equivalent. For the purposes of this analysis, I assume that bachelor's degrees produced from these institutions are roughly equivalent.

As the results show, I find a positive and statistically significant relationship between spending, enrollment, and full-time faculty on bachelor's degree production.[5] However, increases in spending, enrollment, and faculty are not associated with returns to scale at these institutions. If there were returns to scale, it would imply that changes in inputs are proportionally related to changes in bachelor's degrees. Even though an increase in any of these inputs is associated with an increase in the number of bachelor's degrees produced, the impact is much less than a one-to-one match on a percentage basis.

First, the impact of enrollment on bachelor's degree production consistently shows decreasing returns to scale. A 1% increase in enrollment is predicted to result in a one-half percentage point increase (0.47) in the number of bachelor's degrees. Over the range of time in the dataset, the impact of enrollment on bachelor's degrees produced has gone from 0.47% to 0.61%. While this is an improvement, increasing enrollment did not lead to a concomitant increase in bachelor's degrees, a relationship that has stayed more or less stable over time.

Second, the impact of expenditures on bachelor's degrees is even weaker. The predicted impact of expenditures on bachelor's degree production is positive, with a 1% increase in expenditures predicted to increase bachelor's degrees by 0.12%. This indicates that while increased spending is predicted to increase the number of bachelor's degrees produced, the impact is quite small: It would take more than an 8% increase in expenditures to increase degree production by 1%. Over time, institutions have become somewhat less efficient in turning expenditures into bachelor's degrees—a proportional increase in funding in the beginning of the studied period was associated with larger increases in bachelor's degree production than at the end. In other words, over time, more spending at the institutional level has had a reduced impact on the number of bachelor's degrees produced.

Increasing the number of full-time faculty generally is estimated to have a positive effect on bachelor's degree production, but in this case, the estimated impact is even smaller than that for enrollment or spending, and has been declining over time. In the first year of the study, a 1% increase in full-time faculty is predicted to increase bachelor's degrees by 0.2%, while by the last year in this study a 1% increase in full-time faculty is predicted to increase bachelor's degrees by only 0.11%. While most institutions in this sector have rapidly increased their part-time faculty, these changes generally are estimated to have little to no effect on the production of bachelor's degrees.

The full-time share of student enrollment is negatively related to inefficiency, meaning that institutions that have increased the number of full-time students have become more efficient. However, estimates suggest that, for this group of institutions, an increase in the proportion of first-time students correlates to a decrease in bachelor's degree production over time.

Several state-level environmental variables show some compelling results. In particular, institutions that moved under a centralized governing board during this period saw a decrease in their inefficiency—this provides some level of support to those who argue that centralization of state-level governance of higher education improves efficiency. Institutions that have come under the jurisdiction of a statewide governing board are predicted to have become more efficient, while institutions in states where a higher percentage of students have been attending community colleges are predicted to be more inefficient. Last, neither state financial aid nor state unemployment are predicted to impact the technical efficiency of institutions.

It is worth noting that institutions in this analysis may have been subjected to severe and unexpected shocks. This could range from the devastating effects of Hurricane Katrina in gulf coast states to rapid cuts in state appropriations that some public institutions faced, particularly in the aftermath of the Great Recession. While these institutions remained in the analysis, it could be that the results for these individual institutions do not reflect their underlying productive efficiency.

The technical efficiency scores estimated from these results suggest that most institutions are operating close to the efficiency frontier as it is currently defined (see Figure 4.1, which plots the distribution of efficiency scores). According to these estimates, the median technical inefficiency is 0.95, which means that 50% of institutions are producing 95% of the possible number of bachelor's degrees given current policies and practices. In analyses not included here but available from the author, I find that these results are not sensitive to the few outliers in the study.

Figure 4.1: Distribution of Technical Efficiency Scores

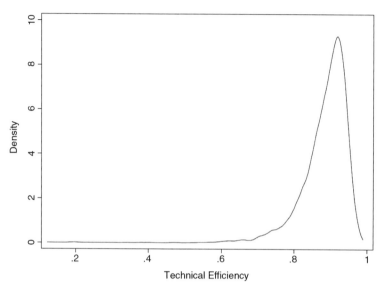

It is imperative to note that the production frontier is derived from the best possible current policies and practices. It does not show what might possibly be done under different policies and practices. Following this analysis, I discuss the implications of these results and why current policy may need to change dramatically in order to avoid major disruption in this sector.

The results provide two key insights into the relationship between inputs and outputs for institutions of higher education. First, the link between all three key inputs—student enrollment, institutional revenues, faculty—and production of bachelor's degrees has grown weaker over time. At the beginning of this study, an increase in any one of these inputs was predicted to increase bachelor's degree production at a higher rate than by the end of the study. In effect, these institutions have become less able to transform these inputs into bachelor's degrees over time. Second, despite this change, most comprehensives are operating pretty close to the most efficient colleges in the sample.

VARIATION ACROSS INDIVIDUAL INSTITUTIONS

Using the results from this study, I can provide a "score" for each institution, showing the relative distance of an institution from the sector's best performers. The best performers (as estimated by this model) will produce the most bachelor's degrees for the fewest number of students, faculty, and dollars. The worst performers will have far fewer bachelor's degrees produced at any given level of money, students, and faculty. In Table 4.1, I list the institutions in the bottom 5% of efficiency scores for 3 years: 1988, 1998, and 2008. I also list the number of bachelor's degrees produced by each institution and the total number of students enrolled for each year. Table 4.2 lists the institutions with the top 5% of efficiency scores for the same years. Across all 3 decades, institutions from a few states dominate low-performing institutions (Indiana and South Carolina) and high-performing institutions (Louisiana and Montana).

As Table 4.1 shows, in 1998, only a few of the same institutions remained low performers, including Indiana University–East and Purdue University–North Central. Institutions from Kansas, West Virginia, and Louisiana dominate the top performers in 1998, with Pittsburg State and West Liberty College remaining as top performers (Table 4.2). By 2008, the list of both high- and low-performing institutions from the perspective of technical efficiency had changed. Four institutions from Missouri are in the bottom 5%, while five institutions from Wisconsin are listed in the top 5%. The Fashion Institute of Technology, a specialized SUNY campus in New York City, went from the bottom 5% in 1998 to the top 5% in 2008. FIT produced 538 bachelor's degrees on an enrollment base of 11,611 in 1998; by 2008 FIT produced 1,196 bachelor's degrees on an enrollment base of 9,736.

These tables of high and low performers only scratch the surface of what could be done with estimated efficiency scores. Multiple analyses could be conducted to compare peer institutions within a state, region, or other grouping. Most important from my perspective would be to go inside the "black box" and better understand the types of practices used in both high- and low-performing institutions that led to their particular score.

IMPROVING EFFICIENCY: POSSIBLE POLICIES

According to the estimates produced in the previous section, most comprehensive institutions are operating quite close to the efficiency frontier as currently defined. Based on current standards and best practices, most public 4-year, broad-access institutions do not have a tremendous amount of room for improvement. This has fairly profound implications for state and federal policy. Simply asking these institutions to do more with less funding, *assuming current policies and practices*, will not result in higher levels of bachelor's degree production.

Table 4.1: Least Efficient Institutions (1988, 1998, 2008)

Institution	State	Bachelor's	Total Undergrads
Low-Performing Institutions, 1988			
California State University–Dominguez Hills	CA	658	5,472
Indiana University–Kokomo	IN	85	2,967
Indiana University–East	IN	21	1,498
Purdue University–North Central Campus	IN	83	2,810
University of Maryland–Eastern Shore	MD	106	1,248
Harris–Stowe State University	MO	57	1,603
Farmingdale State University of New York	NY	28	11,244
University of South Carolina–Aiken	SC	208	2,350
University of South Carolina–Upstate	SC	288	3,083
University of Houston–Downtown	TX	429	5,937
Tarleton State University	TX	576	4,535
Norfolk State University	VA	470	7,047
Low-Performing Institutions, 1998			
Northeastern Illinois University	IL	973	7,524
University of Southern Indiana	IN	676	7,870
Indiana University–East	IN	145	2,309
Purdue University–North Central Campus	IN	125	3,312
Massachusetts College of Liberal Arts	MA	265	1,552
Southwest Minnesota State University	MN	259	2,890
Fashion Institute of Technology	NY	538	11,611
Farmingdale State University of New York	NY	127	5,508
Lincoln University of Pennsylvania	PA	185	1,544
University of Houston–Downtown	TX	901	8,194
Lamar University	TX	903	12,910
Virginia State University	VA	430	3,288
Low-Performing Institutions, 2008			
Indiana University–South Bend	IN	554	6,440
Coppin State University	MD	293	3,242
University of Maryland–University College	MD	2,793	21,853

Table 4.1: Least Efficient Institutions (1988, 1998, 2008) [continued]

Institution	State	Bachelor's	Total Undergrads
Low-Performing Institutions, 2008			
University of Central Missouri	MO	810	8,919
Harris–Stowe State University	MO	106	1,882
Lincoln University	MO	245	2,952
Missouri Western State University	MO	587	5,301
Western New Mexico University	NM	192	2,219
SUNY Empire State College	NY	2,181	12,197
Central State University	OH	170	1,997
Langston University	OK	320	2,531
Lincoln University of Pennsylvania	PA	227	1,904
Angelo State University	TX	780	5,809

Table 4.2: Most Efficient Institutions (1988, 1998, 2008)

Institution	State	Bachelor's	Total Undergrads
High-Performing Institutions, 1988			
Pittsburg State University	KS	753	4,497
McNeese State University	LA	755	6,425
Southeastern Louisiana University	LA	885	7,367
Southern University at New Orleans	LA	254	3,231
Mississippi Valley State University	MS	283	1,848
Montana Tech of the University of Montana	MT	300	2,065
Montana State University–Northern	MT	147	1,387
The University of Montana–Western	MT	135	794
Austin Peay State University	TN	511	4,940
Concord University	WV	366	2,380
West Liberty State College	WV	380	2,450
University of Wisconsin–Stout	WI	1,220	7,069
High-Performing Institutions, 1998			
Fort Valley State University	GA	282	2,407
Emporia State University	KS	748	4,045
Fort Hays State University	KS	766	4,412
Pittsburg State University	KS	875	5,021
Southeastern Louisiana University	LA	1,362	13,571
Southern University at New Orleans	LA	480	3,726
Mississippi Valley State University	MS	285	2,121

Table 4.2: Most Efficient Institutions (1988, 1998, 2008) [continued]

Institution	State	Bachelor's	Total Undergrads
High-Performing Institutions, 1998			
Fort Valley State University	GA	282	2,407
Emporia State University	KS	748	4,045
Fort Hays State University	KS	766	4,412
Pittsburg State University	KS	875	5,021
Southeastern Louisiana University	LA	1,362	13,571
Southern University at New Orleans	LA	480	3,726
Mississippi Valley State University	MS	285	2,121
Oklahoma Panhandle State University	OK	123	1,262
Black Hills State University	SD	473	3,323
Texas A & M University at Galveston	TX	231	1,111
Marshall University	WV	1,168	11,343
West Liberty State College	WV	399	2,397
High-Performing Institutions, 2008			
California State University–San Bernardino	CA	3,779	13,559
Albany State University	GA	505	3,606
Kennesaw State University	GA	2,854	18,272
Fort Hays State University	KS	1,646	8,114
Pittsburg State University	KS	1,058	5,872
The Richard Stockton College of New Jersey	NJ	1,723	6,767
Fashion Institute of Technology	NY	1,196	9,736
Dickinson State University	ND	386	2,670
University of Wisconsin–Eau Claire	WI	1,836	10,189
University of Wisconsin–La Crosse	WI	1,523	8,547
University of Wisconsin–Stout	WI	1,451	7,551
University of Wisconsin–Superior	WI	468	2,497
University of Wisconsin–Stevens Point	WI	1,584	8,694

This means either that states and the federal government must provide more funding and assume that there are no productivity gains to be made, or that public policy must push institutions to implement new technologies and practices in order to shift the technology frontier away from the one currently dictated by common policies and procedures. It appears unlikely that states and the federal government can continue to provide more funding for higher education. This suggests that public policy must push colleges and universities to implement new practices that will re-shape the production frontier.

For comprehensive institutions to remain viable, the changes detailed here must occur—and soon. As Chapter 8 in this volume discusses, it seems that higher education as an industry is ripe for "disruption." It is worth pointing out that massive disruption occurs in industries only when that disruption threatens revenue streams (Christensen & Eyring, 2011). Right now, both states and students have been willing to pay public bachelor's institutions for their products—even in the face of ongoing tuition increases. However, the day may be coming when the current cost and price structure of these institutions proves to be unsustainable.

Comprehensive universities may seem to be the most vulnerable to disruption, and in many ways they are. However, the role of both institutional leadership and state policy will prove to be crucial—given the right actions now, these institutions may be better placed than most to survive the coming wave of disruption from new providers of postsecondary education.

The approach that I advocate in this last, more speculative section posits that the disruption of higher education will occur through the "unbundling" of many of the activities that traditionally have been tied together on campuses. Leaders of comprehensive colleges and state policymakers should take seriously the idea that the set of functions accomplished by the current structure may have to be fundamentally rethought, with some functions disappearing, others occurring in a more networked mode, and some that once may have been peripheral becoming core to the enterprise.

The key functions of a bachelor's–degree–granting institution can be summarized as follows: providing content, delivering learning, supporting learning, providing learning peers, and credentialing learning. I consider each of these in turn.

Providing Content

Providing content is the simple act of making content available to consumers. Institutions of higher education have a huge amount of content available in the form of highly educated individuals, libraries, and other resources. The lecture format is the oldest form of content provision and is still a standard mode of instruction at many of these institutions. Similarly, access to a high-quality library historically has been one of the key services offered by colleges and universities.

It is clear that content provision is no longer the domain solely of colleges and universities. Free, high-quality content spanning a range of topics has become available, with more becoming available every day. The kind of content being made freely available is most appropriate for undergraduates, which means that public bachelor's degree–granting institutions are likely to be the most threatened by the provision of this free content.

Yet only the most highly motivated individuals are likely to be able to take advantage of the high-quality content now available. The vast majority of the population seeking postsecondary education will still need many of the services that comprehensive institutions now provide. One of the key challenges will be for comprehensives to take services that now might be thought of as peripheral to their mission and make them core activities.

Delivering Learning

Delivering learning is a key—and quite separate—activity from providing content, although on many campuses and in many classrooms they are treated as one and the same thing. Providing content simply means directing students' time and attention to content and assuming they somehow will master it. Delivering learning entails using class resources to ensure that students have mastered content.

For example, many learning experts have touted the efficacy of a "flipped" classroom, whereby content is delivered asynchronously and can be accessed by students at any time, while learning activities such as completing exercises or discussion are held only during class time (Hill, Fresen, & Geng, 2012). In a flipped classroom, content is banished from a core activity to a peripheral one, while delivering learning is considered the key role of class time. Similarly, institutions may need to consider becoming "flipped" institutions, in which the provision of content is no longer considered a core activity, but time and effort are reserved for activities that enhance learning.

Supporting Learning

Learning supports denote a wide range of activities undertaken on campuses and designed to enhance student success. These can range from complex interventions such as student success courses, the design of living–learning communities, and professional development for the purposes of increasing student engagement. However, interventions also can be simpler and still effective. In a randomized trial, Bettinger and Baker (2011) found that students who are contacted by a learning coach are more likely to persist and succeed than students who do not receive this intervention. Learning coaches in this study provided students with needed assistance on overcoming real-life barriers such as difficulties with work or transportation and on developing strategies for success. Bettinger and Baker find that this intervention is more cost-effective than other interventions, including student financial aid and incentives for student performance.

Unfortunately, leaders and faculty in many comprehensive institutions still view learning support, such as a learning coach, as a peripheral activity. As I suggest in this section, supporting learning as opposed to simply delivering content should become a core activity of these institutions.

Providing Peer Groups

A key role for many comprehensive institutions is the provision of a group of peers from whom students can receive support and additional learning. It is difficult to see how a student taking advantage of online content could realize the same level of learning as a student interacting with peers in a physical setting. In a randomized study involving community college students, MDRC found that students who are engaged in a learning community are more likely to persist and succeed, at least initially (Scrivener & Coghlan, 2011).

Some comprehensive institutions take their role in developing peer groups and learning communities quite seriously, while others do little or nothing in this area. In the near future, many students may discover that they can easily obtain good content, but finding good learning partners will be difficult. Comprehensive institutions should position themselves to be sites of learning where peer groups and learning communities can easily form.

Assessing Learning

A substantial amount of time and resources on every campus are expended on ensuring that students have learned. Most of this effort is done locally, by individual faculty members in individual classes through homework, quizzes, final exams, and papers. Little of it is systematic, although many individual campuses have made great strides in assessing what students know and are able to do.

As content becomes more widely available, many online providers also will offer assessments of student learning. Yet the need will persist for high-quality and respected assessments of student learning that go beyond simple tests taken on a computer. The role of assessment on college campuses has been taken to be something that most naturally occurs on a course-by-course basis, but institutional leaders and policymakers should begin thinking about how to deploy faculty to assess learning that is taking place both on and off campus. This ability to provide assessments of value to both students and prospective employers may prove to be a key "niche" for these institutions, yet it is currently underdeveloped (Brown & Knight, 2012).

Credentialing

Accredited colleges and universities are the only organizations that can provide students with recognized credentials for learning. For institutions in this volume, the bachelor's degree is posited as the key "product" delivered by comprehensive institutions.

While much may change in the near future, it is unlikely that either the payoff for a credential or the current structure for providing credentials will disappear. Yet, comprehensive institutions must begin thinking differently about their role in providing credentials. Instead of assuming that their role is to provide all of the content and learning environments (i.e., classes) necessary to achieve a given credential, these institutions may need to begin thinking of themselves as sites that offer students high-quality assessment and credentialing for competency-based learning conducted outside of the traditional learning environment. Credentialing may no longer be the responsibility solely of traditional accredited institutions. Nontraditional providers such as Coursera are already beginning to offer credentials, while other alternative providers are working with existing institutions to jointly provide credentials.

The model of Western Governors University (WGU) is an example of this kind of thinking. At WGU, students are provided with a list of online courses that they can take to prepare for a given assessment, but WGU does not provide courses. Instead, it assesses what students know and are able to do, and credentials those students who have completed assessments required to attain a degree (Johnstone & Krauth, 1996).

Comprehensive institutions can go beyond the WGU model by becoming sites where in-person, high-quality assessment of learning that leads to specific credentials can occur, in concert with the kind of delivery, support, and peer group structuring described above. Credentialing should rely on the kind of high-quality assessment learning available on these campuses, yet institutional leaders should not assume that the learning that they assess must happen on their own campus.

From State Systems to State Networks

Earlier, I mentioned the increased efficiency realized by those comprehensive universities that came under a centralized governing board during the time of the study. The rationale for—and implications of—this increased efficiency merit exploration. State policymakers may have to go much further in centralizing institutions of higher education in the future. In the 1950s and 1960s, fundamental shifts in higher education led state leaders to form the first state systems of higher education (Glenny, 1959). It may now be time to begin forming state networks of higher education.

In a state network of higher education, responsibility for the creation of content for students would be distributed across multiple campuses. For instance, in any given state, course design for nursing might be the responsibility solely of a single campus. Yet, this course would be delivered at all campuses in the network, with student learning supports, peer groups, assessment, and credentialing available on each campus. This would share much in common with the design of public television or public radio, where only a few programs are produced at a given station, but programs are shared widely through the network of stations.

A majority of postsecondary students enroll at campuses within 20 miles of their home. In the past, this limited many students to the offerings available at their local institution—which in many cases was a comprehensive. Using a model such as the one proposed here, students would benefit by having wider access to curriculum and learning opportunities, while still being able to stay close to home. These institutions could use such a system to leverage their already high levels of service to local markets.

CONCLUSION

The model of productive efficiency in this chapter shows that business-as-usual is quite similar across institutions in this sector. This is both good and bad news for these institutions. While most institutions are doing about as well as could be expected given the current technologies, it also leaves the field without models of highly productive outliers. It remains to be seen whether models of exceptional productivity within the comprehensive sector will be generated from within the field or imposed by outside actors or forces.

It seems quite likely that comprehensive institutions will see significant disruption of their fundamental model of production over the next decades. The question is whether this disruption will come as the unwelcome result of outside technological changes or the deliberate outcome of changes in state and institutional policies that lead to a fundamental change in the production of learning.

APPENDIX

These data have important limitations. First, as noted earlier in the chapter, there may be variations in quality of bachelor's degrees produced (although I am quite skeptical on this point, at least from the perspective of the labor market). Second, the data do not include some possibly important measures of inputs, and in particular do not include measures of peer effects, which are difficult to measure accurately. The components of the formula used to study these data are as follows (Appendix Table 4.1):

- *Dependent Variable:* The number of bachelor's degrees produced by an institution in a given year
- *Input Variables.* Education and general expenditures, the total number of undergraduate students, the total number of full-time faculty, and the total number of part-time faculty
- *Institution-Level Environment Variables.* Student–faculty ratio, the share of enrollment that is full-time, the share of students who are first time
- *State-Level Environment Variables.* A dummy variable for whether or not the institution is under the control of a centralized governing board, the percent of all students in the state who are enrolled in community colleges, the total amount of state grant aid (need- and non–need–based) per student, and state-level unemployment

Theory and Model Specification

I begin with a description of the equation that I use to measure efficiency.

$$y_{it} = \beta_0 + \sum_{k=1}^{k} \beta_k lnx_{k,it} + \nu_{it} + \mu_{it}$$

In the equation, y_{it} represents the number of bachelor's degrees produced by institution i in year t, while x represents the inputs to institution i. For every institution, there are two additional unobserved components that can affect y. The first is a random error term denoted ν_{it} in the equation. This can be thought of as any random, unobserved shock that an institution may encounter. Some institutions in some years may produce fewer bachelor's degrees due to the family circumstances of students or other circumstances well beyond the control of the institution.

The second component that could affect y is μ_{it}, which is a non-negative inefficiency term. This is assumed to be distributed half-normal. This part of the error term is conceptualized as factors that are within an institution's control that may make it more or less efficient in the production of bachelor's degrees. One simplified example would be to consider two institutions, both of which have the same level of expenditures, the same number of faculty, and the same number of students. If both are operating on the production frontier, they will have the same number of graduates.

Appendix Table 4.1: Means and Standard Deviations for Data in Analysis, Selected Years

	1990	1995	2000	2005	2009
Enrollment	5001.4	5330.7	5335.3	6107.6	7075.7
	(6552.6)	(7722.3)	(7077.6)	(8044.5)	(10097.2)
E&G expend	46469676.2	62730361.5	78416288.7	92798983.3	130895158.8
	(84358090.6)	(129165544.7)	(134254273.0)	(163851147.8)	(248356392.4)
FT faculty	297.6	287.9	300.0	314.8	371.7
	(451.5)	(335.4)	(374.5)	(434.9)	(515.3)
PT faculty	92	145.0	180.9	200.8	275.1
	(151.3)	(457.7)	(573.7)	(517.5)	(695.0)
Student–faculty ratio (100s)	0.176	0.172	0.150	0.152	0.137
	(0.0490)	(0.0485)	(0.0407)	(0.0516)	(0.0549)
FT share of enrollment	0.747	0.745	0.768	0.788	0.790
	(0.152)	(0.145)	(0.133)	(0.125)	(0.132)
Share of faculty FT	0.754	0.702	0.662	0.622	0.570
	(0.190)	(0.190)	(0.185)	(0.162)	(0.143)
Share of students first time	0.184	0.160	0.179	0.175	0.179
	(0.0562)	(0.0481)	(0.0577)	(0.0438)	(0.0454)
Centralized governing board	0.277	0.246	0.223	0.223	0.226
	(0.448)	(0.432)	(0.417)	(0.417)	(0.419)
Percent of state enrollment in CC	0.383	0.408	0.409	0.424	0.430
	(0.142)	(0.146)	(0.140)	(0.125)	(0.120)
State financial aid/student (10,000s)	0.0701	0.0944	0.181	0.205	0.245
	(0.101)	(0.117)	(0.164)	(0.214)	(0.250)
State unemployment	0.0537	0.0589	0.0413	0.0540	0.0561
	(0.0125)	(0.0130)	(0.00927)	(0.00790)	(0.0110)
N	271	248	273	269	217

However, as one or both engage in activities that may make them less efficient, they will deviate from the production frontier, resulting in fewer graduates (even though the inputs have remained the same). This deviation from the production frontier is captured by the term mu_{it}. A transformation of the term in the form $E[exp(-\mu_{it})]$ is what is known as the efficiency score. This score represents the proportion of the total possible output represented by y_{it}. The technical efficiency score reports the ratio of the total number of bachelor's degrees produced by each institution in each year to the total number of possible degrees that could have been produced by that institution given its inputs.

Estimation

There are multiple approaches to estimating technical efficiency. For the purposes of brevity I report on the model with the best fit to the data (Appendix Table 4.2). Results of standard fixed effects models and an alternative specification of the stochastic frontier analysis are available from the author upon request. The following model is used to estimate the production of bachelor's degrees for a given institution:

$$y_{it} = \beta_o + \beta_1 x_{1it} + \beta_2 x_{1it} + \beta_3 x_{1it} + \beta_4 x_{1it}$$
$$+ \beta_5 t + \beta_6 (x_{1it} \times t) + \beta_7 (x_{2it} \times t) + \beta_8 (x_{3it} \times t) + \beta_9 (x_{4it} \times t)$$
$$+ \alpha_i + \nu_{it} + \mu_{it}$$

$$Var(\mu_{it}) = \gamma_1 z_{1it} + \gamma_2 z_{2it} + \gamma_3 z_{3it} + \gamma_4 z_{4it} + \gamma_5 z_{5it}$$
$$+ \gamma_6 z_{6it} + \gamma_7 z_{7it} + \gamma_8 z_{8it} + \eta_{it}$$

Where the key inputs are defined as follows:

y_{it} is the log of the number of bachelor's degrees produced by institution i in year t
x_{1it} is the log of total undergraduate enrollment
x_{2it} is the log of education and general expenditures
x_{3it} is the log of the total number of full-time faculty
x_{4it} is the log of the total number of part-time faculty

In addition, I include several variables that may affect the efficiency with which an institution can accomplish this goal. In this model, the environmental variables z affect the level of inefficiency μ_{it} effectively helping to determine how inefficient a given institution is in its use of resources.

z_{1it} is the student–faculty ratio
z_{2it} is the share of students attending the institution full-time

Appendix Table 4.2: Results from Stochastic Frontier Models: How Technology Affects Inefficiency. Dependent Variable = Log (ln) of Bachelor's Degrees

	(1)	(2)	(3)
Frontier			
ln Enrollment	0.50***	0.60***	0.47***
	(0.02)	(0.02)	(0.02)
ln E&G eExpend	0.12***	0.17***	0.12***
	(0.02)	(0.02)	(0.02)
ln FT faculty	0.17***	0.03	0.20***
	(0.02)	(0.02)	(0.02)
ln PT faculty	0.01***	0.00	0.02***
	(0.00)	(0.00)	(0.00)
Time	0.02	4.09***	−0.04
	(0.61)	(0.68)	(0.62)
ln Expend x time	−0.17*	−0.52***	−0.17*
	(0.08)	(0.09)	(0.08)
ln Enroll x time	0.56***	0.30*	0.63***
	(0.12)	(0.14)	(0.12)
ln FT fac x time	−0.31*	0.09	−0.38**
	(0.12)	(0.14)	(0.13)
ln PT fac x time	−0.12***	−0.03	−0.15***
	(0.03)	(0.03)	(0.02)
Factors Affecting Inefficiency			
Student–faculty ratio	−5.65***	−654.19	−8.50***
	(1.48)	(.)	(1.95)
FT share of enrollment	−9.89***	−880.18	−12.99***
	(0.53)	(.)	(0.78)
Share of faculty FT	1.33***	−18766.50	2.26***
	(0.38)	(.)	(0.48)
Share of students first time	22.95***	−6570.19	30.79***
	(1.13)	(.)	(1.59)
Centralized governing board		85.06	−1.15***
		(.)	(0.19)
Percent of state enrollment in CC		−239.70	5.38***
		(.)	(0.63)
State financial aid/student		−81766.91	−9.92
		(.)	(7.98)

Appendix Table 4.2: Results from Stochastic Frontier Models: How Technology Affects Inefficiency. Dependent Variable = Log (ln) of Bachelor's Degrees (continued)

	(1)	(2)	(3)
Factors Affecting Inefficiency			
State unemployment			−3.39
			(3.12)
Constant	−0.89**	−113.06	−2.34***
	(0.32)	(.)	(0.45)
Constant for Efficiency Equation			
Constant	−4.98***	−4.11***	-4.84***
	(0.04)	(0.02)	(0.04)
Log likelihood	4253.52	3439.63	4333.97
K	296	299	300
No institutions	281	281	281
N	5,422	5,422	5,422

*Notes: ***$p < .001$, **$p < .01$, *$p < .05$.*

z_{3it} is the share of faculty who are full-time

z_{4it} is the share of students who are first-time students—this is a measure of the campuses' reliance on transfer versus starting students

z_{5it} is a dummy variable for whether or not the institution's state has a centralized governing board

z_{6it} represents the proportion of state enrollment that is in community colleges

z_{7it} is the amount of state financial aid (need- and non–need–based) in the state on a per-student basis

z_{8it} is the level of unemployment in the state

Last, α_i is an institution-specific parameter, controlling for each institution in the model. This is known as a fixed effect and controls for every time-invariant characteristic of the institution. Examples of time-invariant institutional features incorporated into this fixed effect include whether the institution is in a certain region of the country and whether it was once a normal school.

I also assume that the error terms are serially correlated and follow an $AR(1)$ pattern. The data is transformed to account for this serial correlation in the residuals.

The interpretation of results from the fixed effects models (as with the other models estimated) has to do only with within-institution changes.

For any coefficient, the correct interpretation is that the dependent variable is predicted to change by a certain amount for a one-unit change in the independent variable within a given institution.

NOTES

1. I use the terms *broad access public 4-year institutions* and *comprehensives* interchangeably throughout this chapter.

2. Returns to scale are a separate concept from economies of scale. Economies of scale refer only to the costs to an organization of providing an output, not the relationship between changes in inputs and changes in outputs. A firm may be in a position to have economies of scale in that it would be cheaper to make more of an output if volume is higher, and yet not have increasing returns to scale because each percentage point increase in inputs does not lead to a more than one percentage point increase in outputs.

3. The criteria for inclusion in the dataset are that the institution must be a public 4-year institution, classified by the Carnegie Corporation as either a public bachelor's–degree–granting or a public master's–degree–granting institution. Flagship institutions are excluded from this group, as are all research institutions. I include only those institutions that are located in a state, leaving out all institutions located in districts or territories. In addition, specialized institutions such as military academies and maritime academies are excluded from the dataset. Military academies include the U.S. Service Academies and the Citadel. Maritime academies include the California, Massachusetts SUNY, and Maine Maritime Academies. Included institutions must have been awarding bachelor's degrees over the entire time period of the study, from 1987 to 2009. This leaves 280 public 4-year institutions, which account for 12% of all public 4-year institutions in the United States, 40% of all public 4-year enrollment, and approximately 24% of all student enrollment.

4. The data in this study are drawn from the Delta Cost Project dataset—which tabulates data from the U.S. Department of Education's Integrated Postsecondary Education Data System—as well as the author's tabulations of state-level variables (Delta Cost Project, 2010; U.S. Department of Education, National Center for Education Statistics, 2013).

5. Results from alternative estimation techniques are also available on the project website.

REFERENCES

Archibald, R. B., & Feldman, D. H. (2010). *Why does college cost so much?* New York, NY: Oxford University Press.

Baumol, W. J., & Bowen, W. G. (1965). On the performing arts: The anatomy of their economic problems. *The American Economic Review, 55*(1/2), 495–502.

Bettinger, E., & Baker, R. (2011). *The effects of student coaching in college: An evaluation of a randomized experiment in student mentoring* (Working Paper No. 16881). Cambridge, MA: National Bureau of Economic Research. Available at ed.stanford.edu/sites/default/files/bettinger_baker_030711.pdf

Bowen, H. R. (1980). *The costs of higher education: How much do colleges and universities spend per student and how much should they spend?* San Francisco, CA: Jossey-Bass.

Breneman, D. W. (2001). An essay on college costs. In A. F. Cunningham, J. V. Wellman, M. E. Clinedinst, J. P. Merisotis, & C. D. Carroll (Eds.), *Studies of college costs and prices 1988–89 to 1997–98* (Vol. 2, pp. 13–20). Washington, DC: National Center for Education Statistics, U.S. Department of Education.

Brown, S., & Knight, P. (2012). *Assessing learners in higher education.* New York, NY: Psychology Press.

Christensen, C. M., & Eyring, H. J. (2011). *The innovative university: Changing the DNA of higher education from the inside out.* San Francisco, CA: Jossey-Bass.

Delta Cost Project. (2010). *Who pays for higher education? Changing patterns in cost, price, and subsidies.* Washington, DC: Delta Cost Project.

Fischer, K. (November 14, 2011). Public-university leaders plan for more hard times ahead. *The Chronicle of Higher Education.* Available at: http://chronicle.com/article/Public-University-Leaders-Plan/129786/

Glenny, L. A. (1959). *Autonomy of public colleges: The challenge of coordination.* New York, NY: McGraw-Hill.

Hill, R. K., Fresen, J. W., & Geng, F. (2012). Derivation of electronic course templates for use in higher education. *Research in Learning Technology, 20,* 1–18.

Johnstone, S. M., & Krauth, B. (1996). Balancing quality and access: Some principles of good practice for the virtual university. *Change: The Magazine of Higher Learning, 28*(2), 38–41.

Kelderman, E. (2011a, January). Colleges to confront deep cutbacks. *The Chronicle of Higher Education.* Available at http://chronicle.com/article/Colleges-to-Confront-Deep/125782/?sid=at

Kelderman, E. (2011b, October). A regional public university scales back its research ambitions. *The Chronicle of Higher Education.* Available at http://chronicle.com/article/Regional-Public-Universities/129570/

Kelly, P. J. (2009). *The dreaded "p" word: An examination of productivity in public postsecondary education.* Delta Cost Project, white paper series. Washington, DC. Available at http://files.eric.ed.gov/fulltext/ED536705.pdf

Kelly, P. J., & Jones, D. P. (2005). *A new look at the institutional component of higher education finance: A guide for evaluating performance relative to financial resources.* Boulder, CO: National Center for Higher Education Management Systems.

Scrivener, S., & Coghlan, E. (2011). *Opening doors to student success: A synthesis of findings from an evaluation at six community colleges.* Social Science Research Network eLibrary.

State Higher Education Executive Officers. (2012). *State higher education finance FY2011*. Boulder, CO: Author.

U.S. Department of Education, National Center for Education Statistics. (2012). *Integrated postsecondary education data system (IPEDS)*. Available at nces. ed.gov/ipeds/datacenter/Default.aspx

Vedder, R. K. (2004). *Going broke by degree: Why college costs too much*. Washington, DC: American Enterprise Institute.

Winston, G. (2000). *The positional arms race in higher education* (Working Paper No. 54). Williamstown, MA: Williams College.

CHAPTER 5

Rethinking Student Outcomes

Constructing Predicted and Adjusted Graduation and Retention Rates for Comprehensive Universities

Michelle Lu Yin

"It is time to stop subsidizing schools that are not producing good results, and reward schools that deliver for American students and our future," President Barack Obama said to a crowded audience at SUNY Buffalo in August 2013 (White House, Office of the Press Secretary, 2013). This call for accountability in higher education—one of many in the President's tenure—followed on the heels of his proposed ratings system, a system that he believes will help students better gauge which colleges and universities serve students well, and which ones do not. College graduation and retention rates are basic consumer facts that would-be students and their families should know when selecting schools. But too few students know—or consider—these measures when choosing where to enroll for their undergraduate education. When students and families have this information, they make better decisions. In one study, the authors found that informing parents of nearby universities' graduation rates increased the probability that they would choose the institution with the better graduation rate by roughly 15 percentage points (Kelly & Schneider, 2011). With the rising call for accountability in higher education, coupled with states' recent disinvestment in higher education appropriations, institutions are under greater pressure to improve their academic performance. Otherwise, they risk monetary sanctions or decreased student demand, both of which ultimately could force them to shutter their doors.

Historically, institutions have relied on two relatively straightforward metrics to demonstrate overall student performance: graduation rates and retention rates. The "Student Right to Know" graduation rate, which is available through the Integrated Postsecondary Education Data System (IPEDS), is the most frequently referenced calculation.[1] Because institutions are required to report it, the definition and data availability remain generally consistent across all institutions and all sectors. This graduation rate for 4-year institutions is the percentage of students in a cohort who complete within 150% of normal time (6 years) regardless of the composition of the student body (with some allowable exclusions, such as transfer students) (U.S. Department of Education, National Center for Education Statistics, 2013). Schools also are required to report their retention rates, or the proportion of first-time students from the previous year who return the next year (U.S. Department of Education, National Center for Education Statistics, 2013). As with graduation rates, this performance metric signals institutional quality to prospective students. Low retention rates could indicate a lack of institutional investment in support services such as academic tutoring or mentorship.

This baseline approach of calculating graduation rates and retention rates offers an easy point of comparison. For example, College X retains 91% of students and ultimately graduates 80% of students, while College Y retains only 60% and graduates only 40% of its students. The value proposition should be relatively clear to the prospective student: College X is a better investment than College Y. But where this approach falls short is in its disregard for institutional characteristics that could impact the overall success of enrolled students. In other words, it provides little in the way of comparing institutions based on the characteristics of the students they enroll or, more broadly, institutional characteristics that vary across schools (such as instructional expenditures or geographic location).

Academic research provides strong evidence that graduation and retention rates are highly correlated with student and school characteristics (Grayson, 1995; Horn, 2006). A recent study by Morrison (2012) found that "key institutional variables that appear to have the largest effect on graduation outcomes include percent of Pell recipients, private college status, and institutional average SAT scores." In other words, the campuses that have opened their doors the widest to serve traditionally under-represented students—that have risen to the challenge of improving college access—will likely perform poorly compared with their more selective peers.

Public comprehensive universities, the nation's 4-year nonresearch institutions, struggle with this exact problem. For years, these largely open-access institutions have been compared with the most selective public 4-year research and private not-for-profit institutions on performance measures. As the calls for accountability grow louder, it is these 4-year institutions that will face the steepest challenge or, if they cannot succeed, suffer the greatest consequences.

Consider this: According to the most recent data from IPEDS, about 24% of public comprehensive universities employ an open admissions policy, which is to say they accept any student who applies. In contrast, only 5% of public 4-year research universities do so. Of those students at public comprehensive universities, over 47% received a Pell grant in 2011. At public 4-year research universities, 35% did. Numerous studies have all found that the proportion of the student body receiving a Pell grant is negatively correlated with the institution's graduation rate. If this is in fact the case, and one campus has a significantly higher proportion of Pell recipients, then it behooves common performance metrics to reflect this variance in student characteristics.

As public interest in institutional accountability continues to grow, the secondary question should focus on whether current official performance measures are appropriate or, more important, adequate. Educating students and helping them complete their degrees is more or less challenging, depending on the characteristics of the entering student body. In some ways, these metrics hardly measure actual likelihood of graduation at all, a point that one academic with years of experience on the topic is quick to highlight:

> Open-enrollment colleges enrolling low-income, first-generation (in college) students with weak academic skills may have profound positive effects on their students yet still have what appear to be low completion rates. Selective colleges populated by well-off students do not have to do much with their students to enjoy strong performance metrics. Comparing the raw graduation rates (or almost any outcome measure) for these two types of colleges makes little sense. (Bailey, 2012)

Calculating graduation and retention rates that fail to account for the academic preparation of the students who arrive on campus all but ensures that these metrics do a better job of reporting the characteristics of the incoming class than the value added by the institution while the students are enrolled.

Which brings the conversation back to President Obama's August 2013 speech, wherein he proposed a new—and many would say radical—way to improve accountability in higher education. His proposal would create a new system that rates colleges based on measures of access, affordability, and student outcomes, and ultimately could allocate federal financial aid based on those ratings. The rating score card, to be launched for the 2015 school year, is expected to include measures such as the percentage of low-income students receiving federal Pell grants, average tuition and student debt, and graduation and transfer rates. It is reassuring to know that the new rating system will consider student financial needs measured by percent of Pell recipients and cost of education. But does it go far enough? A direct comparison of student outcomes across schools without regard for their student body composition and school policies might not result in a fair rating. This is the purpose of the research presented here.

In this chapter, I illustrate how differences in the composition of the student body and certain institutional characteristics might affect graduation and retention rates. I focus on the effects at comprehensive universities, institutions that historically fall into the category of public 4-year nonresearch universities.[2] Because of their open-access mission and the differences in their student profiles, they face a set of challenges that distinguishes them from their more selective and wealthier public research and private not-for-profit peers. Using a "one-size-fits-all" approach when comparing student outcomes between these schools and schools in other sectors neglects the challenges that comprehensive universities face as they seek to educate a less academically prepared and more at-risk student population.

Ultimately, the findings highlight the considerable extent to which institutional characteristics matter when calculating graduation and retention rates. The findings also reinforce the importance of developing a range of measures that encompass institutional characteristics—not just simply the government-mandated ones—when assessing school performance.

THE RELATIONSHIP BETWEEN INSTITUTIONAL CHARACTERISTICS AND STUDENT OUTCOMES

The desire to isolate the impact that various characteristics have on student outcomes has long been at the center of higher education research. Prior studies can be divided into two categories: how student composition affects performance, and how institutional policies affect graduation and retention rates. Research within the first category shows, rather consistently, that student characteristics are significantly related to student outcomes. For instance, colleges tend to report higher graduation rates when their student body is more female, has more full-time students, has a higher average SAT score, and has a higher average family income (Pascarella & Terenzini, 1991), while those with many part-time students have lower graduation rates (Mortenson, 1997; Porter, 2000). In a related study, Goenner and Snaith (2004) found a number of factors associated with lower institutional graduation rates: a high percentage of Native American students, a high percentage of male students, degree of urbanicity, and an older student body.

The second category of studies focuses on whether—and how—institutional policies and financial allocations affect student performance.

Astin, Tsui, and Avalos (1996) found that more selective institutions, measured by admission rate, tend to have higher graduation rates because they tend to enroll better prepared students. On the same note, Goenner and Snaith (2004) found that students' average GPA and SAT scores, which indicate the selectivity of an institution, are both positively related to graduation rates.

Instructional and academic support expenditures also have positive and significant effects on cohort graduation rates (Astin, 1993; Ryan, 2004; Scott, Bailey, & Kienzl, 2006), while expenditures on student services and expenditures on administrative (institutional) support failed to produce any significant impact on graduation rates (Ryan, 2004). William Doyle (Chapter 4, this volume) also considers this question from the perspective of the efficiency of degree production. He concludes that given the current circumstances, most comprehensive institutions are about as productive as they can be.

In a more relevant study, Bailey et al. (2005) developed a model that can be used to adjust community colleges' observed graduation rates based on institutional characteristics. The authors confirmed several hypotheses about institutional determinants of graduation rates at community colleges. They found a consistent negative relationship between enrollment size and completion. Additionally, community colleges with high shares of minority students, part-time students, and female students had lower graduation rates. Finally, greater instructional expenditures were related to a greater likelihood of graduation. A more recent report from the UCLA Higher Education Research Institute attempted to construct predicted graduation rates for 4-year institutions based on student body composition variables, student average high school grades, and SAT composite scores (DeAngelo, Franke, Hurtado, Pryor, & Tran, 2011). Although the study provides further evidence of the importance of taking into account certain institutional characteristics in evaluating institution effectiveness, it omits a few crucial factors that might have altered the results, such as percentage of students who received Pell grants.

Most of the aforementioned studies focus on evaluating factors that might affect graduation or retention rates, but only a few attempt to reexamine school performance by constructing predicted and adjusted performance rates. In addition, of those studies that look at 4-year institutions, none examines how relationships between outcomes and institutional characteristics vary across institutions within a given sector. What performance rates are appropriate for cross-school comparisons? Is the effect of instructional expenditures on graduation rate the same for comprehensive universities and private not-for-profit universities? Does the percent of Pell grant recipients matter as much to performance at comprehensive universities as it does to performance at public research universities? And, moreover, should we expect that the effect of student characteristics is the same across *all* universities? That is, should we use the same relationships to predict graduation and retention rates for comprehensive universities and private universities?

To answer questions like these, the chapter builds upon prior knowledge that certain institutional characteristics are significantly related to student outcomes, then goes one step further to construct both predicted and adjusted performance rates across sectors. To test potential differential effects of institutional characteristics on student outcomes, I also construct corresponding predicted and adjusted performance rates at the institutional level, isolating those comprehensive universities that perform better and worse than expected.

CALCULATING PREDICTED AND ADJUSTED RATES

Calculating predicted and adjusted graduation and retention rates requires first estimating the effects of certain characteristics on performance measures. To do so, I estimate the relationship between graduation rates and retention rates (the outcome variables) and the relevant student and institutional characteristics (the control variables) using a state fixed-effects (FE) model. Using the results of this regression analysis, I then construct predicted and adjusted full-time retention rates and graduation rates at both the sector level and for individual comprehensive universities (see Figure 5.1). The state FE model analysis captures whether an institution's performance measures are influenced by "unobserved" state-level factors that may vary from state to state, but are constant across schools within each state.

Predicted rates can be interpreted as the *expected graduation and retention rates given the school's own characteristics*. These are essentially estimates of how well a school—or group of schools—is expected to do based on the students it serves. To better understand which schools are exceeding expectations and which schools are failing to meet expectations, I then compare these predicted rates with the observed rates. The formula used to calculate the predicted rate is shown in this chapter's Appendix. The full results of the analysis are available in Appendix Tables 5.1–5.3.

Predicted rates provide crucial information for consumers who are choosing among multiple schools. An institution that is highly successful in retaining and graduating its students is expected to have observed rates that are higher than the predicted rates. In other words, based on the students they are serving, these schools retain or graduate *more*

Figure 5.1: Ratings at a Glance

Observed Rate: How well an institution does. For example, six out of every 10 first-time, full-time students at College X graduate within 6 years of entering (or within 150% of the time it takes to complete a 4-year degree). Institutions are required to report their observed graduation and retention rates.

Predicted Rate: How well an institution is expected to do, given the students it serves. For example, 50% of the students at College X are Pell grant recipients. The proportion of students who receive a Pell grant is negatively correlated with an institution's graduation rate. This is reflected in the institution's *predicted* graduation rate, which is only 40%. Because the institution's observed graduation rate (60%) is better than its predicted graduation rate, the institution is performing better than expected given the students it serves.

Adjusted Rate: How well an institution does, given the students it serves and relative to all other institutions. For example, 50% of the students at College X are Pell grant recipients, compared with an average of 30% across all other institutions. Given that College X serves more Pell grant students than the average institution, its observed graduation rate of 60% is increased to an adjusted graduation rate of 70%. This would likely put College X ahead of other institutions that have higher observed graduation rates but serve fewer Pell grant students.[3]

students than the model predicts, which shows up as a positive difference between the observed rate and the predicted rate. In contrast, a less effective institution will likely have an observed rate that is far lower than its predicted rate. Unlike the schools that perform better than expected, these schools retain or graduate *fewer* students than the model predicts, which shows up as a negative difference between observed and expected graduation rates. While the predicted rates essentially provide a way to judge a school against itself, it is not the best way to compare across schools.

To do that, I calculate adjusted rates, which incorporate the difference between an institution's characteristics and the average characteristics across all institutions. This allows for a more fair comparison across institutions and is similar to the approach often used to compare hospitals. A community hospital and a larger regional hospital serve different populations of patients, but outcomes need to be compared for regulatory and insurance purposes. The formula I use to calculate adjusted rates is shown in the Appendix.

DEFINING THE SECTORS AND IDENTIFYING THE
CHARACTERISTICS THAT MATTER

I begin with a sample of 2,311 4-year, degree-granting institutions and accompanying data about the cohort of full-time, first-time students who
entered these colleges in the fall of 2005.[4] Then, I separate these institutions into their respective sectors using the Carnegie classification. The
sectors that I include are: public comprehensive universities, public noncomprehensive research universities, private not-for-profit universities,
and private for-profit universities. This allows for an across-sector comparison of the different performance measures—observed, predicted, and
adjusted—and provides further evidence of the importance of adjusting
for student and school characteristics when constructing performance ma-
trices. In the comprehensive universities sector, there are 364 institutions,
all of which are categorized as either public-4-year-or-above nonresearch
institutions—a definition that mirrors Alisa Hicklin Fryar's contemporary definition in Chapter 1 and is similar to William Doyle's definition
in Chapter 4.[5]

The average graduation rate at comprehensive universities is 43%, and
the first-time, full-time student retention rate is around 72%. In contrast,
public noncomprehensive research universities have the highest graduation and retention rates (58.3% and 79.4%, respectively). Graduation and
retention rates are slightly higher for private not-for-profit universities,
while the numbers are the lowest for for-profit universities. When research universities are excluded from the two private-sector categories,
the numbers do not change significantly. The differences between public
comprehensive and public research universities are almost 20 percentage
points for graduation rate and over 10 percentage points for full-time retention rate.

However, these official rates—all of which the Department of Education reports—do not consider the differences in student body composition
and school policies. In other words, any rating system based on these un-
adjusted rates might change dramatically when taking into account certain institutional characteristics.

Constructing adjusted performance rates requires first identifying the
institutional characteristics that might affect student success and hence
should be included in the prediction model. The explanatory variables
I use draw on the factors that previous studies indicate are related to
student performance, such as the percentage of students who receive a
Pell grant and the demographic composition of the student body. The results begin to tell a story about how the characteristics of an institution's

student body ultimately influence its retention and graduation rates. Students' race and age as well as the institution's geographic location are all correlated with graduation and retention rates. As expected, the percentage of Pell grant recipients, which is considered as proxy for the extent of financial need, is negatively related to performance rates.

Instructional expenses per FTE have a positive relationship to performance rates: Schools that spend more per FTE are expected to have higher graduation and retention rates. While average tuition and fees are positively correlated with student graduation rate, they are negatively correlated with part-time retention rate (although the magnitude of their negative influence is rather small). The variable for tuition and fees is likely picking up other unobserved school characteristics. For instance, the most selective universities tend to have higher tuition and fees.

Because this study focuses on comprehensive universities and how they fare compared with schools in other sectors and one another, I also tailor the set of variables to ensure that the results accurately reflect the differing missions of these schools. For instance, many comprehensive universities are open access; they admit all students who apply. Furthermore, even though academic preparedness of entering students, as measured by standardized test scores, is positively correlated with graduation rates, IPEDS does not include these data for universities with open-access policies. Since the commonly used average SAT scores and admission rates are not available for over 20% of the total sample, this is a problem. The power of prediction is significantly affected when so much of the sample has missing data.

To get around this problem while still allowing for variation based on an institution's admissions policies, which likely influence performance rates, I control for whether an institution employs an open admissions policy. This acts as a proxy for its selectivity. Schools with open admissions policies on average have a full-time retention rate that is 5 percentage points lower than those institutions that do not have open admissions policies. The relationship between whether an institution has an open admissions policy and its graduation and part-time retention rates, however, is not statistically significant. Not accounting for selectivity, through either admission rate or standardized test scores, could lead to less accurate results because of the variance in selectivity across institutions not considered open access: Some of these schools accept the majority of applicants, while others accept less than 50% of applicants. The Appendix presents the mean values of each variable in the model for the full sample, the comprehensive university sample, and the two other sectors studied.[6]

DO SECTOR DIFFERENCES MATTER?

By virtue of its aggregate institutional characteristics—whether selectivity or a focus on research—each sector tends to serve different students. Across all institutions, around 22% have an open admissions policy and slightly less than 50% of enrolled students are Pell grant recipients—similar to the rates for the comprehensives sector (24% and 47%, respectively). Private for-profit institutions serve the most Pell students (73%). In contrast, the proportion of Pell grant recipients is lowest at public noncomprehensive research universities (35%). The cost of attending comprehensive universities is about one-fourth the cost of attending private not-for-profit universities and less than half the cost of attending public research universities. Instructional expense per FTE for comprehensive universities is about half of that for public research universities. I also observe a higher percentage of minority students and older students at comprehensive universities and private for-profit universities.

The observed rates do not reflect the differences in the students enrolled and the different policies that schools adopt—a fact that is reflected in the differences between observed and predicted rates.[7] Once that is accounted for using the adjusted rate, a sector's overall performance changes (see Table 5.1). For the full sample of institutions, the predicted graduation rate is slightly higher than the observed rate (41.9% versus 40%). This indicates that, in general, schools are not getting students to the finish line as well as expected. For comprehensive universities, the observed graduation rate is 39%, while the model's predicted rate is almost 42%. Much like the sample as a whole, this implies that comprehensive universities in the aggregate are doing slightly worse than expected, considering their student body makeup and certain school policies. The same goes for private not-for-profit institutions, although the margin is small (54.4% predicted versus 54% observed). For public noncomprehensive research institutions, the observed graduation rate is almost 5 percentage points higher than predicted (53.6% predicted versus 58.3% observed), which means that these institutions are doing better than expected.

Although not a perfect delineation, as discussed in Chapter 1, the contemporary definition of comprehensive often relies on distinguishing between research institutions and nonresearch institutions. Does the difference between research and nonresearch institutions hold steady across both of the private sectors (last two columns of Table 5.1)? In short, no. Unlike across public universities, there is almost no difference between research and nonresearch universities' predicted rates in these sectors. Much of this stems from the fact that, especially among private not-for-profit

Table 5.1: Observed, Predicted, and Adjusted Graduation and Retention Rates

	All Schools	Public Comprehensives	Public Non-comprehensive Research	Private NFP
Graduation Rates				
Observed	40.0%	39.2%	58.3%	54.0%
Predicted	41.9%	41.8%	53.6%	54.4%
Adjusted	41.1%	41.0%	47.7%	43.1%
Full-Time Retention Rates				
Observed	70.2%	68.8%	79.4%	73.5%
Predicted	69.1%	68.9%	76.2%	73.1%
Adjusted	72.9%	72.3%	75.3%	72.6%

	Private FP	Private NFP Nonresearch	Private FP Nonresearch
Graduation Rates			
Observed	35.1%	52.4%	35.2%
Predicted	33.1%	52.9%	33.2%
Adjusted	45.1%	43.1%	45.1%
Full-Time Retention Rates			
Observed	52.4%	72.4%	52.7%
Predicted	54.4%	72.1%	54.4%
Adjusted	70.5%	72.5%	70.7%

institutions, nonresearch institutions tend to be smaller than more selective colleges. In the public sector, nonresearch institutions vary significantly in size, mission, and student body profiles.

The difference between the observed rates and the predicted rates signal whether a school is doing as expected given its student body. The adjusted rates reflect how well an institution is performing based on how its characteristics differ from the average characteristics across all schools. In fact, calculating the adjusted graduation rate changes the relative ranking of the sectors. For instance, for-profit universities have the lowest observed graduation rate prior to adjustment, but their adjusted graduation rate is 10 percentage points higher (45.1% adjusted versus 35.1% observed). One explanation for this difference is that for-profit universities serve more financially disadvantaged students—a characteristic that the model indicates is negatively correlated with student outcomes, and which is captured in the calculation for the adjusted rates.

Table 5.2: Top 10 and Bottom 10 Comprehensive Universities, by Graduation Rate

Institution Name	State	Observed Graduation Rate	Predicted Graduation Rate	Adjusted Graduation Rate
Top 10				
Maine Maritime Academy	Maine	71%	43%	71%
The College of New Jersey	New Jersey	87%	59%	71%
United States Merchant Marine Academy	New York	80%	56%	67%
St Mary's College of Maryland	Maryland	79%	56%	67%
SUNY at Geneseo	New York	81%	59%	65%
Wright State University–Lake Campus	Ohio	53%	33%	63%
Western Washington University	Washington	73%	54%	62%
James Madison University	Virginia	81%	62%	62%
Institute of American Indian and Alaska Native Culture	New Mexico	34%	17%	60%
Albany State University	Georgia	41%	24%	60%
Bottom 10				
Gainesville State College	Georgia	14%	41%	17%
Midland College	Texas	13%	38%	19%
Louisiana State University–Alexandria	Louisiana	10%	34%	19%
Northern New Mexico College	New Mexico	11%	35%	19%
Texas A&M University–Galveston	Texas	29%	51%	22%
Kent State University at East Liverpool	Ohio	10%	31%	22%
University of Wisconsin–Parkside	Wisconsin	28%	49%	22%
University of Alaska Southeast	Alaska	21%	42%	23%
University of South Carolina–Beaufort	South Carolina	21%	41%	24%
Fort Berthold Community College	North Dakota	11%	31%	24%

Conversely, even though comprehensive universities' adjusted graduation rate is slightly higher than its observed graduation rate (41% adjusted versus 39.2% observed), the sector as a whole has the lowest adjusted graduation rate. While none of the sectors boast an adjusted graduation rate above 50%, the fact that comprehensive universities rank last is an indication that controlling for student profile does not substantially improve their relatively low observed graduation rate.

Similar to the predicted graduation rates, full-time predicted retention rates are comparable to observed rates in all sectors (see Table 5.1).[8] Unlike the graduation rates, adjusting the full-time retention rates did not change the relative ranking of school sectors. The private for-profit sectors—research and nonresearch—have the lowest observed and adjusted full-time retention rates. Compared with how well they are predicted to do, they are exceeding expectations, especially considering that they serve a significant number of financially disadvantaged students.

This sector-level analysis offers a glimpse into why performance measures should account for the student population that an institution serves. Comprehensive universities come out near the bottom both based on the difference between their observed and predicted results, and once adjusted for cross-institutional comparisons. What is still unclear is whether institution-level variance among comprehensive universities is masked by the broader sector-level analysis. I turn to this question next.

STUDENT OUTCOMES AT THE COMPREHENSIVE UNIVERSITY

So far we assume no differential effects of school characteristics on performance measures across sectors. If this is not the case, an independent ranking scheme should be created within each school sector in addition to an overall ranking of all schools. This scheme can then answer questions like: How much variation exists across comprehensive universities? Are some performing significantly better than others? Otherwise, the observed rates might distract from schools that have made significant progress, even if their observed rates are still observationally lower. Learning from the schools that are doing well—and providing additional support for the progress they are making—should be part of any effort to rate schools based on student performance outcomes.

To better understand the comprehensive universities that most dramatically outperform or underperform expectations given their institutional characteristics, I first rerun the prediction models using the comprehensive-only sample of 364 schools. The results indicate that there are indeed differential effects of institutional characteristics in student outcomes when conducting within-sector analysis. The regression coefficients, which are used to construct both the predicted and adjusted rates (see the Appendix), changed significantly on almost all variables. In other words, it is critical to construct predicted and adjusted performance measures within each sector if the purpose is to compare institutions within a specific sector.

What defines a comprehensive university is complicated—an issue at the heart of this volume. Comprehensive universities vary in substantial ways, often as a result of years of mission drift and adaptation. Some comprehensive universities offer master's programs, while others are primarily associate's–degree–granting institutions that have, in recent decades, begun to offer 4-year degrees. Many of the largest institutions maintain their commitment to the mission of open access, while a number of smaller comprehensives are able to drive up the academic profile of their student body by accepting fewer students. In keeping with the open-access mission that historically has defined the comprehensive university, my analysis does not include either admission rate or average standardized test scores. This creates a trade-off between explanatory power and historical mission. Accordingly, adjusted performance rates must be interpreted cautiously. While these rates improve upon the observed rates, they are by no means all-inclusive.

Graduation Rates

Across all comprehensive universities, 52% exceed expectations, which is to say they boast an observed graduation rate that is higher than their predicted graduation rate. The bigger the positive difference, the more the school exceeds expectations. Acknowledging the need to interpret these results with caution, I present, in Table 5.2, the top 10 schools and the bottom 10 schools. When taking into account institutional characteristics, the schools in the top 10 have predicted graduation rates that are significantly lower than their observed rates, indicating that these schools outperform what one would expect based on the composition of their student body. The bottom 10 comprehensive universities have predicted graduation rates that are much higher than their observed graduation rates, which means that they are not performing as would be expected given their institutional and student body characteristics.

The bottom 10 schools, which include a higher percentage of open admissions institutions, serve a student body that has a higher percentage of Pell grant recipients and a higher percentage of Hispanic students. The initial regression analysis indicates that each of these three factors is negatively correlated with graduation rates, which should increase the adjusted rates at schools with a high incidence of these characteristics. But the bottom institutions' relative standing does not improve, even after crediting them for the higher incidence of characteristics that negatively influence performance measures.

The top 10 schools, on the other hand, have higher tuition and fees and higher instructional spending per FTE, both characteristics associated with higher graduation rates. When an institution has higher levels on these two factors, it translates to a higher predicted rate and a lower adjusted rate.

Consider Albany State University, a school with a top 10 graduation rate among its peer comprehensive universities. Although over 80% of the institution's undergraduates received a Pell grant and the instructional expenditure per FTE student was only $5,708, the institution was able to graduate 41% of students. In fact, its predicted graduation rate was much lower—only 24%. After accounting for the prevalence of these characteristics, the adjusted graduation rate was 60%, much higher than either the observed one or the predicted one. Albany State University, then, is doing better than expected and better than most other comprehensive universities.

In contrast, Texas A&M University–Galveston, one of the bottom 10 comprehensive universities, has an observed graduation rate of 29%, but a predicted graduation rate of 51%, meaning that given its institutional characteristics, it should be graduating almost twice as many students as it is. Only around 22% of students at Texas A&M University–Galveston receive a Pell grant, far lower than at Albany State University. But after adjusting for these characteristics using the prediction model's coefficients, the adjusted graduation rate is lower still (22%). In other words, based on its predicted graduation rate, the university is not performing as well as expected. Nor is the university performing well compared with other comprehensive universities.

What's happening here? Are the schools too different to compare, or is Albany State University really exceeding expectations and outperforming Texas A&M–Galveston? While by no means identical in their student body composition, the two schools vary less than do many other comprehensive institutions. Take the size of the undergraduate student body. Albany State University, located in Albany, Georgia, enrolls just under 4,000 undergraduates, while Texas A&M University–Galveston enrolls 2,000. (For context, the largest comprehensive in the sample enrolls well over 20,000 students; the smallest enrolls fewer than 1,000 students.) Albany State University accepts 29% of its students, while Texas A&M University–Galveston accepts 55%. The academic profile at Albany State University is higher than at Texas A&M University–Galveston: The bottom 25% of entering students at the former score 1020 on SAT critical reading and math combined, which is 110 points higher than the 75th percentile at the latter. The model does not control for standardized test scores, but if it did, it is likely that Albany State University's adjusted graduation rate would decline since previous research finds that the academic profile of entering students is positively correlated with student outcomes. Finally, more than 75% of students at both institutions are 24 years of age or younger, a characteristic that is positively correlated with student outcomes.

Despite observed graduations rates that differ by just over 10 percentage points, Albany State performs significantly better than Texas A&M University–Galveston in helping its students reach graduation. Without considering institutional characteristics, it would be easy to assume that neither is doing particularly well.

Full-Time Retention Rates

The same logic applies to retention rates (Table 5.3). The top 10 universities are those with the biggest positive difference between their observed and predicted full-time retention rates, which means they exceed expectations when taking into account the students they enroll. Note that the list is ordered by adjusted, not observed, full-time retention rates (highest to lowest). The adjusted retention rate for many of the schools in the top 10 exceeds 100%, which reflects the impact that student body differences across schools have on the relative standing of these universities. The bottom 10 comprehensive universities are those institutions that are predicted to have higher full-time retention rates than actually are observed. This list also is ordered by adjusted retention rate, from lowest to highest.

Interestingly, the schools listed among the top 10 enroll a higher percentage of Pell grant recipients (a factor that, because of its negative relationship to outcome variables, will decrease the predicted retention rate and increase the adjusted retention rate). These schools also have lower instructional expenditures per FTE and lower tuition and fees, two factors typically associated with lower student outcomes. Schools that enroll more Pell grant recipients and more black and Hispanic students have predicted rates that exceed their observed rates. This is in line with the results from the regression analysis, which indicate that while these factors are positively correlated with full-time retention rates, the relationship is not statistically significant.

Winston-Salem State University boasts an 80% full-time retention rate, which is almost 20 percentage points higher than its predicted full-time retention rate. The university, then, is doing better than expected at retaining its students from one year to the next. After accounting for institutional and student characteristics, its adjusted full-time retention rate

Table 5.3: Top 10 and Bottom 10 Comprehensive Universities, by Full-Time Retention Rates

Institution Name	State	Observed Retention Rate Full-Time	Predicted Retention Rate Full-Time	Adjusted Retention Rate Full-Time
Top 10				
Oklahoma State University–Oklahoma City	Oklahoma	100%	55%	117%
Gordon College	Georgia	100%	63%	110%
Seattle Community College–South Campus	Washington	100%	66%	107%
Dine College	Arizona	100%	66%	107%
Brazosport College	Texas	83%	62%	94%
Glenville State College	West Virginia	78%	57%	93%
Savannah State University	Georgia	71%	53%	90%
Winston-Salem State University	North Carolina	80%	63%	89%
Vincennes University	Indiana	74%	57%	89%
California State University–San Bernardino	California	89%	72%	89%
Bottom 10				
Oglala Lakota College	South Dakota	31%	63%	41%
Texas A&M University–Galveston	Texas	47%	72%	48%
Auburn University at Montgomery	Alabama	50%	73%	50%
University of Hawaii—West Oahu	Hawaii	37%	58%	52%
Gainesville State College	Georgia	56%	73%	55%
Texas A&M University–Texarkana	Texas	47%	64%	56%
Potomac State College of West Virginia University	West Virginia	45%	61%	57%
Abraham Baldwin Agricultural College	Georgia	50%	66%	57%
Kentucky State University	Kentucky	50%	65%	57%
University of South Carolina–Beaufort	South Carolina	54%	69%	57%

goes up to 89%. Gainesville State College, on the other hand, fares differently. The school's observed full-time retention rate of 56% is 17 percentage points lower than its predicted rate. With an adjusted full-time retention rate of 55%, Gainesville State College is among the most egregious underperformers.

Even though their predicted full-time retention rates are roughly similar—a difference of 10 percentage points in Gainesville State College's favor—the schools differ from each other in significant ways. Winston-Salem State University, located in North Carolina, accepts 56% of students and enrolls fewer than 6,000 undergraduates. Gainesville State College accepts 99% of students—making it essentially open access, a characteristic that is not captured in the binary open-access variable—and enrolls over 8,500 undergraduates. While Winston-Salem State University is more selective, Gainesville State College enrolls students with higher SAT scores at the 75th percentile (1080 versus 960). This is likely because submitting an admission test (SAT or ACT) is recommended at Gainesville State College, but required at Winston-Salem State University. Previous research indicates that, if average SAT were included in the model, Gainesville State College would have an even higher predicted full-time retention rate and an even lower adjusted full-time retention rate.

How well an institution retains or graduates its students depends on more than just a snapshot of its students when they first enroll. The most important question, one that observed rates alone cannot answer, is how much value does an institution add to its students' education? And, is an institution finding ways to graduate a significant number of less academically prepared students, even if observed rates remain low? Schools with observed performance rates that are lower than those of their peers can add value. Learning how they do this and transferring these lessons to other lower performing schools is an important step.

CONCLUSION

There are two competing goals in higher education policy right now: graduate more students, and hold institutions accountable for their quality. In some ways, these policy goals are at odds with each other. The same institutions that enroll the greatest proportion of America's public 4-year students are often the ones with the most severe quality problems. Graduating more students from 4-year institutions will require that these low-quality institutions improve. But at the same time, policies that are quick to sanction schools for low retention and graduation rates—with little regard for the composition of their student bodies—may judge quality too hastily. By failing to account for institutional differences, a ratings system inadvertently masks those institutions that are beating the odds. Recall Albany State University: Based on federal definitions, it is graduating 41% of its students, but based on the characteristics of its student body, it is expected to graduate only 24%. Any policy that ignores this fact likely will never ask what it is that Albany State University does to maintain an observed graduation rate that so drastically exceeds its predicted rate.

In this chapter, I explored how higher education accountability efforts might more accurately take into account student body characteristics and their effect on performance outcomes. What I find confirms previous research that shows a strong relationship between certain student and school characteristics and institutional retention and graduation rates. The predicted rates that I construct further reinforce the importance of including such measures to improve the current one-size-fits-all methodology of calculating graduation and retention rates. Observed rates can differ significantly from predicted rates, across both institutions and sectors. The higher the observed rate, especially relative to its predicted rate, the better the institutional performance. Furthermore, institutional characteristics have differential effects on student performance across sectors, as captured in the separate by-sector regression analysis.

While the idea of risk-adjusted metrics often is talked about, such metrics are still relatively uncommon in the analysis of education outcomes. But we have seen that taking into account the risk factors of students served by the institutions can increase performance measures by a dozen percentage points or more. That said, more studies are needed to confirm these findings and to extend the methodology to other measures. And this data leads back to a fundamental policy question: Even after adjusting scores to more fairly represent the challenges of the student population served, is a college—such as Albany State University—with an observed graduation rate much higher than its predicted rate doing well enough to merit accolades? Or are its performance rates still too low, regardless of the composition of its student body?

For a wide range of reasons, student performance rates (specifically graduation rates of full-time, first-time students) can be flawed measures of institutional effectiveness (Adelman, 2006), but their presence in ranking systems, accountability initiatives, and institutional strategic plans has become pervasive. Regardless of whatever useful information these raw rates provide, other important factors related to the probabilities of graduation are not accounted for. Efforts to construct a rating system based on official performance rates without taking into account such factors might harm the population in need by punishing the schools that enroll a higher percentage of students with financial need or lower academic preparation. It might even induce schools to artificially improve their performance measures by employing a more competitive admissions policy, which would leave the most in-need students out of the higher education system.

Overall, the comprehensive universities in this study do no better or worse than other sectors. However, the institutional-level results also suggest that some of these universities might be underperforming relative to the whole body of bachelor's–degree–granting institutions in the nation. This reinforces the importance of constructing better measures. As is well known, first-time, full-time students constitute only a fraction of the students served by these institutions. Yet, there are still tens of thousands of full-time students enrolled in these institutions—and the findings presented here suggest that in many comprehensive universities they could be served better.

APPENDIX

Calculating Predicted and Adjusted Rates

Predicted rates are calculated using the "Predict" command after each regression in Stata (Version 11). The equation used to calculate this rate is:

$$y_{is} = \beta_0 + \sum_1^x \beta_x X_{xis} + \alpha_s + \varepsilon_{is}$$

Where y_{is} is graduation, full-time retention, or part-time retention rate of campus i in state s, X_{xis} is a set of institutional characteristics measuring the extent to which these institutional variables have any effect on graduation or retention rates, α_s is the state fixed effect, and ε_{is} is the error term.

Adjusted rates are calculated using Equation 2 where we subtract the institutional differences from the mean from the observed graduation or retention rates:

$$y_{(adjusted)is} = y_{(observed)is} - \beta(x_{is} - \bar{x})$$

Where $y_{(observed)is}$ is actual graduation, full-time retention, or part-time retention rate of campus i in state s, x_{is} is a set of institutional characteristics, and $\bar{x}$ is average institutional characteristics within a state.

NOTES

1. This refers to the Student Right-to-Know and Campus Security Act (P.L. 101-542), which was passed by Congress November 9, 1990. Title I, Section 103, requires

Appendix Table 5.1: Summary Statistics of Control Variables Included in the Regression Models

	Full Sample	Comprehensive Universities Only	Public Research	Private Not-for-Profit	Private for Profit
Open admissions policy	0.219	0.240	0.0506	0.125	0.521
	(0.414)	(0.428)	(0.220)	(0.331)	(0.500)
Percent received Pell grant	49.76	47.58	35.13	43.55	73.76
	(22.50)	(16.14)	(15.43)	(20.60)	(17.53)
Tuition and fees	17,602	6,302	14,594	23,706	15,251
	(10,556)	(2,280)	(10,953)	(10,190)	(3,930)
Instructional expense per FTE	8,035	6,962	10,574	9,761	3,506
	(7,607)	(2,234)	(4,377)	(9,461)	(2,467)
Percent Black	15.13	14.07	12.05	13.05	22.80
	(20.11)	(20.64)	(17.23)	(19.68)	(19.68)
Percent Hispanic	8.431	8.957	8.574	6.488	13.03
	(11.57)	(13.52)	(10.22)	(8.494)	(14.99)
Percent Asian	3.431	3.036	6.118	3.417	2.763
	(5.570)	(4.735)	(7.120)	(5.467)	(5.288)
Percent American Indian	1.152	2.553	0.460	0.782	1.058
	(6.627)	(12.05)	(1.313)	(4.995)	(3.650)
Percent Native Hawaiian	0.282	0.162	0.0970	0.305	0.401
	(1.773)	(1.072)	(0.482)	(2.199)	(1.237)
Percent two races	1.764	1.938	1.852	1.633	1.887
	(2.030)	(2.237)	(1.670)	(2.056)	(1.803)
Percent race unknown	7.822	4.708	6.004	6.992	14.42
	(10.68)	(5.416)	(8.169)	(8.490)	(16.84)
Percent Asian Hawaiian	3.790	3.278	6.321	3.798	3.222
	(6.140)	(5.225)	(7.332)	(6.187)	(5.748)
Percent nonresident alien	3.423	2.173	6.367	4.393	1.051
	(6.058)	(2.757)	(5.380)	(7.396)	(3.507)
Percent women	55.76	57.70	53.79	55.45	55.90
	(17.27)	(9.065)	(9.200)	(18.70)	(21.15)
Percent (ages 18–24)	66.56	70.07	79.15	74.70	36.12
	(25.30)	(16.43)	(17.36)	(22.18)	(19.37)

Appendix Table 5.1: Summary Statistics of Control Variables Included in the Regression Models (continued)

	Full Sample	Comprehensive Universities Only	Public Research	Private Not-for-Profit	Private for Profit
Percent (ages 25–64)	30.55	25.37	18.49	22.01	63.42
	(25.76)	(14.41)	(17.03)	(22.17)	(19.53)
Percent (age over 65)	0.103	0.109	0.0338	0.130	0.0488
	(0.482)	(0.411)	(0.223)	(0.590)	(0.216)
City midsize	0.111	0.105	0.169	0.106	0.0998
	(0.314)	(0.306)	(0.375)	(0.309)	(0.300)
City small	0.135	0.147	0.165	0.122	0.129
	(0.341)	(0.355)	(0.372)	(0.328)	(0.335)
Suburb large	0.198	0.0974	0.148	0.204	0.313
	(0.398)	(0.297)	(0.356)	(0.403)	(0.464)
Suburb midsize	0.0205	0.0333	0.0169	0.0200	0.00887
	(0.142)	(0.180)	(0.129)	(0.140)	(0.0939)
Suburb small	0.0169	0.0285	0.0253	0.0158	0.00222
	(0.129)	(0.167)	(0.157)	(0.125)	(0.0471)
Town fringe	0.0103	0.0166	0.0169	0.0116	
	(0.101)	(0.128)	(0.129)	(0.107)	
Town distant	0.0941	0.152	0.0506	0.112	0.00222
	(0.292)	(0.359)	(0.220)	(0.316)	(0.0471)
Town remote	0.0602	0.152	0.0506	0.0466	0.00887
	(0.238)	(0.359)	(0.220)	(0.211)	(0.0939)
Rural fringe	0.0789	0.121	0.0295	0.0641	0.0953
	(0.270)	(0.327)	(0.170)	(0.245)	(0.294)
Rural distant	0.0227	0.0238		0.0324	0.00443
	(0.149)	(0.152)		(0.177)	(0.0665)
Rural remote	0.0116	0.00238	0.0127	0.00416	0.0421
	(0.107)	(0.0487)	(0.112)	(0.0644)	(0.201)
Observations	2,242	421	237	1,202	451

Numbers are means; numbers in parentheses are standard deviations.

Appendix Table 5.2: Regression Results Using Full Sample

Variables	Graduation Rate	Full-Time Retention Rate	Part-Time Retention Rate
Open admissions policy	0.0774	−5.159***	−0.263
	(1.120)	(0.969)	(2.192)
Percent received Pell grant	−0.255***	−0.187***	−0.229***
	(0.0332)	(0.0214)	(0.0514)
Tuition and fees	0.000513***	1.16e-05	−0.000209**
	(3.48e-05)	(3.97e-05)	(0.000100)
Instructional expense per FTE	0.000389***	0.000265***	0.000358**
	(6.30e-05)	(5.18e-05)	(0.000177)
Percent Black	−0.0940***	−0.0849***	−0.0851*
	(0.0288)	(0.0223)	(0.0514)
Percent Hispanic	0.0515	0.0244	0.0165
	(0.0479)	(0.0386)	(0.0892)
Percent Asian	0.545	−0.709	−0.938
	(0.816)	(0.909)	(2.018)
Percent American Indian	−0.0626	0.139**	0.0232
	(0.0567)	(0.0627)	(0.148)
Percent Native Hawaiian	0.320	−1.060	−1.289
	(0.815)	(0.932)	(2.089)
Percent two races	−0.457**	−0.368**	−0.0788
	(0.221)	(0.187)	(0.427)
Percent race unknown	−0.137***	−0.0335	−0.0882
	(0.0434)	(0.0334)	(0.0795)
Percent Asian Hawaiian	−0.142	1.118	1.368
	(0.789)	(0.906)	(2.010)
Percent nonresident alien	0.0575	0.0534	0.300*
	(0.0979)	(0.0595)	(0.163)
Percent women	0.0673***	0.0246	0.158***
	(0.0258)	(0.0214)	(0.0598)
Percent (ages 18–24)	0.461***	0.0655	−0.325**
	(0.0668)	(0.0609)	(0.159)
Percent (ages 25–64)	0.313***	−0.118*	−0.324**
	(0.0678)	(0.0602)	(0.157)
Percent (age over 65)	2.206	1.456**	2.587*
	(1.675)	(0.664)	(1.402)
City midsize	2.480*	−1.006	−1.431
	(1.289)	(1.228)	(2.796)

Appendix Table 5.2: Regression Results Using Full Sample (continued)

Variables	Graduation Rate	Full-Time Retention Rate	Part-Time Retention Rate
City small	3.057**	-1.499	-0.657
	(1.217)	(1.197)	(2.807)
Suburb large	0.808	-2.496**	0.185
	(1.078)	(1.054)	(2.482)
Suburb midsize	4.863**	-3.174	-4.813
	(2.103)	(2.456)	(5.254)
Suburb small	3.295*	0.490	3.002
	(1.946)	(2.596)	(5.960)
Town fringe	5.857***	-1.891	4.049
	(1.814)	(3.163)	(7.507)
Town distant	1.992*	-1.101	-9.258***
	(1.097)	(1.340)	(3.358)
Town remote	1.075	-3.860**	-8.640**
	(1.431)	(1.637)	(3.624)
Rural fringe	2.582*	-3.046**	-5.297*
	(1.417)	(1.382)	(3.198)
Rural distant	-4.694**	-2.592	-10.99*
	(2.329)	(2.339)	(6.181)
Rural remote	-0.453	-1.715	-15.50
	(2.896)	(3.481)	(10.32)
Observations	2,242	2,252	1,411
R-squared	0.559	0.419	0.140

Robust standard errors in parentheses; *** p < 0.01, ** p < 0.05, * p < 0.1.

Appendix Table 5.3: Regression Results Using Comprehensive Institution Only Sample

Variables	Graduation Rate	Full-Time Retention Rate	Part-Time Retention Rate
Open admissions policy	-0.790	-2.564	0.832
	(1.714)	(2.346)	(4.529)
Percent received Pell grant	-0.399***	-0.313***	-0.496***
	(0.0587)	(0.0654)	(0.172)
Tuition and fees	0.00180***	-0.000106	-0.00206
	(0.000558)	(0.000516)	(0.00142)
Instructional expense per FTE	0.000351	2.24e-05	0.000813
	(0.000296)	(0.000133)	(0.00108)
Percent Black	-0.0462	0.0252	0.184
	(0.0383)	(0.0383)	(0.116)

Appendix Table 5.3: Regression Results Using Comprehensive Institution Only Sample (continued)

Variables	Graduation Rate	Full-Time Retention Rate	Part-Time Retention Rate
Percent Hispanic	−0.0118	0.106	0.293*
	(0.0671)	(0.0670)	(0.175)
Percent Asian	−0.312	−0.597	2.105
	(1.263)	(1.286)	(3.522)
Percent American Indian	0.0892*	0.152*	−0.230
	(0.0503)	(0.0902)	(0.212)
Percent Native Hawaiian	−1.517	0.981	−5.195
	(1.486)	(1.456)	(3.497)
Percent two races	−1.127***	−0.126	−1.033
	(0.271)	(0.245)	(0.910)
Percent race unknown	−0.0575	0.0266	0.244
	(0.0875)	(0.0980)	(0.284)
Percent Asian Hawaiian	0.366	0.815	−0.982
	(1.260)	(1.273)	(3.461)
Percent nonresident alien	0.189	0.0539	−0.0610
	(0.170)	(0.176)	(0.427)
Percent women	0.0733	−0.00990	0.200
	(0.0653)	(0.0544)	(0.212)
Percent (ages 18–24)	0.198**	−0.00265	−0.337
	(0.0850)	(0.0788)	(0.265)
Percent (ages 25–64)	−0.116	−0.164*	−0.164
	(0.0893)	(0.0876)	(0.266)
Percent (age over 65)	−0.779	−2.881***	−3.292
	(0.956)	(1.082)	(2.511)
City midsize	2.334	−3.862	−11.78**
	(2.060)	(2.642)	(5.680)
City small	2.848	−3.856	−11.60*
	(1.961)	(2.847)	(5.985)
Suburb large	0.889	−6.077*	−10.42*
	(2.216)	(3.138)	(6.303)
Suburb midsize	0.743	−8.423***	−19.97**
	(2.754)	(3.132)	(8.578)
Suburb small	5.022	−2.737	−3.763
	(3.552)	(4.170)	(8.863)
Town fringe	0.225	−4.710	6.081
	(2.853)	(3.494)	(11.47)

institutions eligible for Title IV funding to calculate completion or graduation rates of certificate- or degree-seeking, full-time students entering the institution, and to disclose these rates to all students and prospective students. Full-time student retention rate is defined as the percent of the "fall full-time cohort from the prior year minus exclusions from the fall full-time cohort" that re-enrolled at the institution as either full- or part-time students in the current year. Part-time student retention rate is defined as the percent of the "fall part-time cohort from the prior year minus exclusions from the fall part-time cohort" that re-enrolled at the institution as either full- or part-time students in the current year.

2. Comprehensive university is defined here as a public 4-year nonresearch university.

3. For example, consider an institution whose observed graduation rate is 50% and the percentage of students receiving Pell grants is 60%. The average percentage of students receiving a Pell grant in comprehensive schools is around 44%. Using the coefficient on the Pell grant measure from the regression models for comprehensive schools, –0.512, the adjusted graduation rate equates to 58%, calculated as 50% – (–0.512) * (60% – 44%) = 58%. The adjusted rate is higher than the observed rate because the percentage of Pell grant recipients in this institution is higher than the average across all schools. This single variable example is repeated for all measures in the regression equation using the actual values for each institution.

4. IPEDS is a system of interrelated surveys conducted annually by the U.S. Department's National Center for Education Statistics (NCES), which collects data on institutional characteristics, institutional prices, enrollment, completions, student financial aid, and some other institutional data.

5. Sample size varies slightly when running different regression models, depending on data availability. Sample size is 327 if using full-time retention rate as the outcome.

6. This study is conducted at the school level. Therefore, I am limited to the data available from IPEDS.

7. The formulas for these calculations are located in the Appendix.

8. Note that while the statistical power of the models when applied to graduation and full-time retention is quite high, the same model explains far less variance in the part-time retention rates.

REFERENCES

Adelman, C. (2006). *The toolbox revisited: Paths to degree completion from high school through college.* Washington, DC: U.S. Department of Education.

Astin, A. W., Tsui, L., & Avalos, J. (1996). *Degree attainment rates at American colleges and universities: Effects of race, gender, and institutional type.* Los Angeles,

CA: Higher Education Research Institute, Graduate School of Education, University of California.

Astin, A. W. (1993). *What matters in college: Four critical years revisited.* San Francisco, CA: Jossey-Bass.

Bailey, T. (2012). *Developing input-adjusted metrics in community college performance.* Available at www.hcmstrategists.com/contextforsuccess/papers/BAILEY_PAPER.pdf

DeAngelo, L., Franke, R., Hurtado, S., Pryor, J. H., & Tran, S. (2011). *Completing college: Assessing graduation rates at four-year institutions.* Los Angeles, CA: Higher Education Research Institute, UCLA. Available at heri.ucla.edu/DARCU/CompletingCollege2011.pdf

Goenner, C.F., & Snaith, S.M. (2004). Accounting for model uncertainty in the prediction of university graduation rates. Research in Higher Education, 45, 25–41.

Grayson, J. P. (1995). *Race and first year retention on a Canadian campus.* Toronto, Canada: York University, Institute for Social Research. (ERIC Document Reproduction Service No. ED 418 670)

Horn, L. (2006). *Placing college graduation rates in context: How 4-year college graduation rates vary with selectivity and the size of low-income enrollment.* Washington, DC: U.S. Department of Education, National Center for Education Statistics.

Kelly, A. P., & Schneider, M. (2011). What parents don't know about college graduation rates could hurt. *Education Outlook, American Enterprise Institute for Public Policy Research, 2.* Available at www.aei.org/files/2011/02/08/EduO-2011-02-g.pdf

Morrison, M. C. (2012). Graduation odds and probabilities among baccalaureate colleges and universities. *Journal of College Student Retention: Research, Theory and Practice. 14*(2), 157–179.

Mortenson, T. (1997, April). Actual versus predicted institutional graduation rates for 1,100 colleges and universities. *Postsecondary Education Opportunity,* 58.

Pascarella, E. T., and Terenzini, P. T. (1991). How college affects students: Findings and insights from twenty years of research (1st ed.). San Francisco, CA: Jossey-Bass.

Porter, S. R. (2000). The robustness of the "graduation rate performance" indicator used in the U.S. News and World Report college ranking. *International Journal of Educational Advancement, 1*(2), 10–30.

Ryan, J. F. (2004). The relationship between institutional expenditures and degree attainment. *Research in Higher Education, 45*(2), 97–114.

Scott, M., Bailey, T., & Kienzl, G. (2006). Relative success? Determinants of college graduation rates in public and private colleges in the U.S. *Research in Higher Education, 47*(3), 249–279.

U.S. Department of Education, National Center for Education Statistics. (2013). *Integrated postsecondary education data system (IPEDS).* Available at nces. ed.gov/ipeds/datacenter/Default.aspx

White House, Office of the Press Secretary. (2013, August 22). *Remarks by the President on college affordability—Buffalo, NY.* Available at www.whitehouse. gov/the-press-office/2013/08/22/remarks-president-college-affordability-buffalo-ny

CHAPTER 6

Analyzing Labor Markets in Real Time
Positioning Comprehensive Universities for a Dynamic Economy

John Dorrer

Comprehensive universities are confronting formidable challenges on multiple fronts. They simultaneously must improve access and afford-ability, and better align curricula with labor market needs—all while being held accountable for students' outcomes. Student debt is mount-ing, and new graduates are struggling to land well-paying jobs, fueling criticisms that higher education is losing value. Employers, unable to find graduates with the skills and qualifications needed to fill jobs, voice their frustrations that postsecondary institutions remain unresponsive to labor market needs. Policymakers at both the state and federal levels are calling for new performance measures—such as employment and earnings outcomes for graduates—that would require public higher education systems to become more responsive to employer needs and better align with state economic development strategies. In this envi-ronment, colleges and universities will need to ensure that programs of study align with labor market demands and produce graduates with the skills and qualifications that employers need.

Outside of higher education, the labor market is rapidly evolving. Per-sistent technology innovations, the competitive pressures of a global econ-omy, and the emergence of new forms of work organization have made labor markets more fluid and demanding. In turn, the knowledge, skills, and abilities required for performance in these dynamic work environ-ments have been consistently changing and escalating. Comprehensive universities are expected to respond with enhancements to curriculum and provide evidence that the qualifications of their graduates measure

The University Next Door: What Is a Comprehensive University, Who Does It Educate, and Can It Survive? edited by Mark Schneider & KC Deane. Copyright © 2015 by Teachers College, Columbia University. All rights reserved.

up to these new requirements. In crafting these responses, comprehensive universities will need a deeper understanding of how labor markets work. They will need to constantly assess how market forces assert themselves in the complex environment in which they are operating.

New sources of labor market information and innovative analytics provide a more penetrating look into how the labor market works and the skills employers seek when filling positions. The growing digitization of labor market information—including Internet job postings and resumes, social media sites, and social networks—serve up a constant source of data in real time. These data sources provide timely details of occupational demand, including skills and certifications sought, and on the flip side, the characteristics and qualifications of available labor supply. From these data, and the accompanying analytics, comprehensive universities can shape strategies, guide resource allocation, and enrich the evaluation of programs. By strengthening these functions, comprehensive universities will be able to more tightly align curricula with the requirements of dynamic economies. In doing so, they will become more responsive to the needs of students and employers.

This chapter provides a summary of why labor market information matters in the complex market and policy environment that comprehensive universities must navigate. I begin with a brief review and critique of conventional labor market information sources, and the taxonomies that classify occupations and industries. Next, I review how the Internet has changed the workings of the labor market. Finally, I examine recent experiences of a group of community colleges that have incorporated new real-time labor market information systems. To close, I review how the lessons learned can be of value to comprehensive universities faced with their own set of challenges.

WHY LABOR MARKET INFORMATION MATTERS

As new reports and studies continue to focus on the skills gap and unmet needs of employers, debate on the responsiveness of higher education to labor market needs intensifies. Fundamental to achieving better alignment between what employers need and what our education and training systems produce is a deeper understanding of the short- and long-term labor market needs and trends. Longstanding academic traditions, well-established disciplines, and faculty-centric approaches to shaping curriculum content have provided stability in the academic setting. But forces in the marketplace, including technology innovation, global competitive pressures, and changing forms of work organization, collectively are transforming the work for which graduates are being prepared.

Employer Needs

From the employer side, a number of industry sectors are known for the magnitude and speed of change. Fields such as cyber security, health informatics, and applications development for smart phones are evolving rapidly, while new industries in nanotechnology, life sciences, and composite materials are emerging. All this innovation requires workers with rapidly evolving skill requirements and specialized certifications. However, these emerging requirements too often go unrecognized in established taxonomies and traditional labor market analysis.

Employers become frustrated when they are unable to find qualified workers to fill available positions for these critical new jobs. At the same time, millions of individuals remain unemployed, and university graduates are unable to find jobs. At least for the unemployed graduates, critics point to colleges' and universities' inability to keep up with fast-moving, complex changes in the labor market. A 2011 McKinsey Global Institute study found that half of young graduates are "not sure that their post-secondary education has improved their chances of finding a job" (Manyika et al., 2011). Furthermore, colleges and universities appear to over-rate the preparedness of their graduates. According to the McKinsey survey, 72% of educational institutions felt that their graduates were ready for the job market, but only 42% of employers agreed.

A report released by the Society for Human Resource Management (SHRM) and Achieve in October 2012 echoed this misalignment. "The fact is employers are searching for employees with more training and skills than ever before—a trend that human resource (HR) professionals expect will continue in the future" (p. 2). Their analysis offers additional perspective from the employer side of the labor market, including the following major findings:

- More than 95% of respondents, across all industries, had open positions in 2011. Most job openings required a high school diploma (36%) or a bachelor's degree (36%).
- All industries are projecting that future jobs will require more skills, education, and credentials at all levels, with some variations based on the industry.
- Companies are investing in training for their employees. Most respondents report that training takes place on site (81%), but a significant portion say it takes place on a college campus, either a technical or community college (44%) or university campus (41%).

In the midst of the discontent with our workforce development systems, a more competitive landscape for higher education is emerging.

More private colleges and universities, career schools, and online education and training offerings are introducing competitive learning opportunities. As opposed to traditional public universities, these new competitors enter the market with fewer institutional constraints, greater ability to innovate curriculum and degree offerings, and more flexibility to respond to changing market needs. New, market-driven models for the delivery of education and training also appeal to employers seeking to hire graduates with specialized skills and qualifications. As the labor market favors new providers and delivery models, tradition-bound institutions will continue to be challenged.

Students, Parents, and Third-Party Payers

Employers are not the only ones raising expectations of higher education. Increasingly, parents, students, and third-party payers are demanding more detailed information on the employment and earnings outcomes that higher education produces. The U.S. Department of Education recently introduced a broad set of "gainful employment" rules to strengthen federal student aid programs at for-profit, nonprofit, and public institutions. The rules are designed to protect students from aggressive or misleading recruiting practices, provide consumers with better information about the effectiveness of career college and training programs, and ensure that only eligible students or programs receive aid (U.S. Department of Education, 2011). Under the new, controversial rules, proprietary institutions of higher education and postsecondary vocational institutions must provide prospective students with each eligible program's graduation rate, average indebtedness, and job placement rates.

In 2013, the Obama administration introduced the College Scorecard, a new planning tool designed to help students and their families make better informed choices in selecting a college or university. The Scorecard reports five key pieces of data: costs, graduation rate, loan default rate, average amount borrowed, and employment outcomes. This new transparency on outcomes, in particular employment and earnings, will require that colleges and universities—especially comprehensive universities, which educate a significant number of students and are integral to their local communities—develop a deeper understanding of labor market developments.

Governors, Legislators, and Public Policymakers

A growing number of governors, higher education institution and system presidents, and business leaders are working together to ensure that colleges and universities align their programs with the real-world needs of students. In 2010, the Heldrich Center at Rutgers University, in collaboration with the National Governors Association (NGA), conducted a study of state policies that promote the alignment of higher education with workforce and economic development needs (Sparks & Waits, 2011). Confirming the belief that community colleges, 4-year institutions, and research universities can make a more significant contribution to future economic growth, the report highlighted the value of bringing educational programs more closely in line with fast-changing market demand. Some states—Minnesota, North Carolina, Ohio, and Washington—are already adopting innovative practices and policies in this area.

Policymakers are broadly aware of the strong connection between educational attainment and economic performance, but less often is the unit of analysis a regional labor market. A recent report from the Milken Institute, *A Matter of Degrees: The Effect of Educational Attainment on Regional Economic Prosperity*, provides evidence of this connection in its analysis of the effect of educational attainment on regional labor markets (DeVol, Shen, Bedroussian, & Zhang, 2013). The report associates education with increases in real gross domestic product (GDP) per capita and real wages, linking 1 year of additional education to a 10.5% rise in a region's real GDP per capita and an 8.4% rise in the region's real wages. The report further concludes that the greatest returns are in industries where highly skilled business and information technology workers make up a large share of the labor force.[1]

Understanding the workings of labor markets is key to guiding our investments in education and training. This is especially true for comprehensive universities, which train a significant portion of the nation's undergraduate students for regional labor markets. A deeper understanding of labor market developments at the regional level is essential for comprehensive universities seeking to more effectively compete for students and limited resources in a dynamic economic, demographic, and policy environment. The demands for greater accountability and calls for more performance measures focused on employment and earnings will not subside.

LIMITATIONS OF CONVENTIONAL
LABOR MARKET INFORMATION

To become more responsive to labor market needs, postsecondary institutions first must become more proficient in researching and analyzing labor markets, which community colleges and many workforce development programs have already started to do. However, making more—and better—use of labor market and workforce analysis requires a familiarity with the landscape and limitations of the conventional labor market data sources and the extensive body of research built from these data sources.

Traditional labor market data from state and federal agencies—such as the Bureau of Labor Statistics (BLS), the Census Bureau, and the National Center for Education Statistics (NCES)—include broad measures of key information: employment and unemployment, employment and wages by industry and occupation, indicators of labor supply and demand, enrollments and completions by fields of study, and changes in workforce characteristics over time. Most of the data that institutions work with comes from the following five major sources: census data, employment statistics, industry and occupational taxonomies, administrative records, and occupational employment and projections (U.S. Department of Labor, 2010).

Census Data

Census data provide an excellent source for analyzing trends over time, especially the Decennial Census and the American Community Survey (ACS). For example, the assessment of longer term changes in the occupational and industry structure of a region is essential for strategic planning and institutional investments decisions. The ACS is a reliable source for this analysis. However, this level of data aggregation is too general for more detailed analysis of institutional and program performance or the degree of responsiveness to market needs.

Employment Statistics

Most of us are familiar with the once-monthly announcement of the jobs numbers, namely, the unemployment rate and number of new jobs created. The unemployment rate is an estimate that comes from a monthly household survey of 65,000 households. Data about whether the economy is adding or shedding jobs come from a more elaborate monthly survey of over 200,000 employers. These monthly estimates—published at the national, state, and sub-state levels—primarily serve economic analysts and social science researchers seeking to assess the performance of the economy and conditions of the workforce.

The BLS also surveys 16,000 employers on a monthly basis to determine job openings, new hires, and job separations by industry and by regions. This survey, the Job Openings and Labor Turnover Survey (JOLTS), lacks sufficient data (such as details about occupations and skills) to prepare estimates at the state and sub-state levels. Efforts to expand the survey have been stymied by resource limitations and budget constraints.

While some states conduct supplementary job vacancy surveys at the state and sub-state level, they remain uneven in quality and sporadic in their implementation.

Industry and Occupational Taxonomies

Occupational and industry taxonomies and classification systems help stakeholders effectively interpret data about workers and employers. The O*NET taxonomy defines the set of occupations that are found in U.S. business and industry. Its database, which is the nation's primary source of occupational information, contains hundreds of standardized and occupation-specific descriptors and is updated continually using a survey of a broad range of workers and their supervisors. Based on the Standard Occupational Classification (SOC), the O*NET-SOC taxonomy currently includes 974 occupations that have, or are scheduled to have, data collected from job incumbents or occupation experts. To keep up with the changing occupational landscape, the taxonomy is revised periodically; the latest revision was in 2010. The North American Industry Classification System (NAICS) is used by business and government to classify business establishments according to type of economic activity (process of production) in Canada, Mexico, and the United States.

These classification systems provide the foundation for how we view and measure jobs and industries. However, two problems plague their utility. First, the rapid deployment of new technologies and the diffusion of innovation outpace these classification systems' ability to keep up. Second, this problem could be fixed, but underinvestment in the nation's statistical infrastructure remains a serious impediment to more effective institutional planning and human capital investment.

Administrative Records

Employer compliance with state employment laws and regulations, and education and training institutions' compliance with administrative reporting requirements, yield large volumes of quarterly data on worker earnings and the dynamics of job gains and losses. With a longitudinal record of worker earnings and employment, analysts can accurately and reliably track the labor market experiences of workers and new graduates. For instance, interested parties could use these records to explore the characteristics that are common to unemployed workers in a given occupation or industry.

While state wage records—which indicate industry, employer, and earnings—provide a more complete labor market footprint, the links between graduates and their employment record are made only sporadically. A number of states (Florida, Connecticut, Tennessee, Virginia) and institutions have moved toward a more complete system that integrates student data with longitudinal data on employment and earnings outcomes.[2] The result is the first step toward a more robust understanding of the intersection between institutional performance and labor market success.

Similar efforts at the federal level are hamstrung by partisan gridlock, which leaves only existing sources of information. The Integrated Postsecondary Education Data System (IPEDS) is the primary source of enrollment data for colleges, universities, and technical and postsecondary vocational institutions in the United States. IPEDS provides descriptions of the broad qualifications of the emerging labor supply, such as enrollments and degrees conferred by program of study. The U.S. Department of Labor (DOL) has established the Wage Records Interchange System (WRIS) database where employer-provided wage records of participating states may be examined for purposes of tracking employment and earnings of a workforce that moves across state lines in pursuit of job opportunities. Unfortunately, these federal infrastructures lack program-specific data on a student's subsequent success in securing a job and the application of credentials gained.

Efforts from the U.S. Department of Education to invest in and establish state longitudinal data systems linking K–12, postsecondary, and workforce data are underway but will require more time to reach their goals before they become fully functional. While there are calls for greater accountability and evidence-based decision making in education, there is also political resistance on privacy grounds. This has the potential to thwart our ability to more deeply understand relationships between education and training investments, academic performance, and labor market outcomes. But, if harnessed effectively, this storehouse of administrative data has the potential to help institutions analyze students' educational and training investments and their associated labor market outcomes.

Occupational Employment and Projections

Higher education institutions, community colleges, and workforce development programs place a heavy reliance on occupational projections to gauge the labor market outlook. The BLS funds and coordinates a sample survey of state-level employers to determine detailed estimates of occupational employment and wages. Every 2 years, the DOL updates occupational projections to provide a rolling 10-year occupational outlook. State employment statistics agencies assume an important role in preparing these projections at the state and sub-state levels. However, surveys of occupational employment and projections of future employment are based on standard taxonomies, which update more slowly than the economy evolves. Consequently, we are much less likely to capture emerging occupations and changing job performance requirements in occupational data.

What Next?

As analysts begin to use these labor market data sources as a guide for job seekers, students, and the institutions that serve them, the limitations become clearer. These data were never intended to meet the needs of planning or curriculum improvement, or to assist students in making more informed choices about which program of study to pursue. Their initial development as a support for macroeconomic analysis and policymaking do not lend themselves to microanalyses of local labor market performance and evolution.

Too often, institutional researchers and program developers are unable to find the evidence in these data sources to justify their proposals. As a result, bold reforms and increased responsiveness to market forces—both critical to the future of comprehensive universities—often are limited in scope and may take longer to implement. Limitations of the data suggest that users need to be cautious as they apply it to critical analysis designed to guide institutional direction and investments.

THE INTERNET AND REAL-TIME LABOR MARKET INFORMATION

Among the early adopters of Internet technologies were employers and job seekers: Employers seeking new hires began to post openings to Internet job banks, while workers looking for jobs posted resumes to advertise themselves. This digitization of the job search process spread rapidly over the past 2 decades as commercial and public job boards gained prominence. In essence, how employers and employees engage in the job search and match process has been transformed. And, when harnessed effectively, the large volumes of new data can improve our understanding of labor market evolution.

Rise of the Internet as Labor Exchange

Jobs and resumes find their way to the Internet through many digital routes. Some routes are less structured, such as social media sites and digital information exchanges. For example, most states offer free job boards to employers and job seekers as a public service of their workforce agencies. Other sites, such as Craigslist, provide low-cost means of entering jobs at the lower end of the skill and wage spectrum. There are also growing numbers of specialty sites. Dice Holdings, Inc., is a leading provider of specialized websites for professional communities, including technology and engineering, financial services, energy, health care, and security clearance. Additionally, most firms use their company websites to post jobs and recruit employees.

As early as 2001, surveys conducted by the Society for Human Resource Management found that more than 90% of job seekers used Internet job postings as part of their job search strategy. While the Internet is not the only method used for job search and recruitment, it typically plays a part in most recruiting and hiring transactions. A recent study from the Rand Corporation concluded that Internet use increased the likelihood of 12-month re-employment for unemployed job seekers (Suvanulov, 2010).

By a wide margin, the most common avenue for posting or finding a job listing is via an online job board, such as Monster.com or CareerBuilder. Every day millions of job seekers scan Internet sites looking for jobs posted by employers, who have a collective 3 million monthly job openings they hope to fill. CareerBuilder, for example, claims 36 million active resumes on file, with 15,000 new resumes added on a daily basis.

Aggregating Job Postings

The posting of job ads and resumes on job boards and social media sites has spawned new services that aggregate the job ads from these sites. Sophisticated data aggregation technologies accompanied by advanced artificial intelligence algorithms can detect new job postings from thousands of sites (spidering); assess whether they are duplicate ads (de-duplication); and add them to a database that is updated on a daily basis. One of the most popular aggregator sites is Indeed.com, which reports 80 million unique visitors and 1.5 billion job searches per month. The website collects its job posting data from over 25,000 unique job boards and websites. Another firm, Wanted Technologies, claims that it maintains a database of 800 million unique job listings assembled over time from multiple sources.

Burning Glass Technologies uses its job aggregation technology to search for job listings from over 17,000 sources, including employer websites, job boards, newspapers, and government agencies. From this aggregation process, Burning Glass compiles a database of over 7 million current job listings, updated daily, taking special care to de-duplicate the gathered job postings. The ultimate goal, reports Burning Glass Technologies (2014), is "to populate a comprehensive database of real-time job opportunity information in a manner that provides as accurate a representation as possible of the full scope of advertised labor demand." Such claims, however, are not independently validated.

We also have witnessed explosive growth in employers' use of social media sites for job postings and employee recruitment. Simply Hired (2012), an aggregator of job postings across the Internet, reports significant growth in the use of social media services, especially Facebook and LinkedIn. These aggregators quickly realized that the vast volumes of data not only make job searches more convenient, but provide a source for more timely labor market information and new labor market analytics. Regular tallies of which industries are hiring, which occupations employers are looking to fill, and what skill sets are being sought, provide effective and timely signals of labor market demand that can be used for workforce development guidance.

Real-Time Labor Market Information

Until recently, the concept of real-time labor market information existed primarily in the abstract. At a 2009 Brookings Institution forum on labor market information, participants discussed the significance, opportunities, and challenges associated with this newly emerging data source. In the course of their conversations, they agreed to the following definition of real-time labor market information (LMI), which I adopt for the purposes of this chapter:

> Real-time LMI is labor market intelligence derived from the analysis of job postings and resumes placed into public and private labor exchanges. It is "real time" because it can be pulled from the Internet daily. It is labor market intelligence because it can include supply and demand trends, emerging occupations, current and emerging skill requirements, and market demand for education and certifications. (Vollman, 2011)

Aggregating digital information generated by Internet users as byproducts of market transactions often can be superior to traditional methods of data collection, which are more expensive and less timely. This is particularly true of market research, consumer behavior, and other economic exchanges where timeliness of the data is critical to capturing current market trends and conditions.

Additionally, technological advances in reading and analyzing these data have added a new dimension to labor market analysis. For example, most of the Internet-generated data—such as job postings and resumes—are in text formats as opposed to numerical codes. In order to make these data into meaningful labor market intelligence, however, careful parsing of words and phrases must take place to discern important factors such as skill requirements and performance traits associated with job postings.

The new systems and sources of real-time labor market information are not without limitations. Real-time data comes from private providers with proprietary interests, but with minimal regulation and uneven monitoring. These providers protect their sources and methods of data gathering and manipulation, which results in a lack of transparency. This is in stark contrast to public providers of labor market information, who must explain data gathering and estimating methods. However, as the use of real-time labor market information grows, users will likely assert themselves more in seeking greater transparency.

Real-time labor market information and new analytical tools are contributing to enhancing the quality of labor market analysis. We are able to see in greater detail the qualifications, skills, and certifications that employers want and job seekers offer. Once based mostly on quantitative information, labor market analysis now includes rich qualitative details that can inform how colleges and universities, in particular comprehensive universities, respond to trends in their local labor markets.

NEW LABOR MARKET ANALYTICS

Rich and timely data about supply and demand conditions in the labor market have given rise to innovative strategies for conducting labor market analysis. These new data sources and tools fill a number of critical gaps that traditional labor market information has not been able to overcome and allow for analysis in new categories such as trends in occupational demand, emerging skill and certification requirements, job seeker characteristics across industry, and supply and demand for a given skill set.

At the forefront of these new developments in analytics are proprietary software companies, career services providers, and job boards that aggregate and code data from job postings and resumes. Some of these providers also use sophisticated technologies to convert unstructured data (text, images, etc.) into meaningful analytics, which they can then license to state and local governments, workforce boards, educational institutions, and economic development and research organizations. Some examples of the new analytical tools' capabilities include tracking Internet job postings against official labor market data; capturing labor supply and demand by occupation; monitoring demand for various credentials, skills, and certifications; and tracking movements in the labor market, which can help job seekers chart their career paths.

Tracking Internet Job Postings Against
Official Labor Market Data

One of the most basic questions about new real-time LMI is whether it has the capacity to outperform traditional indices of labor market developments and trends. Take the Help Wanted Advertising Index, developed by the Conference Board. For years, the Index served as a leading economic indicator describing labor market developments and trends and the direction of U.S. businesses in hiring new workers. But as employers moved away from using newspapers for help wanted advertising, the value of this index as a predictor of hiring plans began to erode.

As more users turned to the Internet for job postings and the job search, the Conference Board (2012) responded by establishing the Help Wanted OnLine Data Series (HWOL). First published in 2005 and expanded in 2006, HWOL provides data on job demand captured through total levels of new and outstanding job postings. The index also controls for duplicate entries, which reduces the count of overall ads from above 13 million to around 4.5 million.

Because of the level of detail that HWOL can provide, it is a particularly useful tool for national, state, and regional labor market analysis. National estimates of occupational detail are published at the major occupational group level, and state and regional estimates are published at higher level aggregates. Using 6-digit SOC occupational level, HWOL produces time series data for the United States, geographic regions, states, metropolitan statistical areas, counties, and cities. Furthermore, users seeking more detail may purchase historical HWOL time series data on 6-digit occupations by local geographies.

HWOL's connection to and reference of the BLS data series is one of its most distinguishing features. After removing duplicate ads and controlling for coverage and definitional differences, the resultant unduplicated ad levels for the HWOL program compare favorably with those produced by the BLS JOLTS program. For instance, data from HWOL are comparable in timing and geographic detail to the BLS monthly measures of labor supply (unemployment) and employment. The Conference Board then releases these data on a monthly basis.

A recent analysis from the Upjohn Institute found that job openings data from JOLTS and HWOL generally move in the same direction over time (Watts, 2011). However, researchers noted differences in magnitude of job openings between the two series, with HWOL significantly higher than JOLTS (3.9 million versus 3.2 million, respectively, in September 2011). More independent examinations such as this one are needed from researchers and market analysts.

Labor Supply and Demand by Occupation

In order to understand the competitive aspects labor markets, analysts need to assess supply and demand balances. With a market share of 34% of help wanted websites and 24 million unique visitors each month, Career-Builder is the largest employment and recruitment website in the United States. Through its network of integrated Internet career sites, employers can directly solicit and target job seekers. The job seekers can access job postings and use available tools to find, explore, evaluate, and compare job opportunities.

CareerBuilder has moved forward in capitalizing on its large volumes of digital information by creating the Supply and Demand Portal, which permits users to search for data about the supply and demand for specific jobs and skills (CareerBuilder, 2014). Trends in these areas are available across detailed sub-state geographies. Analytics develop ratios of supply to demand that help employers identify the best regions in which to recruit talent with specific skills. But there are limitations. For instance, supply data come from the CareerBuilder resume files and thus are not a comprehensive count of available supply.

Credentials, Skills, and Certifications in Demand

One of the weaknesses of traditional labor market information is the lack of good data about credentials, skills, and certifications that currently are being sought by employers and how these are changing over time. Burning Glass Technologies, another of the industry leaders in real-time labor market information, was founded in 1999 by a group of artificial intelligence scientists focused on developing computer-based searches of large volumes of unstructured data. Since then, the company's primary mission has changed and is now to match people with jobs. When it first began to shift its focus, Burning Glass aimed its technology at major corporations and staffing companies confronted with large volumes of resumes that needed to be matched with detailed job specifications. Now, the company works more closely with workforce agencies, schools, and colleges.

Burning Glass uses its data extraction and analysis technologies to mine and code detailed data from each job listing, such as the specific skills, skill clusters, educational credentials, certifications, experience levels, and work activities required for a given job, as well as information about salary, number of openings, and job type. Users can then access this data with the Labor Insight tool, filtering by geography, time period, industry, occupation, or level of educational attainment. Users also may purchase services to develop customized data runs and analytics (Burning Glass Technologies, 2014).

Without real-time labor market data and associated analytical tools, analysis at this level of detail and responsiveness—particularly when examining an emerging field such as health informatics—could not be conducted. The traditional occupational taxonomy provides just one occupational category for health informatics and offers very limited data about how relevant skills are being integrated with other health care occupations.

Tracking Movements in the Labor Market and Charting Career Paths

Too little is known about the entry of new graduates into the labor market and the subsequent movement from one job to the next, and traditional labor market information provides only static snapshots of reported employment over time. Monster.com, one of the early entrants in providing digital job postings on the Internet, has developed new technologies to assess career paths and labor market movements using the more than 50 million resumes it has stored. These resumes contain vast amounts of job seeker data, including job titles, skills, certifications, credentials, experience gained, and special knowledge offered. Furthermore, the resumes in the database offer detailed employment histories and documented career paths of registered job seekers.

To exploit this storehouse of information, Monster.com is applying new artificial intelligence technologies that can parse resume data and develop new analytical tools to document career pathways and employment history (Monster.com, 2014). For employers looking for qualified candidates, the ability to tap into resume files and extract only those resumes that meet exact requirements enhances recruitment. Another use of the data permits a more systematic investigation of how job seekers move from one job to the next. More specifically, the analysis reveals the role of skills, credentials, and experience in successfully navigating the labor market.

Using this storehouse of data, Monster.com developed a new analytical tool that allows job seekers to better understand the employment pathway required for their desired career. With the company's Career Path tool, job seekers select an occupation that they seek to enter or have some experience in beforehand. Then, based on the analysis of experiences contained in the resume files, the job seekers are able to see "most likely next steps" or occupational titles reported by those with similar employment experiences. Job seekers looking to map career paths can extract details such as credentials, certifications, and skills reported by those navigating the labor market across occupations, industries, and employers.

But That's Not All

These examples of analytics are indicative of some of the capabilities available from the leading providers of real-time labor market information. They are not exhaustive and, given the state of this industry, innovations are being introduced regularly. Comprehensive universities stand much to gain by exploring how this emerging technology can be incorporated into planning, evaluation, and program development functions.

WHAT COMPREHENSIVE UNIVERSITIES CAN LEARN FROM COMMUNITY COLLEGES

Job creation in the coming decades will transform the landscape of emerging occupations, escalate skill requirements, and create new occupational certifications. These developments in the labor market will require swift and more focused actions from comprehensive universities if they are to respond to market demand. Comprehensive universities will be expected to have better alignment of curriculum with job performance requirements and the timely availability of programs of study that respond to these new labor market demands. Such responsiveness is essential to ensure students get jobs, employers find the workers with the requisite skills and qualifications, and policymakers continue to support needed investments in higher education.

For the past 2 years, Jobs for the Future, with funding from Lumina and Joyce Foundations, has been leading a major national effort to introduce real-time LMI tools and data systems to a select group of community colleges. The aim was not simply to transfer this technology but to explore ways that it could be applied to advance the community college mission of aligning services and outcomes with regional economies.

Among the significant accomplishments of the project were several illustrations of how real-time LMI assisted community colleges with difficult challenges. These examples offer comprehensive universities important guidance as they consider applying new technology and data analysis to the labor markets in which they operate. Examples of how community colleges utilize real-time LMI include capturing data on emerging occupations, analyzing the market and incorporating performance-based funding, responding to employer needs, aligning curricular content with regional economies, and tracking occupational supply and demand.

Capturing Data on Emerging Occupations

When "green" job advocates pushed for the development of programs that train workers for employment in green occupations and industries, LaGuardia Community College, an urban institution with over 18,000 students, made use of real-time LMI. Traditional labor market data lacked relevance since new job titles, skill sets, and certifications associated with green jobs were not yet found in these data sources. By using real-time LMI data tools, LaGuardia staff incorporated previously unavailable information about emerging occupations, skill requirements, and certification needed to qualify for employment in new industries. The outcome was a more targeted and responsive program design along with a more prudent use of limited resources.

Labor Market Analysis and Performance-Based Funding

Texas State Technical College (TSTC), the state-supported technical college system in Texas, serves nearly 30,000 students in traditional degree programs, short-term continuing education, and corporate training programs. Its role and mission are to help Texas meet the high-tech challenges of the global economy, in partnership with business and industry, government agencies, and other educational institutions. In response to a shift in its funding model—from one dependent upon enrollment and contact hours to the new model, which relies on student placement/transfer and graduates' earnings—TSTC is now examining how real-time LMI can be used for program and curriculum development. TSTC has implemented multiple real-time tools, including Wanted Analytics, CareerBuilder, and Burning Glass Labor Insight. In addition, TSTC is working closely with other providers such as the Texas Workforce Commission to develop new tools to link job seekers with complementary job openings based on competencies.

By harnessing real-time LMI, TSTC can improve a number of important metrics, most of which fall into two categories: fostering curricular alignment and strengthening job placement. Fostering curricular alignment requires that TSTC identify skills that are in high demand, and make comparisons of skills between resumes, job postings, and curriculum. Strengthening placement requires accurately forecasting emerging employer demand, providing insights into which employers are actively hiring and whether this demand is location-based, and identifying and recruiting

employer partners for advisory committees. TSTC's improvements using
real-time LMI provide an excellent illustration of how institutions should
approach the integration of real-time technologies into ongoing work.

Responding to Pressures from Employers

Cerritos College, a public community college serving southeastern Los
Angeles County, offers degrees and certificates in 87 areas of study in
nine divisions. When regional employers called on the Executive Dean
for Workforce Development to train more graduates with advanced manufacturing skills, he first turned to traditional sources of labor market
information. But these sources indicated long-term trends of declining
employment in manufacturing.

Using multiple real-time LMI tools and data sources, Cerritos analysts
conducted additional research to determine whether there was demand
for advanced workers and, if so, what skills and certifications were required. The use of real-time LMI revealed that there was in fact growing
demand in niche areas of manufacturing that were hidden within traditional industry codes. The real-time data provided stronger and more detailed evidence to move ahead in developing new programs in advanced
manufacturing occupations.

Aligning Curriculum with Regional Economies

Kentucky has opted to pursue job creation in targeted sectors and industry clusters, with particular emphasis on linking economic and workforce development strategies and investments. As part of this statewide
initiative, Kentucky Community and Technical College System (KCTCS),
a statewide multicampus system enrolling over 100,000 students in 600
credit programs, engages in self-assessment of its programs and courses.
As the largest provider of postsecondary education and workforce training in Kentucky, KCTCS has an incentive to ensure that its students graduate with the skills and qualifications employers need.

In August 2012 the Chancellor of KCTCS launched the Dynamic Skills
Audit (DSA) and called on every college in the system to determine the
key growth occupations that make up employment in the targeted economic sectors and to extract the knowledge and skills required for these
jobs using Internet job posting data. Then, the colleges were to conduct the
same analysis at the program level and use the results to improve course
content and learning objectives within those programs of study linked
with targeted occupations.

The DSA, which frequently yielded new insights about the changing
nature of occupational labor markets, was introduced not as a substitute

for established efforts at curriculum refinement and industry advising, but as a complement to them. The DSA relied on both real-time and traditional sources of labor market data, including details about skills and certifications. Technical support is provided to all campuses from the Chancellor's office, external consultants, and data systems providers.

The DSA is a cost-effective approach with a replicable structure that is enhanced by streaming labor market data. It is a sustainable, inclusive process that involves faculty, employers, and administrators in the quest to align programs of study with dynamic regional economies. This process will be ongoing as part of a larger transformation of how Kentucky community colleges respond to economic change, and is a strong example for other colleges and universities seeking to respond to changes in the labor market with dynamic and more detailed information.

Institutional Collaboration

The Bay Area Workforce Funding Collaborative (BAWFC), which focuses on health care and life sciences, covers 10 counties in the San Francisco Bay Area, a region of more than 6 million residents. The San Francisco Bay Area has multiple community colleges, universities, and workforce development programs engaged in training workers for the health care and life sciences industry. The region also has thousands of employers with a wide range of employment opportunities and needs. BAWFC served as a catalyst to bring together the region's education and training providers with employers to examine how well existing training programs were responding to employer demands in this critical sector.

On the supply side, analysts gathered data on program-specific characteristics, such as enrollments, completions, certifications, licensure, and job placement results. On the demand side, analysts gathered data on occupational employment levels, occupational wages, long-term occupational projections, current occupational demand from Internet job postings, and skill requirements and certifications data by occupation (also from Internet job postings). Using these data, the Collaborative then identified program duplication, excess of graduates in relation to employer hiring patterns in some instances, and the emergence of new certification requirements not captured by training programs.

PRACTICAL LESSONS FOR COMPREHENSIVE UNIVERSITIES

Comprehensive universities, if they are not already engaged in labor market research, will have to acquire the capabilities, tools, and new technologies to assess complex markets for talents and skills. Traditional sources of labor market information offer a starting point for developing a broad overview of labor market performance and trends. These sources, however, lack specifics or actionable intelligence that comprehensive universities need if they are to improve curricular content and develop market-responsive programs of study.

As comprehensives adapt to the changing demands of the labor market and increasing political pressure to train students, there are several lessons that we have learned, mostly from observing how community colleges have moved to more successfully tap real-time LMI.

Collaboration Is Key

Comprehensive universities do not have to pursue labor market research as individual institutions. In fact, there is much to be gained if institutions collaborate to frame the research and share investments in new labor market tools and systems. In our work with community colleges, we established a network of professionals at the outset of the project and convened this group regularly. Members of the group communicated their needs and shared their experiences and expertise with one another. They provided important feedback about technology and data deficiencies and contributed suggestions for improvements in data, systems, and technologies. Comprehensive universities should consider self-organized networks or use institutional or professional associations to support their collaborative efforts.

Learning Through Practical Applications

Comprehensive universities are confronting formidable, practical challenges that could benefit from the application of real-time labor market data and tools. In working with community colleges, we found that while the new technology offered enticing analytical functions, its value was not confirmed until each participating institution applied the technology to a practical problem of immediate relevance. Sharing practical applications of real-time technologies with colleges—and providing technical assistance for replication—proved most helpful in lifting the comfort level of new users.

Sustained Focus

New innovations often struggle to gain widespread acceptance across complex institutional settings. They are easy to put aside as the mounting daily workload intrudes. Comprehensive universities, like their community college counterparts, will need to plan for and effectively manage the introduction of real-time LMI tools. When real-time tools and technologies became better integrated with ongoing work and job functions of colleges, they received more intensive and extended use. These patterns of use ultimately helped to quicken acceptance of the technology.

Acquisition Costs and Budgeting Innovation

Comprehensive universities and community colleges alike face budget challenges and resource constraints. For this reason, when Jobs for the Future first began working with community colleges to adopt real-time LMI tools, we provided the tools at no cost, with the expectation that colleges would assume future responsibility for licensing fees and other associated costs.

Ongoing software license fees, training costs, and expenses associated with data analysis can be an obstacle for investing in new technology. Fortunately, providers of real-time tools have demonstrated a willingness to provide volume discounts, which can help participating campuses reap considerable savings through multicollege or cooperative procurement arrangements. Because the adoption of new real-time technologies also signals an important commitment to tracking labor market demand, private contributions could be solicited from employer groups to support such efforts.

Not a Panacea, But an Important Next Step

New real-time data, tools, and technologies are not a panacea but can contribute to improved decision making and program development. These new technologies provide a significant innovation that can be applied to support strategic planning, program development, and curriculum improvements. While they will not replace the power and influence of faculty, administration, boards, and employers in guiding the future of comprehensive universities, they are an important complement to these efforts.

CONCLUSION

The rise of the Internet as a labor exchange has created vast volumes of digital information from employers and job seekers. These postings have given rise to new real-time LMI, analytical tools, and data systems that provide a richer and more timely view of how labor markets work. This technology permits the capture of up-to-date information on occupations in greatest demand and data on new and emerging occupations, while allowing for a more in-depth examination of detailed skills, certifications, and job performance requirements that are valued by the market.

Until recently, colleges and universities have been unable to utilize the information provided by these new data sources and analytical tools. Recent work with a consortium of community colleges has yielded some important lessons that may be of value to comprehensive universities. These colleges demonstrated how new data and analytical tools can be applied to guiding alignment with regional economies; assist in examining the responsiveness of their programs of study; and help with curriculum review to ensure they are teaching the right skills.

Comprehensive universities must constantly reassess their programs of study and curriculum content to meet the demands of a dynamic economy and the transforming workplace. Furthermore, regulatory pressures such as those generated through "gainful employment" regulations certainly will require that comprehensive universities, in a highly competitive environment, place greater emphasis on controlling costs and monitoring the labor market outcomes of their graduates. The rapid emergence of data-based information systems such as College Scorecard for students and their families will allow students to incorporate labor market outcomes into the college and career decision-making process.

State and regional economic development strategies also will be more reliant on comprehensive universities. Graduates, along with their skill sets, will be a vital ingredient to support economic growth and innovation. Comprehensive universities must look to relevant labor market information as one critical source of input if they are to remain responsive to the power of market forces and consumer choice.

Comprehensive universities are integral to the national effort to provide graduates with the skills needed for our evolving economy. But they are under considerable pressure to produce graduates that can perform effectively in more demanding work environments. For comprehensive universities to continue to succeed with this important mission, they must have the capacity and tools to assess complex labor markets and understand the rapidly changing work environments their graduates will enter.

NOTES

1. Milken draws its findings from data going back more than 30 years. The data shows educational attainment by age, state, metropolitan area, and occupation, along with real wages and real GDP per capita.

2. College Measures is working with Florida, Tennessee, Virginia, Colorado, and Texas to make these links more easily available. Arkansas is also on the list, but it eschewed any publicity, and Nevada has supplied College Measures with the data, but is less engaged in making the data public.

REFERENCES

Burning Glass Technologies. (2014). Labor/insight market analysis. Available at www.burning-glass.com/products/laborinsight-market-analysis/
CareerBuilder. (2014). Supply and demand portal. Available at www.careerbuilder.com/JobPoster/Products/page.aspx?pagever=SupplyDemandPortal
Conference Board. (2012). Conference board help wanted online. Available at www.conference-board.org/data/helpwantedonline.cfm on February 1, 2012.
DeVol, R. C., Shen, I., Bedroussian, A., & Zhang, N. (2013). *A matter of degrees: The effect of educational attainment on regional economic prosperity.* Washington, DC: Milken Institute.
Manyika, J., Lund, S., Auguste, B., Mendonca, L., Welsh, T., & Ramaswamy, S. (2011). *An economy that works: Job creation and America's future.* Washington, DC: McKinsey Global Institute.
Monster.com. (2014). Career mapping. Available at my.monster.com/Career-Planning/Pathing.aspx#path=&tabIndex=0&eview=H
Simply Hired. (2012). Available at www.simplyhired.com
Society for Human Resource Management & Achieve. (2012). *The future of the U.S. workforce: A survey of hiring practices across industries.* Washington, DC: Author. Available at http://www.achieve.org/files/Achieve-SHRM-Survey.pdf
Sparks, E., & Waits, M. J. (2011). *Degrees for what jobs? Raising expectations for universities and colleges in a global economy.* Washington, DC: National Governors Association for Best Practices.
Suvanulov, F. (2010). *Job search on the internet, e-recruitment and labor market outcomes.* Santa Monica, CA: Rand Corporation.
U.S. Department of Education. (2011). Obama administration announces new steps to protect students from ineffective career college programs [Press release]. Available at www.ed.gov/news/press-releases/gainful-employment-regulations
U.S. Department of Labor. (2010). *Catalogue of workforce information sources: Decision making assistance for workforce and economic development.* Washington, DC: U.S. Department of Labor.
Vollman, J. (2011). *Brookings Institution LMI forum on real time labor market information.* Washington, DC: Brookings Institution. Available at http://

www.brookings.edu/~/media/research/files/speeches/2010/9/27%20
labor%20statistics%20reamer/0927_labor_statistics_vollman.pdf.

Watts, B. (2011, December, 19). Tracking job openings and employment. Available
at www.upjohn.org/node/678

CHAPTER 7

Opportunities for Innovation
Reimagining the Next Decade of Higher Education for Public Comprehensive Universities

Jeffrey J. Selingo

In October 2012, 2 weeks before the presidential election, some 130 leaders of regional public institutions gathered in New Orleans for the annual meeting of the American Association of State Colleges and Universities (AASCU) (Selingo, 2013). On the agenda were the usual conversations about state budgets, accountability, demographics, and access. But sprinkled throughout the 4-day meeting were discussions about innovation in higher education. The world had changed since the group last met the previous fall. MOOCs (massive open online courses) were now a household word. The governors of Florida and Texas were prodding their colleges to create a $10,000 bachelor's degree. And Western Governors University was shopping its competency-based model in other states, fresh from setting up shop in Indiana, Texas, and Washington.

At one session—aptly titled, "Warning: Edupreneurs in Rear View Mirror May Be Closer Than They Appear"—presidents engaged in a vigorous conversation about the balance between serving their institution's mission and innovating too quickly. Several complained that the public was questioning the value of their degrees at a time when their states needed more highly educated and highly skilled workers. While many in the room said they understood that change was necessary, they pointed out that their institutions had already been transformed by lawmakers and a public pressuring them to cut costs and still deliver a high-quality product. As the session came to a close, one of the panelists, Judith A. Bense, president of the University of West Florida, summed up the mood of many in the room: "Innovation might be the flavor of the moment," she said, "but our institutions have been around for generations and every year asked to do more with less money. New technology can't solve every problem we face."

Talk of disruption and innovation was fairly new territory for this crowd. Regional comprehensives have long been considered the undistinguished middle child of higher education—squeezed on one side by flagship research universities, on the other by community colleges. In recent decades, many of these former teachers' colleges have been known to simply copy what universities ahead of them did. They added dozens of master's and PhD programs that soaked up money and personnel, hired faculty members who pushed for research opportunities, and pumped money into research and expensive graduate programs. Few of the strategies were particularly innovative, and many just added new costs to the bottom line. Some educators believed the expansion was nothing more than "mission creep" (Selingo, 2000).

Now with those ambitions constrained by anemic growth in the economy, and institutions searching for new sources of revenue (or at least ways to cut costs), the time is ripe for regional comprehensive universities to consider adopting new ways of financing their operations, delivering courses, and utilizing technology. But just because the financial underpinnings of these institutions are collapsing does not mean that doing business differently will be easy, fast, or inexpensive, or suddenly bring a windfall of new dollars.

Skepticism of anything new and opposition to change run deep throughout higher education, and the public comprehensive sector is no exception. Just ask George Mehaffy. He is a vice president at AASCU and in charge of its Red Balloon Project, a national initiative to re-imagine and redesign undergraduate education for the 21st century. As part of that project, he has traveled to more than 40 regional campuses since 2010, talking to administrators and faculty members about the current state of higher education and the need for innovation. "One of my first presentations was at Fresno State in California," he told me. "Everybody from students to faculty were there. I laid out this notion that the money was not going to come back from the state. And at the end, a woman stood up and told me she didn't like anything I said and that I was flat-out wrong."

The reaction was similar as he visited other campuses. "They were hostile to change because they thought the current economic situation was temporary," Mehaffy said. Then in late 2011, he started to notice a difference in the response he received on campuses. "The MOOCs really captured their attention that they were vulnerable," he said. "They got it. Now they wanted to know what to do."

Unfortunately for those academic leaders, there is no playbook outlining exactly how to create an entrepreneurial university. But exemplars do exist in the sector, a handful of institutions that have carved a new path by embracing innovative strategies, and in many cases technology, to improve retention and graduation rates and deliver courses in different and cheaper ways to a new generation of students. This chapter draws on the experiences of those leaders in driving change on their campuses, based on interviews, campus visits, and my reporting for *The Chronicle of Higher Education* and my book on the future of higher education, *College (Un) bound: The Future of Higher Education and What It Means for Students* (2013). I start with a very brief overview of the barriers to innovation at public comprehensive universities (which mirror higher education generally). I then profile the most successful innovation efforts at seven regional public universities. I close with concluding thoughts on why these universities were able to pursue a change agenda when so many others find the prospect difficult, and sometimes impossible.

BARRIERS TO CHANGE

When Steve Jobs introduced the "Think Different" advertising campaign on his return to the helm of Apple in 1997, the slogan was not aimed at consumers alone. It also was meant to inspire those inside the struggling company to innovate for the future. Of course, what followed is now the story of one of the most successful companies in American history: a decade when Apple transformed the music industry with the iPod, the mobile phone industry with the iPhone, and now the publishing industry with the iPad.

Apple succeeded partly because it decided to take a different path from its competitors in the tech industry, and consumers followed. The history of business is filled with similar tales. Just look at what happened to Detroit's Big Three after the arrival of Japanese automakers in the United States. Regional comprehensives face a litany of challenges right now: rising costs; low completion rates; and delivery systems, curricula, and teaching methods that show their age. A desperate need exists for some big ideas to emerge that will reform entire institutions and transform how colleges do business.

Instead there is more sameness to regional comprehensives as a consequence of several key influences at work. These forces are so strong on many campuses that reformers often find it is just easier to build new institutions from scratch (Marcus, 2011). That is why what the seven institutions chronicled here have achieved in pushing for reforms on their campuses is significant.

Positioning for Prestige

College and university leaders often brag about the diversity of American higher education. Despite the rhetoric, colleges and universities "are eerily similar in vision," writes Doug Toma in *The Organization of Higher Education* (2012). "Their common goal is legitimacy through enhanced prestige" (p. 118). This race for prestige leads institutions to be risk averse, to innovate only on the edges, and for those who cannot afford to compete, to take on large amounts of debt to look like everyone else. Few institutions step away "from the herd in meaningful ways," Toma writes, because the "pull of legitimacy" is so powerful (p. 118).

Mission Creep

Mission creep is the result of positioning for prestige, and everyone on campus is to blame, not just presidents and boards. Bruce Henderson, a psychology professor at Western Carolina University, has been studying mission creep among regional comprehensives for 20 years. What Henderson found in his research is that everyone from the president on down through the faculty at these universities wants to recreate the schools where they trained as academics, yet they are not working with the same caliber of students. "We all got our doctorates at research universities, we learned how to behave there, and we wanted to teach at places where we could clone ourselves," Henderson said.

Governance

Faculty and departments have a significant role in making decisions, sometimes even more so on regional public campuses because they are mandated to do so in collective-bargaining agreements. Shared governance is not unique to higher education, but the way it is practiced in academe often leads to inefficiency and redundancy because leaders find it easier to simply delay decisions. Jeffrey Denneen, who leads the higher education practice at Bain & Company, said that in higher education "there's not a lot of clarity about roles and rights. Faculty choose to participate in some decisions, and ignore others. It's completely ad hoc and depends on how much they care. The fear of faculty backlash really tamps down on the ability of presidents to change universities" (Selingo, 2012, p. 93).

Funding Mechanisms

For the most part, regional comprehensive universities are more dependent on state funds than their flagship counterparts because many lack large research operations and medical centers, which bring in federal research dollars, or immense fund-raising arms. Without incentives to change from their chief funders—that is, major inducements tied to appropriations—the institutions will continue to operate the way they always have, namely, chasing student enrollment by which they are funded.

AUSTIN PEAY STATE UNIVERSITY: A COMPUTERIZED MAP FOR COLLEGE

During the summer of 2010, Tristan Denley, then provost at Austin Peay State University, about an hour northwest of Nashville, was facing a problem that perplexed academic leaders at many regional public comprehensive universities like his: how to keep students on a timely path to a credential. Only about a third of Austin Peay's 9,800 students graduate within 6 years, according to federal data (*Chronicle of Higher Education*, 2004). Although the university's completion rate had hovered around that mark for a decade or so, the problem was now front and center because the institution was about to take a financial hit for failing to graduate more students. Tennessee lawmakers had just passed a bill to make the state the first one in the nation to appropriate nearly all of its higher education budget based on student outcomes, including graduation rates. Getting students in seats was no longer good enough to qualify for state funds. Now public institutions had to be sure they graduated.

On a trip to Europe to visit family that summer, Denley read two books that would shape his thinking on how he could get more students to complete a degree. One was *Moneyball*, the precursor to the movie of the same title, about how the Oakland Athletics used player data to field an inexpensive, yet competitive baseball team. The other was *Nudge*, which argues people need to be gently encouraged to make better decisions in life. As he read the books, Denley wondered whether he could nudge students to choose courses that would lead to a degree, if they knew in advance how well they might perform.

The problem, as Denley came to see it, is that students have too many choices of pathways through colleges, entire course catalogs full of classes from which to choose with very little information about how they might do in the class beyond a generic description and comments on websites, such as ratemyprofessors.com. As a result, students often make bad decisions based on convenience or ease that lead them to classes that are a bad fit—either they do not need the class for their major or they end up failing. "The best analogy is that you're walking down a cereal aisle at the supermarket," Denley says. "You're overwhelmed with choices and you don't know the best one unless you open the boxes. Picking the wrong cereal is a low-stakes decision. Picking the wrong class is not."

Denley figured he could predict grades by matching current students to similar students who previously took the classes. The university had years of grade data just sitting in databases waiting for alumni to request transcripts. "We do a great job of collecting data in higher ed, but then not using it," Denley said. When he returned to campus from his vacation, he started putting his ideas to work. Prior to becoming provost, Denley had an active career as a programmer and math professor. Taking a page from the algorithms that power the suggestions Netflix and Amazon spit out to customers based on what similar customers purchased, Denley designed software that would do the same for college classes.

The following spring, Austin Peay unveiled Degree Compass. To see how it works, let's take a hypothetical student, Leslie, who is a nursing major constructing her schedule for the fall of her junior year. The system has access to her grades from the classes she took her first 4 semesters, plus her high school records. She is thinking about taking a statistics course to satisfy a math requirement. The software searches the records of students who have taken similar classes, sorting through some 500,000 grades to find appropriate matches and correlations between grades. How well Leslie or students like her did in calculus, for instance, has direct bearing on how she will do in statistics, Denley says. Such correlations lead the system to figure out predicted grades. The system recommends courses to Leslie based on her predicted grades and how those courses might satisfy degree requirements or general education credits (just in case she changes majors, so the classes still count for something). The software then creates a list with star ratings showing how well suited Leslie is for a particular course.

The software is incredibly accurate. It has predicted performance within a half a letter grade, on average. In more than nine out of 10 classes in which Degree Compass predicted that students would get an A, B, or C, they actually received one of those grades, Denley said. As a result, more students are taking recommended classes. In the fall of 2011, nearly half of the classes on the student schedules were from recommendations in the top 10, and nearly 60% in the top 15 (Parry, 2012). Overall, the number of students on campus earning A, B, or C grades has increased steadily since Degree Compass was put in place. What is more, the percentage of Pell grant recipients earning a top grade rose 4% during that time. For Candace Windle, a sophomore biology major at Austin Peay, Degree Compass gave her the confidence that she could persist in her major. "I didn't do as well as I thought I would my freshman year," Windle told me. "I was thinking about switching majors or taking a break, but when it matched me up with the courses I needed this year knowing my grades, I decided to keep going."

For those who see college as the last chance in life to explore by taking random classes, Denley's software might seem limiting, as if it is funneling individuals into a particular line at a supermarket. But Denley sees the platform as empowering students. On Netflix or Amazon, he said, most users click on the movies or books recommended to them because they are unaware of the titles. The same is true of Degree Compass. As in previous years, students still discover classes they otherwise might not have taken, but now they are empowered with information about how well they might perform and how the class fits in with their overall degree plan.

Most people who give advice, whether doctors, lawyers, or college professors, are heavily influenced by the advice they have given in the past, Denley said. When he tested his software at the University of Texas at Austin, it recommended a hypothetical student take Arabic. A university advisor wondered why it did not suggest Spanish. "I asked him why he would think that," Denley recalled. "He told me, 'Because most of the time I recommend Spanish. Most people take Spanish.'"

One problem with human advisors is that their knowledge of an inch-thick course catalog with hundreds of thousands of classes and dozens or perhaps even hundreds of majors is limited. They often know their field the best. When students need guidance on classes outside the major or even other majors, advisors struggle and sometimes make bad recommendations. The student, of course, ends up suffering the consequences. One result is that students are forced to take extra classes. On average, students who earn an associate's degree graduate with 19 more credits than the 60 they need. For recipients of bachelor's degrees, it is 16 credits beyond the 120 needed (Complete College America, 2011). That's fine if the student ends up graduating (although the degree still costs more than it should), but plenty of students end up dropping out because they got off track as a result of poor advice.

Three other Tennessee colleges have already adopted Degree Compass, which has attracted a $1 million investment from the Bill & Melinda Gates Foundation to modify the platform for other institutions. And because more students at Austin Peay are staying enrolled as they earn better grades, the university's retention rate has improved, resulting in a projected $3 million in performance funds from the state. Degree Compass has the potential to pay even larger financial dividends in the future. The university's graduation rate is critical to receiving new appropriations when the state fully implements performance funding. Denley also is working with corporate partners on further scaling the software platforms for use by other universities.

Meanwhile, Denley has moved on to his next project, applying the concepts of Degree Compass to another key decision in college: choosing a major. By looking at historical grade trends, Denley has isolated the courses that indicate success in a particular major—"fingerprint courses," as he calls them. He has linked those courses to the Degree Compass software, allowing students to see majors where others like them performed well. The university unveiled the software, called My Future, in the fall of 2012. About one in five students come to Austin Peay without a major, and Denley suspects many more are undecided but have picked their current major because a relative or guidance counselor suggested it.

Degree Compass and My Future are two innovative tools that use data found on any college campus. So why were they developed at a mid-sized comprehensive institution few people outside of Tennessee have ever heard of? What encouraged innovation on this particular campus? After all, when Denley first dreamed up the idea of Degree Compass on his trip to Europe, similar institutions were facing the same problems, and many of them still do today. Denley credits the change in the state funding formula and inspirational leadership on campus. "From the president on down, we talk a lot on our campus that if you want last year's results, then do this year what you did last year," he said. "But if you want something else, do something better. Don't muddle around the edges."

TEMPLE UNIVERSITY:
PROFESSIONAL ACADEMIC ADVISORS

Jenna Nicolosi changed her major three times in as many years at Northampton Community College in Bethlehem, PA, before she transferred to Temple University in 2011. She arrived at Temple as a philosophy major but switched to criminal justice during her first semester on campus. "I was lost," Nicolosi recalled. "I didn't know what I wanted to do. I was afraid I'd never finish."

That is when she met Rashidah Andrews, who helped put Nicolosi on the road to a bachelor's degree. Andrews is a professional academic advisor in Temple's College of Liberal Arts, part of a cadre of 60 full-time advisors hired by the university since 2006, whose sole job is to better guide students through the sometimes confusing, meandering, and increasingly expensive path to graduation.

"I come here quite a bit," Nicolosi said as she stood outside Andrews's office on a recent morning. "Faculty in criminal justice don't know everything about what I need to complete my degree requirements or about courses I might want to take outside the major. Rashidah understands me and my interests better than my professors."

Academic advising is one of those services on a college campus that students rarely think about until that frantic moment when they furiously search for a professor to sign a form allowing them to register for next semester's classes.

That is how academic advisors largely are seen by undergraduates: as administrative gatekeepers. The result is that professors find advising a burden that takes time away from research and teaching, and students seek advice elsewhere about majors, courses, and career options.

Only four out of 10 students consider academic advisors their primary source of advice regarding academic plans, according to the National Survey of Student Engagement (2012), an annual poll of freshmen and seniors. About one-third of freshmen said friends or family were their main advisors, and, overall, one in 10 students said they never even met with an academic counselor.

While students may consider academic advising an afterthought, the cost of acting on bad advice could negatively affect an undergraduate's prospects for graduating. Take the advisor who recommends the wrong class to satisfy a requirement and prevents the student from graduating on time, or another who suggests withdrawing from a course, putting a student's financial aid in jeopardy because he or she is not taking enough credits in a semester.

In the past, professors shrugged off extraneous courses and circuitous routes to a degree as the price of once-in-a-lifetime opportunities for students to explore a wide array of academic disciplines. But as the cost of college has spiraled upward—making it more important than ever to get students out on time—colleges and universities increasingly have taken the job of advising away from professors and put it in the hands of professional academic advisors.

"When it comes to helping students be engaged, to give them advice about what they need to do outside the classroom, faculty are not always the best," said Charlie L. Nutt, executive director of the National Academic Advising Association, which represents professional academic advisors. "It's not because they don't care, but because they are hired to teach a specific set of courses. So they end up advising like they were advised in college—they give students a schedule and send them on their way."

About 80% of colleges today use professional counselors in some capacity, according to a survey by the National Academic Advising Association (2011). A majority of those institutions still use faculty to advise students but rarely in the critical first 2 years of college when students are more likely to transfer or drop out. Professional academic advisors have become more common because colleges are more focused than ever on seeing students graduate, Nutt says, largely prompted by federal and state officials who are trying to tie taxpayer dollars to outcomes, like graduation rates.

To increase the number of returning first-year students and of graduates, Temple University introduced an extensive initiative in 2006 to improve academic advising. Since then, the Philadelphia institution, with 27,000 undergraduates, more than doubled its professional advising staff. During the same time, the proportion that returns for their sophomore year has remained relatively steady at around 88%. Meanwhile, those graduating in 4 years has risen to 43%, from 35%—the average 4-year rate for public colleges nationwide is 32%—and students report a higher satisfaction with advising.

For one thing, professional advisors are easier to find and have more time to dedicate to counseling than do faculty members. "It's a one-stop shop," said Irina Veramidis, a professional advisor at Temple. "We're always here. We're less intimidating than faculty, who are inaccessible to a certain extent."

One morning near the end of the Fall 2013 semester, Veramidis met with a sophomore who was still trying to decide on a major after she dropped her initial choice, biology. The student was debating between marketing and tourism. Veramidis mentioned that the marketing major requires a calculus course for business students. "You already took calculus for science and math and that didn't work out so well," she said, looking over the student's academic record on her computer monitor. The student asked about the difference between the two calculus classes. The advisor read the course descriptions and then recommended an online tutoring tool and suggested she talk to a peer advisor—a current student who worked in the advising center—who had taken the business calculus course.

Before the student left, Veramidis took one last look at her transcript and noticed she had taken enough Spanish classes to come close to qualifying for a minor. "Keep that in mind," she said. "We don't want you to be here longer than you need to be."

The appointment lasted half an hour—more time than the student would likely spend with a professor during limited office hours—and the conversation extended beyond the initial reason for the appointment: advice on registering for spring classes.

"Our hope," Veramidis said, "is that students see us as more than just clerical workers who help them register for classes."

Often, however, that is exactly how students see advisors and wait too long to seek help. As a result, colleges and universities are developing "intrusive advising" strategies that weed out students who need help the most but never seek it. "An advisor's role shouldn't be like a librarian who waits for students to come in for help," said Peter R. Jones, Temple's senior vice provost for undergraduate studies. "Too often by the time students realize they need help, it's too late."

Temple uses a computer algorithm to pinpoint students most at risk of dropping out in their first year of college. In the first semester of the freshman year, the algorithm is based on factors like their high school records, whether they plan to work a job more than 20 hours a week, and whether they are the first in their family to attend college.

Of its incoming class of 4,300 students, Temple identifies about 650 at-risk students and contacts them at least five times during the semester, twice in person. The second semester, the algorithm is based on first-semester grades and the number of credits completed. Since Temple put the system in place, the proportion of students who return for their sophomore year has risen, but only slightly, to 89% from 85%, Jones said.

"It is important for us to be realistic about how much opportunity for improvement exists," Jones said. "Many of our students are first generation, and many face significant challenges and stop attending simply because they cannot afford to continue."

CAL STATE MONTEREY BAY: SUCCESS COACHING TO IMPROVE RETENTION

When Ronny Hicks arrived at Cal State Monterey Bay in 2007, the university was "losing freshmen at an alarming rate." The institution's freshman-to-sophomore retention rate was a dismal 65%, the lowest in the 22-campus California State University system, where the average was 80%. "The problem was staring us right in the face, but there was no office that took this on," Hicks said. "There was no champion of retention here."

So Hicks turned to InsideTrack for help. InsideTrack is a 12-year-old company that provides one-on-one executive style coaching to students. It has worked with some 350,000 students across a range of colleges. Coaches from InsideTrack assist students in planning their career, in getting around obstacles that might get in the way of school, and with life skills such as time management, setting priorities, and financial challenges. An independent study of InsideTrack's work by Stanford University in 2011 found that students who received coaching were much more likely to stay enrolled, and graduate, than students who did not get coached, and that one-on-one coaching was the most cost-effective retention strategy (Bettinger & Baker, 2011).

In 2009, the first year Monterey Bay worked with InsideTrack, it assigned the coaches to freshmen most at risk of dropping out: first generation, low income, and those in remedial courses or with low grade point averages. That cohort equaled about a third of the freshmen class of 900 students. Half of the at-risk group of students received coaching from InsideTrack, and the other half served as the control group, using the university's traditional advising services.

At the beginning of the semester, coaches met with the students, helping them register for classes, meet with advisors, and understand what college was about. Throughout the first half of the semester, the coaches continued to talk with students through email and text messages. In the middle of the semester, the coaches returned to campus to meet with the students. When the coaches learned of problems students were having with specific departments on campus or about students thinking about dropping out, they passed that information on to the appropriate university officials. The coaches returned at the end of the semester for a final check-in with the students. The result: The retention rate was 5% higher for the students who were coached compared with those who continued through the traditional advising system.

Since then, the university has expanded the program and changed the composition of its at-risk groups. It also has added a bevy of services in response to the information it gleaned from students through the coaches: an office of retention, learning communities where students who take classes together also live together, and an early-warning system, which alerts students when they are at risk of failing.

When campus officials first proposed the idea of using outsiders to coach students, there was resistance on campus, especially among faculty members. InsideTrack charges anywhere from $400 to $700 a student, and professors wondered why the institution needed to spend money on a function that they believed was already served by existing resources on campus, including their own advising of students. "Once the president issued an ultimatum that retention matters, people started to take notice," Hicks said. "It took about a year and a half, but we changed the culture so that everyone on campus felt it was part of their job." Instructors no longer need prompting, for instance, to alert the appropriate campus offices when their students are having difficulty with a class; the retention office regularly gets email messages now from faculty members. "You won't find that on many campuses," Hicks said. "Faculty started to pay attention when they realized they wouldn't have any students to teach if they didn't get on the retention train."

University officials, meanwhile, were motivated by the financial rewards. The Cal State system provided performance funds to campuses that improved their retention rates, and cut the appropriations of those institutions where rates fell. By 2011–2012, Monterey Bay had boosted its retention rate to 81%, a dramatic rise from 65% in 2007–08. The campus now ranks above the system average. "It was all about gaining the insight into why these students were leaving," Hicks said. "InsideTrack gave us a window on the issues we were missing and showed us how to keep these at-risk students engaged."

SAN JOSE STATE UNIVERSITY: MOOCs AS A TEACHING TOOL

San Jose State University sits in the middle of California's Silicon Valley, just minutes from the headquarters of Google, Apple, and Facebook. With 26,000 undergraduates, San Jose State is the sixth largest campus in the sprawling California State University system, which enrolls nearly a half million students at two dozen campuses.

Long known as the university system for California's working class, Cal State has been turning more and more students away in recent years, the result of $1 billion in budget cuts that have eliminated more than 20,000 seats. In 2013, San Jose State received 78,000 applications for just 7,000 open spots.

Even for those students lucky enough to get in, an acceptance rarely guarantees seats in the classes they need to actually graduate. Students line up early for registration each semester, as if they were waiting to buy the latest iPhone at an Apple store. Courses often fill up with students who had been closed out in previous semesters, leaving everyone else to fill out their schedule with electives and making the route to graduation day even longer.

The classes with the most availability are usually those held in cavernous lecture halls, stuffed with 300 students. Sitting near the back of those sloped classrooms, students barely can make out the professor at the front of the room and often resort to surfing Facebook or texting during class. It is their own unique experience with "distance education."

Engineering students at San Jose State fear the one course they often have left to fulfill their graduation requirements: electronic circuits. The class is the most hated among engineering undergrads. Nearly half the students in the course receive a C or lower, and many students have to repeat it at least once.

In the fall of 2012, when engineering students went to register for the course, they were given the option of taking a section taught using materials from edX, a partnership between MIT and Harvard.

A few months earlier, four San Jose professors traveled to Cambridge, MA, to see how edX, one of the major providers of MOOCs, could help them remake their failing circuits course. The result would be a new way of teaching the class. San Jose students would watch edX lecture videos at home and attend face-to-face classes twice a week with a San Jose professor to practice what they had learned and ask questions.

More than 80 students signed up for the course. Another 160 students registered for the traditional version of the course. By the midterm, the San Jose professors teaching the edX version knew they were on to something. Grades in that section were significantly higher than in traditional classes. Nine in 10 students ended up passing the MOOC-powered course. The pass rate in the traditional courses was just 50%.

Those numbers caught the attention of San Jose's president, Mohammad Qayoumi. To serve increasing numbers of students with less money, he needed to move those already on campus through faster and more efficiently, and improve the quality of the academic experience, all at the same time. If the MOOC approach worked in engineering, why couldn't it work in philosophy, political science, or physics? Could he save money and improve results if he outsourced the teaching function to the best universities and then hired faculty to act more like coaches?

"We must seek new ideas and approaches from other industry sectors and promote audacious thinking through carefully reviewing and adapting effective innovations," the president wrote in a report.

Qayoumi did not know it yet, but he had happened on an emerging school of thought in higher education, one where human professors churning out commoditized information would be partly replaced by machines. It is an idea that would raise hackles among his faculty and end up putting him at the center of a national debate about the role of online learning. In the subsequent months, San Jose State administrators partnered with another MOOC provider, Udacity, to jointly create three introductory mathematics courses open to anyone whether they were enrolled or not, and urged the philosophy department to adopt an edX class in its curriculum. But neither experiment worked out as administrators initially had hoped.

Philosophy professors responded by publishing an open letter criticizing the notion of "one-size-fits-all, vendor-designed" courses and refused to incorporate the edX class into their courses, worried that the experiment would both put them out of work and provide a substandard education to their students. Meanwhile, the three Udacity courses had pass rates between 24% and 51%, much lower than their traditional face-to-face classroom counterparts. The following semester the rates improved for the Udacity courses, sometimes exceeding the pass rates for the face-to-face courses, thanks partly to the fact that they enrolled better prepared students.

The conflicting results and uproar over the courses on campus caused San Jose administrators to pause the experiment with Udacity for a semester to tweak the offerings. When the Udacity-powered courses returned, they were offered for credit to a limited number of students at San Jose State and among the other California State University campuses. The abrupt change was seen by some critics as proof that the MOOC experiment failed, but officials at San Jose State and Udacity saw the move as a pivot. MOOCs could be useful tools within the context of a larger face-to-face course (but not a replacement for it) or with experienced students motivated to learn a skill.

"We have found our niche in helping people find employable skills," Sebastian Thrun, Udacity's founder, said. "The basic MOOC is a great thing for the top 5% of the student body, but not a great thing for the bottom 95%."

CAL STATE NORTHRIDGE: HYBRID COURSES POWERED BY THE OPEN LEARNING INITIATIVE

In the fall of 2008, encouraged by university administrators, the math department at Cal State Northridge started offering hybrid courses for its introductory statistics course. As at many large universities, this is a course with large enrollments—800 a year at Northridge—and numerous sections taken mostly by non-math–majors. Rather than create their own online content, Northridge instructors used materials provided for free from Carnegie Mellon's Open Learning Initiative (OLI). "I wanted to try a hybrid course but I never really liked the attempts at materials until OLI came along," said Mark Schilling, a math professor at Northridge.

The OLI is the Cadillac of online courses. The classes take months to build and are designed by teams of professors in the field, along with learning and data scientists, who constantly are searching for clues in the student data they collect and track in order to improve the product. The OLI has designed 2 dozen courses this way in statistics, biology, and other core subjects using the latest research on how people learn instead of relying solely on the intuition of professors. The result is virtual simulations, labs, and tutorials that provide immediate feedback to students and information to faculty members to help them spend their face-to-face time with students in the most productive way. With the financial backing of charitable foundations, Carnegie Mellon provides the courses free to more than 100 colleges.

That includes Northridge, where students in four sections of introductory statistics use OLI materials 2 hours a week outside of class, with the remaining 2 hours for in-class discussion and problem solving. The idea behind hybrid courses is twofold. First, with fewer classroom meetings, the time spent face-to-face is focused on higher-value concepts, rather than just lectures. And, second, with fewer sections meeting face-to-face every week, professors potentially could serve more students as their role changes to one more akin to a coach than a revered figure at the head of the class. "A good coach figures out what makes a great athlete and what practice helps you achieve that," Carl E. Wieman, associate director of the White House Office of Science and Technology Policy, told *The Chronicle of Higher Education.* "They motivate the learner to put out intense effort, and they provide expert feedback that's very timely" (Berrett, 2012).

There is beginning to be a body of evidence that hybrid courses can produce student learning outcomes equal to those of face-to-face instruction, and do so in significantly less time. The most noteworthy of these studies was conducted by Ithaka S+R, a nonprofit think tank focused on technology in teaching. In the fall of 2011, Ithaka put OLI's statistics course to the test. Researchers asked undergraduates at six different public universities taking a face-to-face introductory statistics course whether they would participate in a study (Bowen et al., 2012). Some of them would stay in the class and others would be assigned to a hybrid version of the course using OLI materials. More than 600 students took part in the research and were randomly assigned to either the blended course, which had an hour of face-to-face instruction each week and the rest online, or the traditional course, which met for 3 hours once a week or an hour and a half twice a week.

The group turned out to be a diverse set of learners. This was an important factor for researchers since the commonly held assumption is that those who perform best in online classes are self-motivated, high-achieving students. Half of the students in this study came from families with incomes less than $50,000, and half were the first in their families to go to college. Fewer than half were White, and the group was almost evenly split between students with grade point averages above and below 3.0.

At the beginning of the semester, all the study participants took a test of statistical literacy. They took the same exam at the end of the semester, along with a questionnaire. How faculty members taught the course varied from campus to campus. In general, the professors tended to lecture more often in the purely face-to-face sections (without the online component to pick up that task), and attendance was lower in the weekly meetings for the hybrid sections (where students appeared only when they needed extra help). The bottom-line finding of the study was that students learned just as much in the hybrid format as they would have in the traditional course. What's more, the study found that the students in the hybrid sections took about a quarter less time to learn just as effectively, a discovery that has the potential to significantly reduce costs for large introductory courses. William Brown, a former president of Princeton University and one of the architects of the study, said, "The most important single result" of the research was that "it calls into question the position of the skeptic who says, 'I don't want to try this because it will hurt my students'" (Wessel, 2012).

At Northridge, however, students and professors remain split on efficacy of the hybrid statistics course. Schilling, a math professor, said class evaluations are almost evenly divided on whether they like the format. The professors in the department who use the OLI material "tend to be the early adopters and were motivated." The other instructors either do not have the time or do not see the benefits. "Given this is the math department, most professors teach it like a traditional math course," Schilling said. "It's a lot easier to go into the classroom every day and teach the way you always have."

NORTHERN ARIZONA AND U. OF WISCONSIN SYSTEM: COMPETENCY-BASED DEGREES

Like many new ideas in higher education, Western Governors University grew out of frustration with the status quo. In 1995, nearly 20 governors from western states gathered for a meeting and agreed it was easier to form a new college than try to reform their existing ones (Gravois, 2011). Their idea was to create an institution that would measure learning and award credentials like no other on a massive scale. The idea behind Western Governors was simple and practical: Degrees should be based on how much students know, not how much time they spend in a classroom. Western Governors is built on a competency-based system where students demonstrate mastery of a subject through a series of assessment tests, instead of following a prescribed set of courses.

Western Governors now boasts 25,000 students and is growing at a breakneck pace of 40% a year. The average student at Western Governors completes a bachelor's degree in about 2½ years for a price tag in the neighborhood of $15,000. Its teacher education program is the largest supplier of math and science teachers in urban schools. Since 2010, three states—Indiana, Texas, and Washington—have created official spin-offs, allowing residents to access state financial aid programs to pay for tuition. Despite these successes, the idea of competency-based education often is met with skepticism within academic circles. Few colleges want to risk defying the financial and academic model that has long defined higher education.

But with colleges under pressure from the public and politicians to create more low-cost degree options—and with Western Governors being courted by other states—at least two comprehensive universities were willing to take the gamble: Northern Arizona University and the University of Wisconsin system. Both announced plans to launch competency-based degree programs in 2013.

In January 2013, Northern Arizona rolled out three competency-based bachelor's degree programs in business administration, computer information technology, and liberal studies, aimed at working adults. Built in conjunction with Pearson, the major textbook publisher, the self-paced courses rely on materials from books and online lectures, not traditional professors. While the university's full-time faculty have a hand in constructing and maintaining the courses, the cost savings for Northern Arizona come from abandoning the traditional faculty role in teaching and advising. Instead, the university plans to hire full-time, coach-mentors only as they are needed when enrollment grows. These coach-mentors reduce costs from the traditional model because they will serve many more students by focusing only on those who truly need help. The university pays Pearson $875 for every enrolled student every 6 months (Kolowich, 2012). "The cost of the faculty is a major cost," said Fred Hurst, Northern Arizona's senior vice president for extended campuses. Those cost savings have been passed on to the students in the form of lower tuition: Students pay a flat fee of $2,500 every 6 months. The university anticipates the average student will finish the program, called Personalized Learning, in 3½ years, for a total price of just $17,500.

The University of Wisconsin–Milwaukee launched UW-Flex, its competency-based program, in the fall of 2013, with four degree and one certificate program (nursing, diagnostic imaging, information science and technology, and professional and technical communication), as well as an array of general education courses offered through the university's extension service. As at Northern Arizona, the competency-based degrees are built off current programs using existing faculty members who design the learning outcomes and assessments needed to prove competency.

Officials at both universities said the time was right to introduce competency-based degrees aimed at adult students who have some college credits, but no degree, because of the advances in technology. "Our students have all the information that we have as professors," said Aaron Brower, special assistant to the president of the University of Wisconsin system. "So there is no premium on access to information. The question now is how do you build an educational system around that providing the opportunity for individual instruction."

The biggest hurdle for Northern Arizona and the University of Wisconsin in starting these programs was not with faculty members or others on campus, but with off-campus accreditors and the federal government, which design many of their rules and regulations around the "credit hour," which mandates direct faculty instruction. The U.S. Department of Education released a "Dear Colleague" letter in March 2013 to provide guidance to institutions on using federal aid for competency-based degrees (Fain, 2013). "We are working closely with the Department of Education," Brower said. "They are eager to help us figure this out."

Both Wisconsin and Northern Arizona have set aside initial dollars to get the programs off the ground, but expect them to be self-supporting within a few years. Given that the institutions project large enrollments—Northern Arizona expects 8,000 students in 5 years—it is probable that the programs could generate a healthy profit. Even so, Hurst, the Northern Arizona senior vice president, said questions remain about the unexpected costs that typically crop up with any new project. "If we could control those costs, then this could be generating real revenues for the university in a few years to help offset our losses elsewhere."

A RECIPE FOR SUCCESS

While the work of these seven comprehensives to change how they deliver courses to improve outcomes, boost efficiency, save money, or generate revenue, is significant, each one taken alone is a small drop in the bucket in the effort needed to position these institutions for the future. For example, none of the projects profiled here are generating for the universities new revenue streams that even come close to supplementing the dollars that will likely disappear from the federal government, state coffers, and students in the decade ahead. For now, the projects have allowed the universities to find needed efficiencies or improve productivity. Those improvements should be applauded, but whatever has been gained, has flowed largely to the bottom line. In other words, the cost savings have not been passed on to the students and the efficiencies have not led to greater access for students, at least not yet.

All these endeavors are in their early stages. But as I talked with those academics deeply involved in the projects, I discovered there are common themes as to why these efforts succeeded when so many others in the sector have failed. In further exploring the reasons for success, we can discover clues about what might shift the dynamics across the entire sector, so that it will be more open and likely to embrace innovation in the years ahead.

One key ingredient to success is leadership. It was the one common response mentioned by all the project participants—they were leading these enterprises because someone at the top had inspired them, asked them, or encouraged them. But it is not just about rhetoric. On many of the campuses, there was a key champion—a Tristan Denley at Austin Peay, a Ronny Hicks at Monterey Bay—whose day-to-day responsibility included making sure project goals were met.

Financial incentives helped, of course. Many campus officials said they were motivated by innovation or performance funds that encouraged them to figure out solutions to nagging problems (or punished them by taking away dollars if they did not). On a small scale, such dollars did not seem to make that much of a difference, but in the case of Tennessee, where the institution's future appropriation from the state depends on improving student success, the presence of money obviously played a large role.

Playing an almost equal role to money is the academic culture and its rewards structure. As discussed in an earlier section, the race for prestige matters to most campus leaders and faculty members these days. There is no ranking as well-known as that of *U.S. News & World Report* for the nation's most innovative universities. So there is more risk than reward right now for college leaders who follow a different path than or look radically different from the institutions ahead of them.

Finally, the education innovation arena is evolving at a very fast pace. MOOCs were a fringe idea at the start of 2012, and by that summer the president of the University of Virginia was ousted by her board because she was not moving fast enough to position the institution for a rapidly changing world. Academics are, by their nature, skeptical of anything new and want an abundance of evidence before changing course. But given their sometimes precarious position in the marketplace, comprehensive universities might find it best to adopt an iterative approach to innovation rather than wait for others to figure it out. "We may not have all the evidence we need," said Denley of Austin Peay, "but we need to take more risks if we're going to change the performance of our institutions."

REFERENCES

Berrett, D. (2012). How 'flipping' the classroom can improve the traditional lecture. *The Chronicle of Higher Education.* Available at chronicle.com/article/ How-Flipping-the-Classroom/130857/

Bettinger, E. P., & Baker, R. (2011). *The effects of student coaching in college: An evaluation of a randomized experiment in student mentoring.* (NBER Working paper). Available at ed.stanford.edu/spotlight/stanford-study-shows-college-student-coaching-improves-retention-and-graduation-rates

Bowen, W. G., Chingos, M. M., Lack, K. A., & Nygren, T. I. (2012). *Interactive learning online at public universities: Evidence from randomized trials.* New York,

NY: Ithaka S+R. Available at www.sr.ithaka.org/sites/default/files/reports/
sr-ithaka-interactive-learning-online-at-public-universities.pdf

Chronicle of Higher Education. (2004). College completion. Available at
collegecompletion.chronicle.com

Complete College America. (2011). *Time is the enemy.* Available at http://
completecollege.org/docs/Time_Is_the_Enemy.pdf

Fain, P. (2013). Beyond the credit hour. *Inside Higher Ed.* Available at www.
insidehighered.com/news/2013/03/19/feds-give-nudge-competency-
based-education

Gravois, J. (2011, September/October). The college for-profits should fear.
Washington Monthly. Available at www.washingtonmonthly.com/magazine/
septemberoctober_2011/features/the_college_forprofits_should031640.php

Kolowich, S. (2012, July 11). Competency loves company. *Inside Higher Ed.*
Available at www.insidehighered.com/news/2012/07/11/northern-arizona-
u-partners-pearson-competency-based-degree-programs

Marcus, J. (2011). Old school: Four-hundred years of resistance to change. In B.
Wildavsky, A. P. Kelly, & K. Carey (Eds.), *Reinventing higher education: The
promise of innovation* (pp. 41–72). Cambridge, MA: Harvard Education Press.

National Academic Advising Association. (2011). *2011 NACADA national survey.*
Available at http://www.nacada.ksu.edu/Resources/Clearinghouse/View-
Articles/2011-NACADA-National-Survey.aspx

National Survey of Student Engagement. (2012). Available at nsse.iub.edu/

Parry, M. (2012, July 18). Big data on campus. *New York Times*, p. ED24. Available
at   http://www.nytimes.com/2012/07/22/education/edlife/colleges-
awakening-to-the-opportunities-of-data-mining.html?pagewanted=all&_r=0

Selingo, J. (2000, November 17). Facing new missions and rivals, state colleges
seek a makeover. *The Chronicle of Higher Education.* Available at chronicle.
com/article/Facing-New-Missions-and/31282

Selingo, J. J. (2013). Bain goes to college: Rethinking the cost structure of higher
education. In A. P. Kelly & K. Carey (Eds.)., *Stretching the higher education dollar*
(pp. 87–104). Cambridge, MA: Harvard Education Press.

Selingo, J. J. (2013). *College (un)bound: The future of higher education and what it means
for students.* New York, NY: New Harvest.

Toma, J. D. (2012). Institutional strategy. In M. N. Bastedo (Ed.), *The organization of
higher education: Managing colleges for a new era* (pp. 118–159). Baltimore, MD:
Johns Hopkins University Press.

Wessel, D. (2012). Tapping technology to keep lid on tuition. *Wall Street Journal.*
Available at online.wsj.com/article/SB10001424052702303942404577534691028046050.html

CHAPTER 8

Learning to Do

Anchoring a State Comprehensive University in Mission Drift

Michael B. Horn, Michelle R. Weise, Lloyd Armstrong

Alongside community colleges, state comprehensive universities (SCUs) are the broad-access institutions that together educate nearly 80% of Americans (Carey, 2010). The People's University, as Bruce Henderson (2009) calls it, "opened higher education to the masses in the middle class" (p. 5). Distinct from flagship universities and private colleges because of their vocational orientation geared toward specific regions, SCUs originated as schools that were entrenched in the community. Roughly half started as teachers colleges that prepared and educated elementary school teachers in the region. Although they have moved more broadly into other realms, they continue to have a significant impact on teacher preparation; in 2009–10, as an example, SCUs awarded 54,705 (77%) of the 70,761 bachelor's degrees in education (National Center for Education Statistics, 2014). Today SCUs vary greatly in size, selectivity, and the range of disciplines and majors they offer.

There's an economic urgency to the current challenges and competition: State budgets for higher education are shrinking; the costs for traditional institutions to stay competitive with their peers continue to rise—in an effort to control costs, many are being forced to drop out of the race; the price of tuition has soared; and, for many SCUs, there exists an increasing number of students who wish to enroll but cannot for the lack of space. SCUs also face competitive threats from an emerging group of online organizations, ranging from for-profit universities (FPUs) to massive online open courses (MOOCs).

This chapter uses the theory of disruptive innovation to bring into sharp relief the nature of the disruptive threat to SCUs from online innovators. An in-depth review of the key players in the field and their effect on the current business models of SCUs illuminates a need for administrators and faculty to think more critically about the missions of their institutions. Exploring why students "hire" an SCU through the "Jobs to Be Done" theory—a way of looking at the higher education market from the student's point of view—shows why many SCUs should return to their regional and vocational roots and develop stronger relationships with industry clusters in the area.

WHAT IS DISRUPTIVE INNOVATION?

The theory of disruptive innovation helps explain why it is so challenging for organizations to sustain success. Organizations tend to innovate faster than their customers' needs evolve. As a result, most organizations eventually produce products or services that overshoot their customers' needs (Christensen, 1997). Companies pursue these *sustaining innovations* at the higher tiers of their markets because this is what historically has helped them succeed: By charging the highest prices to their most demanding and sophisticated customers at the top of the market, companies achieve the greatest profitability; however, by doing so, companies unwittingly open the door to disruptive innovations at the bottom of the market. An innovation that is disruptive allows a whole new population of consumers at the bottom of a market to gain access to a product or service that historically was accessible only to consumers with a lot of money or a lot of skill.

Generally, the original disruptive entrant does not offer a breakthrough improvement, nor does it even offer a "good" product from the established organization's perspective. Characteristics of disruptive businesses, at least in their initial stages, can include lower price points or unattractive cost structures, from the perspective of the established organizations; smaller—or seemingly nonexistent—target markets; and simpler products and services that may not appear as attractive as existing solutions when compared against traditional performance metrics. Existing customers will not buy it, and industry leaders will not use it; they might even mock and deride the new product that, as a result, entrant organizations often pioneer. To gain traction, these underwhelming products do not compete head-on with the established names in the field.

Instead, disrupters serve nonconsumers—people for whom the alternative is nothing at all. Disruptive innovations tend to be simpler, more convenient, and more affordable than any of the other options in the market, which allows nonconsumers to benefit from the new product. In the case of Sony transistor radios in the 1950s, for example, teenagers were fine with the perceived lower quality because, from their perspective, the radios were delightful, cheap, and portable. Over time, the disrupters predictably improve their products. Ultimately, as the mainstream customers flock gradually to the disruptive solution that develops enough to meet their needs, disrupters serve a much wider audience more affordably.

WILL SCUs BE DISRUPTED NEXT?

The disruption of the print newspaper is a fitting analog for the potential disruption of SCUs. Newspapers are general-purpose products that try to do lots of "jobs"[1] for lots of people: They help you stay up-to-date with current events; they help you find a job, a career, a relationship; they amuse you with puzzles and help you find a home. In doing so many different jobs, however, they struggle to do everything well. With so many roles to defend, print newspapers were quite susceptible to disruption. Thus, it was not a single business but a multitude of them, including Google, blogs, CNN.com, Cars.com, Monster.com, Craigslist, and others that together disrupted the print newspapers. Piece-by-piece, each led to the unbundling of the jobs for which we formerly hired a newspaper.

Much like the newspaper, universities have long operated as institutions with multiple value propositions. In the 17th and 18th centuries, universities emerged primarily as teaching institutions, but most evolved gradually to help different people with different jobs: research for society, teaching and imparting knowledge to students, a social experience or a transition to adulthood, and access to a network, job, career, or promotion. With many parts of the organization to defend and by doing many different jobs for different people, the university, like the newspaper, also could be disrupted on a job-by-job basis.

To deliver on these multiple value propositions, universities have cobbled together fundamentally different business models, which have turned them into very complicated and expensive institutions. Research is organized into what we call a solution shop model; teaching is done as a value-adding process activity; and universities run a multitude of facilitated networks, within which students work with one another, career staff, or even alumni to succeed and have fun (Stabell & Fieldstad, 1998).[2] These business models are not only fundamentally different, but are also incompatible within the same organization. A typical state university today is the equivalent of a merger of the consulting firm McKinsey (a solution shop) with Whirlpool's manufacturing operations (a value-adding process activity) and Northwestern Mutual Life Insurance Company (a facilitated network). Having multiple business models housed in one university complicates its operations and creates conflicts and competition between the different models over resources.

One of the critical reasons for climbing administrative costs in traditional universities is the complexity of managing under one umbrella the fundamentally different business models of research, teaching, and social growth (Christensen, Horn, Caldera, & Soares, 2011). For a university, the precise costs of producing different parts of an education are in many ways unknowable because these bundled services are interdependent and inseparable. All revenues are spent on increasing the size and quality of some mixture of the multiple business models.

Costs become even more convoluted as colleges and universities—similar to their peers in the business world—act on their desire to go up-market, what Gordon Winston (2000) describes as the "arms race" and Kaplan CEO Andrew Rosen (2011) calls "Harvard envy." A joint report from Bain & Co. and Sterling Partners describes the fallout of what they call the "Law of More": "Institutions have become overleveraged. Their long-term debt is increasing at an average rate of approximately 12% per year, and their average annual interest expense is growing at almost twice the rate of their instruction-related expense" (Denneen & Dretler, 2012, p. 4).

The quest for prestige, in Rosen's opinion, has led to experiences that have nothing to do with learning, not to mention the misallocation of resources that drives up tuition and consumes large sums of taxpayers' money. Research becomes a priority over teaching, and socially oriented student services trump academic efforts. (Consider the resort- or country–club–like university with sushi bars, climbing walls, ice cream trucks, and more and newer buildings.)

SCUs have not been immune to Harvard envy. In his brief history of SCUs, Henderson (2009) uses the phrase "in theory" when describing the original missions of these universities: "In theory the SCUs are distinguishable from the rest of the public colleges and universities by having a distinctive mission . . . a special responsibility for providing teaching, research and public service with a vocational orientation" (p. 6). SCUs are known for providing access to affordable higher education to all students. At the same time, however, these comprehensives are spread thin by the need to "be responsive to . . . government officials, parents, students, and people in the private sector, who desire an increasingly broad array of activities, from curricula and courses to services and entertainment" (p. 9). Pulled in multiple directions, SCUs have lost sight of their original missions.

In their attempt to distance themselves from their vocational orientation, SCUs have found themselves mission-adrift without, according to Henderson, "a model that fits their situation" (p. 15). Because SCUs prioritize access to education, it is virtually impossible to mimic the selective admissions standards of research institutions. According to IPEDS data on all enrolled undergraduates for 2012, out of the four-year non-doctorate-granting public institutions, 49.6% of students are enrolled exclusively full-time. Many of these students work while enrolled full-time: 13.8% work 26 to 39 hours per week while 12.8% work 40 or more hours per week. Out of all students enrolled full-time, 29.4% are first-generation college students whose parents have a high school diploma or less, and 15.2% of first-generation students work 26 to 39 hours per week while 15.8% work 40 or more hours per week. The pressures on an SCU to prioritize research do not align well with a student population that, with its wide range of skill sets, is in need of strong pedagogy and mission-oriented instructors.

This drift into research increases overall costs and exacerbates the financial pressures on SCUs. For example, even though the University of California (UC) system fights to block the California State Universities (CSUs) from morphing into research universities, the CSU system has developed research facilities in a range of fields, including agriculture and biotechnology. A 2002 report estimated that faculty members spent about 20% of their time on scholarly and creative work; additionally, 50% of faculty reported that they wanted to do less teaching and 85% reported that they wanted to do more research (Social and Behavioral Research Institute & California State University, San Marcos, 2002). When faculty members interact less and less with students, inevitably the value of student learning diminishes in favor of research. This is problematic for a sector that serves a student population so different from that of a more selective research institution.

KEY PLAYERS AND THE NATURE OF THE DISRUPTIVE THREAT

This up-market phenomenon displayed by SCUs is common to all sectors we have studied. It is a key reason why incumbent organizations struggle so much with disruptive innovation; they prioritize becoming bigger and better, overshoot their customers' needs, and inevitably cede more and more ground to the disrupters. In this particular case, SCUs no longer have a clear mission; they have become less specialized and more generic over time, which has increased their overall costs in ways difficult to reverse. In addition, these institutions typically have a brand that is weaker than that of the flagship institutions in their states. The combination of weak brand and generic but diverse products is what makes SCUs a tempting target for both the earliest generation of potential online disrupters and developing educational innovations.

Historically, disruption in higher education was impossible because there was no scalable technology driver capable of disruptively carrying the business model of low-cost universities up-market.[3] Now, however, a perfect storm seems to be brewing. College tuition and fees have leapt 439% from 1982 to 2007 after inflation (Kamenetz, 2010). As university administrators, lawmakers, and state and federal officials frantically look for solutions, online learning has emerged as the technology enabler of disruptive innovations. Even the most dominant of traditional universities are scrutinizing the opportunities that online education affords.

State investments in higher education will continue to be strained in the years ahead. In February 2013, Louisiana Governor Bobby Jindal proposed a budget that would slash higher education funding in his $200 million. If this trend continues, it will imperil SCUs' traditional operations. They would have to either raise tuition substantially or cut back dramatically on their traditional services—or some combination of both. Either option would render them less competitive and open the door to greater competition from online universities and other educational options, as well as the likely loss of students.

The First Disruptive Wave

There is a growing number of online learning players emerging in higher education. The first group, fully online learning universities, developed 2 decades ago. Many of these were for-profits, such as the University of Phoenix and DeVry University—institutions focused exclusively on teaching and learning, not research. Although in many cases these online universities had physical campuses, the creation of fully online degree programs allowed them to scale rapidly. As many have observed, however, these first online universities tend to charge tuition that is higher than in-state tuition at a comparable public institution. As a result, people have questioned their disruptive nature.

Disruption, however, tends to unfold in stages. Often, the first wave of a disruption promises a new value proposition around convenience and accessibility before future waves innovate on price. In the case of the first online universities, they offered a more convenient value proposition for their target students—adult learners with a job or other commitment that made commuting to a campus difficult. Before this, many "nontraditional students" had been nonconsumers of higher education. Online programs offered two valuable opportunities: convenience and lower opportunity costs, both of which allowed students to go to school without leaving the workforce. Indeed, students flocked to these online for-profit institutions.

The disruptive strategy for these online universities seemed relatively straightforward: target historical nonconsumers of higher education and offer programs that helped them advance their careers or find a job, typically in fields with established career paths that do not rely on institutional brand or reputation. These disruptive upstarts with weak brands planted themselves in the market and improved their ability to teach and place students, without adding an expensive research function. Although a lack of research affected their prestige (according to the traditional metrics of performance), investing in it would have increased their costs and thus affected their profitability, a bigger concern for for-profits and a comparative advantage they have over SCUs as they move up-market. Even though the price of the first online universities was higher than the in-state tuition of SCUs, their overall costs were lower. SCUs struggle to balance decreasing state subsidies with increases in tuition, which leads to operating budgets with razor-thin margins. Conversely, for-profits tend to have high operating margins. This suggests that as online universities compete, they will be able to appeal to consumers on price (through keeping prices constant or lowering prices), while SCUs will be forced to increase tuition given rising costs and falling state subsidies.

Unfortunately, the first wave of online universities relied heavily on the federal government's Title IV loan dollars. For many years, this funding stream provided easy money to institutions almost regardless of how well they taught and placed students into jobs. Now, with threats of a student loan bubble and a fragile economy, the government has tried to crack down on these institutions. Senators Tom Harkin (D-IA) and Dick Durbin's (D-IL) most recent series of inquiries publicized the questionable and sometimes predatory practices of leading for-profits.[4]

The Second Disruptive Wave

Even before these revelations came to light, a second wave of disruptive online programs began emerging. Many of them are pushing innovation on price, which, according to the Parthenon Group, increasingly is displacing convenience as the most important factor for many students considering college. Groups like American Public University System (APUS, which includes American Public University and American Military University) and Grand Canyon University are for-profit, low-cost models. Others, such as Western Governors University (WGU), Southern New Hampshire University (SNHU), and UniversityNow (UNow, which includes New Charter University and Patten University), are even lower priced models that incorporate competency-based learning, in which mastery of a subject is more important than the seat time to gain that mastery.

Like the wave of disrupters before them, these institutions offer programs that help students find jobs and advance their careers. They are attempting to reach both nonconsumers of higher education as well as price-sensitive students who historically have attended community colleges, SCUs, and the first wave of disrupters. Interestingly enough, when community colleges in some states, like California, have experienced budget woes and run up against capacity constraints, they have effectively abandoned their open-access mission and gone up-market by limiting the number of people that can attend. UNow's Initiative California emerged to offer enrollment to the 470,000 students on community college waitlists at a price of $46 a month for unlimited courses.

A separate set of disrupters has taken a different tack. Rather than replicate all of the trappings of a university, they instead focus only on offering courses. StraighterLine has been doing this for several years, and, more recently, MOOCs have emerged to provide a different set of experiences.[5] Over time, this wave of disrupters might offer micro-credentials in their own right by charging for competency-based certificates. For this to work, employers would have to value the credentials.

The disruptive threat also could assume a more insidious form, as these groups gradually take over universities one course at a time. Consider the story of the disruption of Dell Computer by ASUSTeK. ASUSTeK first suggested to Dell that it outsource circuit board manufacturing, which made sense to Dell because ASUSTeK could manufacture the circuit boards at 20% lower cost. Dell could increase profits by continuing to charge consumers the same prices for its computers. A couple of years later, ASUSTeK suggested that it manufacture the motherboards for, once again, 20% lower cost. Dell happily complied. ASUSTeK returned a third time to tell Dell that it should turn computer assembly over as well because ASUSTeK could do it at 20% lower cost. Dell gladly did, and both companies thrived.

A few years later, ASUSTeK returned and suggested that it manage Dell's supply chain so that Dell could focus on design and marketing. Once again, both companies increased profits; Dell had almost no assets on its balance sheet by now but had the same revenue. Soon ASUSTeK returned with an offer to design the computers for Dell. Once again, this worked well for both parties. But the final time that ASUSTeK returned with an added-value proposition, it did not go to Dell. It went directly to

Best Buy and proposed that it could build new, inexpensive personal computers for them at 20% lower cost without Dell's brand. Best Buy leapt at the opportunity, and Dell was disrupted.

The early scenes of a similar story may be playing out in higher education. StraighterLine and MOOC providers have approached various colleges and universities to provide certain classes. Some institutions, including SCUs, have signed contracts with the MOOC providers. This provides potential relief for both parties. The MOOC providers could get revenue, and the traditional institutions could lower their costs without hurting profitability. Critics of MOOCs tend to belabor the unexciting quality of the learning experience: the lack of intimacy, the poor quality of videos, or the clunkiness of the various learning platforms. But as is true with all disruptive innovations, in an effort to improve their product and increase profitability, successful MOOCs will invest in improvements to the functionality of their platforms: how they teach online and assess student performance. Through careful use of the massive amounts of data that they collect about their students and how they learn, the MOOC providers' products will likely become better at delivering a high-quality learning experience that is both less costly and simpler to use. As they improve, MOOCs will likely increase their market share, and the decision facing the universities will be the same as the one that faced Dell. With state budgets tightening and, in many cases, professors retiring, they will be able to offer yet another "MOOC"[6] at lower cost and maintain their revenue stream.

The California State University system has explored partnerships such as these. In January 2013, in an effort to attend to the more than 50% of entering students who do not meet basic requirements, San Jose State University (SJSU) partnered with Udacity to offer introductory and remedial three-credit courses for a discounted tuition rate of $150/course. The courses included remedial algebra, college-level algebra, and introductory statistics. The pilot program was limited to 300 students—half from SJSU and the other half from other community colleges and high schools (Lewin & Markoff, 2013). Although the initial pilot did not produce great results and the partnership was temporarily paused, both sides plan to learn from their mistakes and keep innovating.

This kind of partnership could play an important role in remediating students and evening out the wide-ranging preparedness of students in an SCU classroom. For many teachers, it may be a welcome relief not to have to teach these lower level classes and focus instead on a more advanced course. Particularly at SCUs where the range of subjects might be more limited, leveraging existing courses from MOOCs would enable departments to teach a wider range of courses. As Duke Provost Peter Lange said about Duke's partnership with Coursera: "No university can deliver the full range of courses that both might be interesting and useful and enlightening to our students" (Seligson, 2012). For many lower tiered universities with more constraints on the subject areas and majors that they offer, licensing introductory course materials might alleviate staffing issues and enable certain institutions to save money by hiring non-PhDs to mentor students. By licensing the content from Coursera, edX, and Udacity, or from e-publishers, such as Pearson and McGraw Hill, SCUs might be able to leverage existing content to deal with gaps in their curricula.

Although in the short term, the decision to partner with a MOOC will always appear to be the right one, institutions unwittingly may be handing over their value propositions to the improving and quality-conscious MOOC providers. One of the major vulnerabilities of SCUs is that they have no competitive edge when it comes to general education courses. Companies such as StraighterLine specifically target courses common to the first 2 years of general education. The twisted logic of all of this is that most professors prefer to teach more specialized courses versus the remedial and introductory courses in their fields. For university administrators, however, these courses often represent the profit centers—large classes, few teachers. Should some significant portion of that fall away, administrators would need to consider alternatives.

At some point, MOOCs just might go directly to consumers through a different distribution channel. As with newspapers, which are being disrupted on a job-by-job basis by multiple competitors, perhaps it will not be just the MOOCs that provide all of a university's different jobs; however, through a collection of disruptive offerings, including co-working spaces and opportunities to build networks, universities might find themselves ultimately disrupted.

Hope in Jobs to Be Done

Although the outlook certainly appears bleak, the collapse of SCUs is not inevitable. There remains a significant opportunity for SCUs as the incumbent institutions. Although disruptive innovations transform sectors, they do not always result in a complete disintegration of the old order. A key insight is that the incumbents that are being disrupted can focus their efforts on defending the parts of their business that are beyond the *extendable core* of the disruptive innovator's product. The extendable core is "the aspect of the business model that allows the disrupter to maintain its performance advantage as it creeps upmarket in search of more and more customers" (Wessel & Christensen, 2012). This is what enables a technology driver such as online education to scale and be capable of disruptively carrying the business model of low-cost universities up-market.

Even though e-learning institutions gradually are improving the effectiveness of their programs while maintaining the cost and convenience advantages, online universities' extendable core is not of much use to those students who value face-to-face interactions with a community of peers or networking opportunities. Moreover, most upstart online providers today cannot boast the valuable alumni networks that an SCU might.[7] Signaling and brand recognition within a geographic region still maintain an edge over for-profit competition. One of the biggest criticisms of the growing use of online education is that technology removes an important aspect of socialization that occurs on a college campus. Many commuting students may not crave the social peer-to-peer interactions that a residential 18- to 22-year-old population might, but they may value the potential for frequent face-to-face interactions with professors, advisors, and mentors.

The key for comprehensive institutions is to figure out where they are likely to succeed—or perhaps more important, where what they offer ultimately will not be as valued. As Kevin Kiley (2013) writes in his summary of the recent Moody's report, "The 'buffet model' of higher education—where institutions try to be all things to all people—is over." These institutions must ask themselves: What is the most indispensable "job" that our students—many of whom are commuting and already employed—hire us to do for them?

As the great marketing professor Theodore Levitt taught, "The customer doesn't want a quarter-inch drill. He wants a quarter-inch hole." Hence, when a customer hires a product to do one job, she may be delighted with its quality because the product did that particular job well. Another customer with a very different job to be done might hire the same product and judge it to be very low in quality—not because the product is different, but because the job is different.

The job we hire an SCU to do is—and should be—different from the job we hire a Harvard or Yale University to do. Ascertaining this job will be crucial and will enable SCUs to make critical resource allocation decisions to defend their campuses. Understanding the different reasons why students pursue higher education in general is an important starting point.

Broadly speaking, students choose to consume higher education as an employment enhancer, employment changer, employment launcher, employment preserver, a transition to adulthood, and a way of broadening their views and conceptual understanding of the world. Many of these jobs include elements of learning, engaging in research, socializing, and networking; they shift depending on the particular circumstances of a student. When we narrow the scope to SCUs, the priorities of the student population—often nontraditional, working commuter students with families or ties to the geographic area—shift away from a transition to adulthood and gaining broad conceptual knowledge, and move toward *learning to do*. Those students who desire a residential social experience will likely choose a different kind of institution. Many of the students attending SCUs are already immersed in the working world and observe firsthand the immediacy of economic uncertainty.

Even as the economy recovers slowly, high unemployment persists. According to the Bureau of Labor Statistics, as of July 2013 the national unemployment rate teetered at 7.6% while 3.8 million jobs remained unfilled nationally. The Associated Press analysis of data from 2011 reported that 53.6% of recent college graduates were unable to secure jobs, which implies that high unemployment rates may stem from an economy that is not healthy enough to produce jobs *and* from a workforce that is improperly trained for the jobs that are available. Few universities or colleges can aver that their programs and majors match the needs of today's labor market. When such a labor mismatch exists, job seekers tend to look for programs that can prepare them for available jobs and careers.

BACK TO REGIONAL AND "VOCATIONAL": LEARNING TO DO

SCUs should return to their original missions of serving the regional economy. Such focus would help meet the needs of the students and make a positive economic contribution, which ultimately would strengthen taxpayer support. By helping students learn industry knowledge and gain specific skill sets for the workforce, universities and colleges can stave off disruption. As the joint Bain & Co. and Sterling Partners' report affirms, "The worst case scenario for an institution is to be relatively expensive and completely undifferentiated. Who will pay to go to a school that is completely undistinguished on any dimension?" (Denneen & Dretler, 2012, p. 5).

Using real-time labor market information (LMI), SCUs could reach out to regional businesses to assess the qualifications they seek in a new hire. A university could strategically position itself by entering into partnerships with regional employers to retool curricular offerings and train students for high-demand jobs. Internships for credit would enable employers to try out potential employees and simultaneously provide students a bird's-eye view into a certain company. Through a co-op model, students could complete coursework while serving as interns or apprentices at local businesses.

Fairfield University announced a new internship program in January 2013 to connect its students with employment opportunities in Bridgeport, CT; jobs range from positions in city departments to the local animal shelter (Harney, 2013). Although this is a good start for the Jesuit university, it is unclear whether more-selective colleges and research institutions will be able to emulate such programs with their nearby communities. The matriculated students at these colleges might not desire gainful employment in their college town, where they have no intention of staying. Moreover, most faculty at more-selective, research-focused institutions do not necessarily envision an interrelationship between their scholarship and workforce training for students.

The student populations of SCUs, on the other hand, tend to prize nearby employment opportunities, as many are already somehow tied to these geographic areas. This is a prominent trend in higher education. In UCLA's Higher Education Research Institute's (2012) American Freshman Survey, 87.9% of college freshmen—approximately 17 percentage points higher than in 2006—cited getting a better job as a vital reason for pursuing a college degree. This suggests that students would value tailored offerings more closely aligned with their career objectives. Comprehensive colleges therefore should avoid squandering resources in an effort to defend parts of their organization that can be easily disrupted.

Such a dramatic shift in strategy for SCUs requires academics, administrators, employers, as well as students to move beyond the derogation and conflation of *vocation* with low-skill, factory-line jobs. Unfortunately, as Henderson (2009) points out, many SCU faculty members in liberal arts disciplines scorn the way their institutions "are too much like glorified trade schools" (p. 6). At this critical juncture of increased global economic competition, however, all universities need to consider the alignment of education and job training. By focusing on their job-seeking students, SCUs have a chance of staving off disruption. Coupling *learning knowledge* with *learning to do*—through on-the-job, in-person training, or on-the-ground projects integrated tightly with regional clusters of employers—is vital.

A DELIBERATE CORE MISSION

This refocus of mission forces SCUs to resolve two issues. First, they will need to find ways to provide quality education with a career focus to larger numbers of students in times of increasing state fiscal constraints—in other words, lower the cost per student while increasing the efficiency of the learning process. Second, they will need to adopt many of the desirable attributes of the innovators, including convenience in scheduling and location, as well as varied approaches to shortening time to degree completion.

Regional universities therefore must reconsider their current strategies that divert resources away from better teaching and learning. In a recent article in *The Chronicle of Higher Education*, Scott Carlson (2013) details the elaborate country–club–like amenities blossoming at less selective universities. Based on the findings of a new report by the National Bureau of Economic Research, Carlson summarizes how in an effort to increase student enrollment, these universities actually are *de-prioritizing* instruction and academic quality. The perils of soaring tuition, shrinking state budgets, high student loan default rates, and the labor mismatch call into question whether this strategy will continue to be effective in the future.

These less selective universities also must question their aspirations to move up-market toward greater prestige. Is it even possible? And, is it worthwhile for an SCU to hire more expensive research-oriented faculty, give them lowered teaching loads, and divert institutional funds to research? Comprehensives will need to re-evaluate the traditional roles of faculty members in light of the explosion of new online resources and approaches. Greater outreach to industry and convenience for students may require a more established presence off campus (without the large capital expenditures usually associated with physical expansion).

In short, these less selective universities will require a very different model from the one they use today. Such a shift in priorities will not be easy or even feasible for many institutions. Educating students with different resources, processes, and priorities is not a simple, overnight task. For those regional colleges up for the challenge of emboldening their missions, priorities must shift toward closing the gap between their newly minted bachelor's graduates and the potential employment opportunities.

BRACING FOR DISRUPTION BY CREATING AUTONOMOUS ENTITIES

In our research on innovation, we have witnessed time and time again that the only companies able to pioneer a successful disruptive transformation were those that created independent entities separate from the organization. The key dimensions of autonomy relate to processes and priorities. The disruptive business needs to have the freedom to create new processes and to build a unique cost structure in order to be profitable—or, in the case of nonprofits, sustainable.

SCUs must develop new organizational structures—autonomous units potentially under a different brand or, more likely, with an additional brand that makes clear their new purpose—that free them from the bureaucracy, slow decision making, and high fixed costs of the existing brick-and-mortar university operations. Traditional universities that successfully invested in online education made it a priority to separate their online ventures from the original institutions. At SNHU, President Paul LeBlanc used his presidential authority to create an autonomous division, SNHU Online, which potentially one day could disrupt the parent university. SNHU Online maintains control overall aspects of the new online programs to the point that SNHU faculty members do not have veto power over decisions that SNHU Online makes—and now LeBlanc is doing it again with SNHU's latest venture, College for America. The presidents at universities that have created these autonomous entities established their new organizations' missions before anyone joined, which allowed for the creation of relatively autonomous organizations with defined roles up front. This was the most efficient way to achieve agreement.

Autonomy is vital given the complex relationships between the various stakeholders—faculty, boards, and the administration—on a campus. At traditional institutions, faculty governance is most often at odds with rapid innovation, as the creation of new programs or even new courses must undergo extensive vetting from faculty committees. Furthermore, most faculty do not necessarily believe that employers know what a student needs to learn. Such dynamics stifle the prioritization of innovative, cost-effective programs. As a consequence, when new programs or courses ultimately do get approved, they have little to do with employment opportunities.[8]

Creating an autonomous unit, although certainly challenging, is critical in ensuring that the group is allowed to function independently and away from the tensions and politics of the university. Administrators such as those at SCUs would be able to move rapidly and adapt more nimbly in order to match graduates with the appropriate skills necessary for their career goals. The success of for-profits is due in large part to their structure as private and flexible entities. They are better positioned because they are unburdened by faculty governance, formal procedures, and historical hierarchies that are embedded within most traditional institutions. Many have technology teams devoted to implementing improvements, building courses, and creating online content. In addition, they do not always hire full-fledged PhD candidates to teach; rather, they hire teachers specifically for the online arena.[9] Professors at most traditional universities, on the other hand, have little or no experience building online courses. But what the SCUs potentially do have over their for-profit peers are stronger brands. If they can harness the power of true autonomy to unleash those brands, then they may have a leg up on their competition. The opportunity exists for certain SCUs to do what SNHU has done and, through an autonomous unit, create low-cost, competency-based, degree-completion programs in high-demand fields.

A TEMPERED OUTLOOK

The years ahead for SCUs will be challenging, to say the least. Unfortunately, there is no completely defensible value proposition for any SCU; there is nothing that an SCU does that an FPU or MOOC—or even another public institution with an autonomous unit—could not do. Each institution must anticipate that it may be competing for students choosing between a for-profit, MOOC, or other regional institution.

Some institutions may wish to marshal their efforts toward implementing new competency-based learning experiences. WGU, UNow, SNHU, the University of Wisconsin, and Northern Arizona University are all exploring competency-based learning as alternative pathways to college credit. Companies such as Knewton are experimenting with student-centric learning that adapts specifically to a student's distinct knowledge sets.

Ultimately, however, the major pathway to profit seems to be in developing employer relationships. As the up-market pull for greater profits has led many FPUs to deliver fully online degree programs, an area of nonconsumption has reopened around students who are already working for different companies that, to enhance their own employee pool, offer employees tuition assistance to gain certificates, degrees, and more training. Many of these employees wish to gain college credentials for either a change in career or a move up the ladder. As Rosen (2011) writes, college is increasingly "a place you return to at periodic intervals, to retool and reload for the next phase of life's journey" (p. xxvi).

This new distribution channel should excite SCUs intent on increasing their focus on *learning to do*. SCUs have an opportunity to attend to these students. SCUs can take advantage of their regional positions by directly feeding student talent into the industries in the area. If an SCU is bold enough to strengthen relationships with employers in the area and create better pathways that equip students for the skills needed in the region, employers will begin to rely on the institution in a way that they could not with a global or even national for-profit provider.

Within each region, there are different skills gaps that need to be addressed. Detroit, despite its 11.3% unemployment, faces a shortage of machinists. Jon Marcus (2013) describes how in this particular case, the

Workforce Intelligence Network (WIN) and a coalition of employers, incubators, workforce development boards, and community colleges are using technology "to comb through real-time online help-wanted advertisements and analyze what jobs are open and what skills or education they require."

Schools in the region would be the fastest and most adept at training prospective employees for these unfilled jobs. That being said, however, SCUs must move quickly. The MOOC provider Udacity is already doing something similar through its creation of the Open Education Alliance (OEC), which facilitates outreach between learners and employers. If Udacity can successfully attend to the skills gap for an employer, it will put enormous pressure on traditional institutions of higher education. This is where the opportunity lies for SCUs: to combine brand power with the intimacy of regional contact in order to meet the demands of the labor market.

CONCLUSION

In President Barack Obama's 2013 State of the Union address, he alluded to the need for faster paths to employment: "Right now, countries like Germany focus on graduating their high school students with the equivalent of a technical degree from one of our community colleges. So those German kids," he said, are "ready for a job when they graduate high school. They've been trained for the jobs that are there." The goals of higher education are changing slowly from retention and graduation to postgraduation employment opportunities.

We believe that there is significant reason for hope in the face of the unknown. No single for-profit, MOOC, or even elite institution has it all figured out. Even prestigious business schools are pausing to think about how to compete with disruptive entrants, such as corporate universities. The rapid-fire advancements in technology make it impossible for institutions to remain complacent about the state of higher education and its interaction with the U.S. workforce. All of this competitive pressure perhaps can lead our students more directly to their intended careers.

What will SCUs do to make a change? By removing themselves from the rat race of resembling an institution they are not, SCUs would be able to focus on doing fewer things well instead of offering a vast array of educational services that they cannot deliver. Instead of fighting the disruption head-on, wise SCUs could develop innovations aimed at completing their still-defensible jobs: serving a highly unmet need for their graduates' gainful employment.

NOTES

1. See www.therewiredgroup.com/jobs-to-be-done/ for more information on the concept of "Jobs to Be Done."

2. We are deeply indebted to our friend Øystein Fjeldstad of the Norwegian School of Management, who developed and taught us this framework.

3. Community colleges that have become 4-year institutions and then research universities offering graduate degrees have not been able to carry their low-cost business models up-market. They have had to transform from their original form and replicate the cost structure of the institutions they are striving to emulate by competing with them on the basis of sustaining, rather than disruptive, innovation.

4. These revelations had questionable effects on the for-profit industry. While those within the education industry viewed the hearings as damaging of the for-profit brand names, Parthenon found in a recent report that 90% of prospective students had no awareness of the negative press. See Ross (2012).

5. For example, StraighterLine offers a robust, live 24/7 tutoring support to help students through courses, whereas MOOCs do not offer nearly this level of personal touch today.

6. Although today these are called MOOCs, over time what may emerge is something that looks very different from a MOOC today. Facilitated networks or adaptive learning platforms—like Khan Academy and Knewton—actually may be better positioned than MOOCs (in their current forms) to improve learning and serve massive numbers of students with tailored offerings. See Horn & Christensen (2013).

7. This, of course, could turn out to be a short-term problem, as many of these online providers become more adept at facilitating interactions between their thousands of graduates and degree candidates. For-profits like the University of Phoenix have graduated over 500,000 students, while places like Ashford University have approximately 80,000 students currently enrolled in their classes. There are opportunities for such institutions to develop new formats for creating dynamic social connections among their numerous students.

8. When disruptive technologies are deployed under the auspices of a traditional institution, the results lead to sustaining and costly innovations only. Given that many MOOCs have been born directly out of institutions—most of them research institutions that are not as focused on pedagogy—in many cases, they may not be all that disruptive. As an example, see Waldman (2013).

9. Udacity makes a point of hiring and training excellent teachers, which means turning away many qualified professors in favor of training people who can create better learning experiences for this particular setting. According to Amanda Ripley at *Time Magazine* (2012), "Udacity has turned down about 500 professors who have volunteered to teach, and it has canceled one course (a math class that had already enrolled 20,000 students) because of subpar quality" (See Ripley, 2012, October 18). http://nation.time.com/2012/10/18/college-is-dead-long-live-college/print/

REFERENCES

Carey, K. (2010). Education sector. In A. Kamenetz (Ed.), *DIY U: Edupunks, edupreneurs, and the coming transformation of higher education* (p. 69). White River Junction, VT: Chelsea Green Publishing.

Carlson, S. (2013, January 28). What's the payoff for the 'country club' college? *The Chronicle of Higher Education*. Available at chronicle.com/blogs/buildings/whats-the-payoff-for-the-country-club-college/32477

Christensen, C. M. (1997). *The innovator's dilemma: When new technologies cause great firms to fail.* Boston, MA: Harvard Business Review Press.

Christensen, C. M., Horn, M. B., Caldera, L., & Soares, L. (2011). *Disrupting college: How disruptive innovation can deliver quality and affordability to postsecondary education.* Washington, DC: Center for American Progress.

Denneen, J., & Dretler, T. (2012). *The financially sustainable university.* Boston, MA: Bain & Company.

Harney, J. O. (2013, January 31). *Practical internships in southwestern Conn.* New England Board of Higher Education. Available at www.nebhe.org/newslink/practical-internships-in-southwestern-conn

Henderson, B. B. (2009). The work of the people's university. *Teacher-Scholar: The Journal of the State Comprehensive University, 1*(1), 5–15.

Higher Education Research Institute. (2012). *The American freshman: National norms fall 2012.* Los Angeles, CA. Available at www.heri.ucla.edu/monographs/theamericanfreshman2012.pdf

Horn, M., & Christensen, C. (2013, February 20). Beyond the buzz, where are MOOCs really going? Available at www.wired.com/opinion/2013/02/beyond-the-mooc-buzz-where-are-they-going-really/

Kamenetz, A. (Ed.). (2010). *DIY U: Edupunks, edupreneurs, and the coming transformation of higher education.* White River Junction, VT: Chelsea Green Publishing.

Kiley, K. (2013, January 17). Nowhere to turn. *Inside Higher Ed.* Available at www.insidehighered.com/news/2013/01/17/moodys-report-calls-question-all-traditional-university-revenue-sources

Lederman, D. (2013, January 14). MOOCs assessed, modestly. *Inside Higher Ed.* Available at www.insidehighered.com/news/2013/01/14/assessing-moocs-higheredtech-conference

Lewin, T., & Markoff, J. (2013, January 15). California to give web courses a big trial. *New York Times.* Available at www.nytimes.com/2013/01/15/technology/california-to-give-web-courses-a-big-trial.html?_r=0

Marcus, J. (2013, January 1). Motown rising. *United Hemispheres Magazine.* Available at www.hemispheresmagazine.com/2013/01/01/motown-rising/

Moody's Investors Service. (2013). Moody's: 2013 outlook for entire U.S. higher education sector changed to negative. [Press release]. Available at www.moodys.com/research/Moodys-2013-outlook-for-entire-US-Higher-Education-sector-changed--PR_263866

National Center for Education Statistics. (2010). *Profile of undergraduate students: 2007–08*. Washington, DC: U.S. Department of Education.

National Center for Education Statistics. (2012). *Integrated postsecondary education data system*. Available at nces.ed.gov/ipeds/

Obama, B. (2013, February). *State of the Union address*. The White House. Washington, DC. Available at www.whitehouse.gov/the-press-office/2013/02/12/remarks-president-state-union-address

Ripley, A. (2012, October 18). College is dead. Long live college! Can a new creed of online megacourses finally offer a college education to more people for less money? *Time Magazine*. Available at http://nation.time.com/2012/10/18/college-is-dead-long-live-college/print/

Rosen, A. S. (2011). *Change.edu: Rebooting for the new talent economy*. New York, NY: Kaplan.

Ross, C. (2012). *Where have all the students gone? Enrollment trends in private sector higher education*. Boston, MA: Parthenon Group.

Seligson, H. (2012, November 15). University consortium to offer small online courses for credit. *New York Times*. Available at www.nytimes.com/2012/11/16/education/duke-northwestern-to-offer-semester-online-classes.html

Social and Behavioral Research Institute & California State University, San Marcos. (2002, February). *CSU faculty workload report*. Available at www.calstate.edu/acadres/docs/csu_facwrkldrpt.pdf

Stabell, C. B., & Fieldstad, Ø. D. (1998). Configuring value for competitive advantage: On chains, shops and networks. *Strategic Management Journal, 19,* 413–437.

Waldman, S. (2013, January 16). SUNY to develop a 3-year degree plan. *Times Union*. Available at http://www.timesunion.com/local/article/SUNY-to-develop-3-year-degree-plan-4196074.php

Wessel, M., & Christensen, C. M. (2012). Surviving disruption. *Harvard Business Review*. Available at hbr.org/2012/12/surviving-disruption/ar/1

Winston, G. (2000). *The positional arms race in higher education*. Williamstown, MA: Williams College.

Conclusion

KC Deane and Mark Schneider

In 1994, David Breneman, then professor and former dean of the education school at the University of Virginia, posed a scandalous question to the higher education community: Is the demise of the liberal arts college imminent? His book, *Liberal Arts Colleges: Thriving, Surviving, or Endangered?*, examined whether these intellectually driven niche colleges could withstand the market pressures of an increasingly technical world.

His question now pertains to a broad cross-section of America's postsecondary institutions. Public comprehensive universities—the institutions whose missions, histories, performance, and challenges are at the heart of this volume—must answer for themselves the question that Breneman first asked 2 decades ago: At a time when the labor market requires skills that too many of our colleges and universities seem unable to teach, are comprehensive universities thriving, surviving, or endangered?

When our nation's leaders point to the value of higher education, they applaud a small subset of selective institutions. Likewise, when policymakers call on higher education to improve its value, they wag their finger at no institution in particular. In this volume, we have done our best to dissect the comprehensive university. Instead of relying solely on the common trope about these universities—that they are hard to define, but easy to overlook—we instead sought to build a better understanding of their place in American higher education. These institutions are, in many ways, the bedrock of postsecondary education in the United States.

When change is demanded of higher education, industry spokespeople nod their heads agreeably, but it is the comprehensive universities that are left to deliver. First, in the 1800s, it was teacher training. Normal colleges, which in their current form constitute almost 50% of comprehensive universities, opened in response to the demand for more elementary and secondary education teachers. Then, in the 1960s and 1970s, as a college education became a rite of passage for low- and middle-class students and the federal government established student financial aid programs to propel college access, comprehensive universities absorbed the growing enrollments. And now, as attention shifts to graduating more students equipped with the skills necessary for a 21st-century job, once again comprehensive universities are being called on to respond.

If these institutions have such a rich history of picking up the proverbial slack in higher education, why are they relegated to the shadows? Those at comprehensives do little to help their cause; spokespeople for the sector turn first to self-degradation. "I won't lie to you. I know that if you take a job at an institution like mine, people in your field will ask you what your institution's letters stand for, and your adviser won't brag about where you were placed," said one professor in an essay on state comprehensive universities (Olwell, 2011). Internally, professors spar over mission drift—chasing prestige—and whether their foundation as teaching institutions remains intact. Stakeholders outside of comprehensive universities know not what to do with these debates; for their purposes, all that matters is whether the institutions are delivering. Are students enrolling? Are they graduating? Are the bills paid?

It is unsurprising that these institutions struggle to position themselves in higher education, and in the higher education industry's evolution. Higher education historically has been defined by either elite institutions that garner praise for their quality (and use this powerful position to their advantage) or community colleges, many of which came about during nationwide initiatives to improve college access. Whenever the goals required of higher education change, the institutions at the forefront—particularly selective colleges and universities—give lip service to the new goal, but do little to respond. Comprehensive universities are always one step behind in the public relations game, but are the ones forced to deliver.

THE COMPREHENSIVE UNIVERSITY'S LEARNING CURVE

For the nation to rise to the call for improved baccalaureate degree completion, the institutions that educate the majority of 4-year students must take the lead. Similarly, improving labor market readiness matters most to the institutions that function as the training grounds for local communities. Comprehensive universities operate in this intersection; they serve a disparate and laudable mission. Likewise, within this mission are all of the contradictions that call their future into question.

There are those institutions that have joined the prestige race, others that have become outspoken champions of their role as teaching universities, and those that have fallen behind. The consequence of this diverse adaptation to ever-changing demands is a relegation to second-tier status within higher education. Simply put, we ignore what we do not understand, and we do not understand comprehensive universities.

First, there are the comprehensive universities that, after the 1960s–1970s enrollment swell, never stopped evolving. With higher quality as the end goal, they added master's, and often doctoral, programs. In the name of increased respect for the doctoral programs, the faculty continues to angle for additional research opportunities. Or, the institutions play the reputation game so as to compete with state flagship universities directly. Recruitment of highly qualified students increases and, if possible, the acceptance rate decreases. These institutions "begin to look like lesser versions of their states' flagship universities" and the historical focus on open access loses out to the competitive drive to go "up-market" (Selingo, 2000).

A smaller subset of comprehensive institutions remains committed, in both word and deed, to their position as teaching universities. Says one professor of his teaching at Eastern Michigan University, "Working at a regional public institution is mostly about teaching students with a wide range of backgrounds and preparation." He goes on to explain these students' motivations: "They are at the university to succeed, graduate, and get a job. They expect capable, relevant instruction for their future paths" (Olwell, 2011). The professors at these institutions define their job by its proximity to students: first teach, then research. Within the institution, there might be disagreement about the appropriate balance of teaching and research, but, overall, these institutions shun prestige in favor of their historical commitment to access and teaching.

The third group of comprehensive universities sits in a more tenuous position. These are the underperformers. Unable to attract academically well-prepared students with the same success as their peers that have gone up-market to compete with the more prestigious state flagship universities, they accept all who enroll, but graduate only a fraction of those who enter. They educate a significant number of adult and transfer students, but do little to ensure that these students have the resources they need to succeed. They play an integral role in their local labor markets, but rarely respond by incorporating local needs into program offerings or, more important, curricular content. Of all the comprehensive universities, these institutions are the most endangered. They risk losing students to more flexible and lower cost options such as community colleges and online universities, losing state appropriations to the state flagship universities, and losing federal dollars if the Obama administration's efforts to tie institutional performance to Title IV eligibility are successful.

These universities historically have done exactly what was asked of them, the consequences of which are steep. Namely, the result is a group of institutions that, "able to view themselves only according to the model of the academic procession . . . [are] quick to discard their past" (Ogren, 2005, p. 3). But, in fact, this tendency to embrace America's dynamic needs is also their greatest asset as the country once again needs higher education to bolster progress. Comprehensive universities have long been at the center of their communities, integral to the local labor market, and a source of identity for the citizens. Now, they must become an exemplar for how to rethink and respond to new changes in higher education.

Comprehensive universities need to capitalize on the characteristics that separate them from other institutions and, in doing so, clarify their purpose and value. Distilled into three central lessons, the chapters in this volume tell the story of a set of institutions that, if willing to respond, can lead the charge in ensuring that higher education provides its customers—communities, students, and the companies that employ them—with what they need to flourish.

Lesson #1: Historical and Contemporary Positioning Matters

By now it should be abundantly clear that comprehensive universities' histories are varied and frequently utilitarian. To accommodate these histories, author Alisa Hicklin Fryar ultimately settles on two separate definitions of the comprehensive university. The first relies on the historical development, and the second caters to a modern interpretation of the state comprehensive university.

But understanding how these institutions define themselves is just the beginning. Even a modern interpretation yields a set of schools with drastically different histories and missions. Some of these are branch campuses, Historically Black Colleges and Universities, or, more recently, Hispanic-serving Institutions. And many of them are not serving their students well. When compared with students at public research universities, as well as private for-profit and nonprofit institutions, comprehensive university students graduate at slightly lower rates. Author Michelle Lu Yin advises us, however, to interpret these "observed" student performance rates—the same ones that state and federal governments use as cues for quality—with caution. Because the composition of student bodies differs across institutions, a school's performance is relative—an important caveat for a group of schools with this degree of diversity. (The same argument has been made for community colleges, and rightfully so.)

We learn from Awilda Rodriguez's chapter that middle-ability traditional students who enroll at comprehensive universities want to stay close to home and want a lower cost education—although not to the same degree as their middle-ability peers who opt to attend public 2-year colleges. And, unlike their peers who attend similar noncomprehensive public 4-year institutions, these students are not reputation-sensitive.

Successfully enrolling more middle-ability students could help improve student performance outcomes (the observed rates, at least).

But a significant number of the students enrolled at comprehensive universities are nontraditional or part-time learners. They are returning to college later in life, or they are transferring in from a community college. The existing measurements exclude these students. In other words, there is an incentive to hyper-focus on the students who will improve the metrics that matter, which distracts from efforts to improve the education that *all* students deserve.

Here again, historical context should inform future decisions. Normal schools enrolled students that were viewed as "nontraditional" long before the term held its current meaning. "While their official mission was preparing teachers, the characteristics of their student bodies forced the normal schools to expand their unofficial mission to include welcoming unsophisticated students into an engaging intellectual and public life" (Ogren, 2003, p. 642). Even then, educating the nontraditional student required a different approach, but they did it well, a lesson that Ogren points out contemporary comprehensive universities would be wise to remember.

Because of their position as educators of *all* cross-sections of students, comprehensive universities undermine their own efforts if they attempt to respond just like the rest of the 4-year colleges and universities. Nor should those who hope to harness higher education to solve new goals dismiss this set of institutions. Instead, comprehensive universities can chart a new course by successfully navigating the tension between two disparate student populations.

Lesson #2: Growing Tension Between the Old and New

If you listen to the pundits, higher education either is going the way of the dodo or will rise from the ashes like the phoenix. Whatever happens, change is coming. MOOCs threaten to steal students with free, online courses taught by the best professors (although this threat has faded in the past year or so). Moody's stirs the pot with ominous downgrades for individual institutions and the industry more broadly. And the headlines on student loan debt deepen concerns that the value of a college education is not what it used to be. In other words, the traditional model of higher education is showing signs of erosion.

It is likely that selective colleges and universities, with their hefty endowments and loyal alumni, will weather the coming decades of change without much trouble. Comprehensive universities do not have these luxuries. For years, they have continued to adhere to the generic set of expectations laid out for 4-year, degree-granting institutions. And up until this point, they have done well enough. In his chapter, William Doyle illustrates that, given the current policy environment, these schools are doing about as well as we can expect. But the profusion of new initiatives, tight budgets, and a growing focus on student success could expose their productivity as nothing more than the by-product of outdated policy.

What more creative comprehensive universities could and should look like, not surprisingly, is up for debate. Author Jeffrey Selingo cites big initiatives happening at comprehensive universities across the country to show how these schools can survive, if they focus. But others fear that this tinkering is ultimately a strategy that will likely require more tweaking later, until eventually the universities flounder. The potential consequences of this mentality, as Michael B. Horn, Michelle R. Weise, and Lloyd Armstrong describe, could be dire.

Comprehensive universities have a choice to make: Will they modify their existing structure, or do impending challenges call for a more fundamental change? Many universities will find Jeffrey Selingo's solutions appealing. These innovations are practical and, especially for those universities that have successfully rebranded as more-selective research universities, will not require major disruption. But many of these universities just will not survive without a more systemic change. In the past, change at comprehensive universities has come about only through a shift in the national dialogue. This time, these universities should move first.

Letting go of the old model will not be easy. Until recently, it has helped sustain these universities, whether the incoherence of transfer credits, the black box of credit hours, or the ever-rising tuition rates, traditional models have worked in their favor. But low-cost providers are nipping at the heels of higher education, and students who prioritize cost, convenience, and employment—in other words, the student of the comprehensive university—will be the first to go. Staying nimble as these changes set in will improve student outcomes and help ensure financial stability (if not overall survival).

Lesson #3: Improving the College Progression from Enrollment to Employment

Fortunately, many comprehensive universities already have the makings of successful change. This starts with the nontraditional students, who now constitute nearly 40% of all students (McCann & Laitinen, 2014). The public and private 4-year schools that are the spokespeople for higher education have had, up to this point, no reason to consider whether their own model is sufficient to educate the nontraditional student. Comprehensive universities, on the other hand, have grappled with the challenges of educating a diverse student population since their founding. Because of their history, and because of their willingness to change, successful comprehensive universities can do what very few 4-year universities know how to—or try to—do well: educate the nontraditional student.

Take the transfer process between community colleges and 4-year universities. As Alison Kadlec and Mario Martinez chronicle in their chapter, students are told that it is a wise decision to save money by enrolling at a community college for their first 2 years, then transferring to a state university. But the transfer process is far from clear. "It is as though students blame themselves for the roadblocks they hit—even for those problems that, from the outside, appear to result from the clear failure of institutions and systems to collaborate effectively." What matters most to a seamless transition is a well-articulated pathway, complete with resources and communication. Someone has to lead this charge and encourage state policymakers and institutional leaders to respond. With their diverse student populations and the need to find a new approach to the higher education business model, comprehensive universities are in a good position to do so.

As students prepare for graduation, comprehensive universities once again have an opportunity to retool the existing model. The student who graduates with little sense of where to go next, and unaware of the skills required to get there, has been let down by higher education. Here again, comprehensive universities can become the model for what is required to ensure that students succeed after graduation. John Dorrer encourages comprehensive universities to move beyond outdated (and slow to update) labor market resources to data sources that are more in-tune to local needs and national trends. Colleges can use this information to inform the development of program offerings and curricular content.

Eventually, all of higher education will need to consider how to better serve students that do not fit the traditional narrative of the college student. Community colleges know intimately the challenges associated with educating students that are not all newly minted high school graduates with basic academic knowledge. And they continue to reflect on how to better serve these students because they know with certainty that serving these students is core to their mission. Comprehensive universities are not there yet; they serve both the traditional and the nontraditional student, which creates tension within the university. Do they model themselves on the community college, or the traditional 4-year university? Both, and that will not be easy.

POLICY AT THE HELM

Because all of higher education is in the midst of an identity crisis, comprehensive universities are not alone. The renewed call for higher completion rates and better job preparedness will require industry-wide collaboration. With that said, many of the reform efforts developing at both the state and federal levels are initiatives that, unless comprehensive universities respond, could lead to their demise. In other words, their survival depends on their ability to redefine their role in the landscape of higher education.

Speaking up on behalf of themselves—and the students they educate—historically has not come naturally to many comprehensive universities. The puzzle, then, is first deciphering how comprehensive universities can support policies that position them in the reform movement. And second, figuring out what policies state and federal policymakers can support that will encourage *all* of higher education to respond to the changing reality facing the industry. Tinkering at the edges, especially for comprehensive universities, is not enough.

For Institutions

Senior administrators at comprehensive universities have a number of tools at their disposal that can be used to create a university that is more responsive to the shifting needs of higher education, especially the changing demographics of college-going students.

In their chapter, Alison Kadlec and Mario Martinez explore firsthand what it takes to create a coherent transfer pathway between community colleges and 4-year institutions. Will a community college class count toward a 4-year degree and, if so, will it fill a required course or just a general requirement? How does transferring affect financial aid eligibility? And most important, who can answer these questions? Successful initiatives are anchored by similar characteristics, the most important of which is a leadership team at both the community college and the 4-year university devoted to improving the process. This is an integral first step if comprehensive universities hope to better serve their nontraditional students.

There is a growing debate in higher education about whether the industry is shifting too far toward vocational education. Gubernatorial calls for the $10,000 bachelor's degree, along with other efforts to improve graduates' career readiness, fuel the fire. By virtue of the students they educate and the communities they serve, comprehensive universities are caught in the middle. Anchoring the nontraditional student in their institutional mission and policies might displease those who view changes to curriculum and sensitivity to labor market needs as "career oriented," but that is a short-sighted response. As John Dorrer articulates in his chapter, making these changes will help ensure that these institutions graduate more students who successfully start their careers. It will not, as some might fear, turn these universities into glorified trade schools.

Implementing new institutional policies begins with self-reflection. Perhaps the first and most obvious question is simple: Are students succeeding? And, if not, what can be done to fix the problem? Recall Jeffrey Selingo's story of Austin Peay State University. Compelled by changes in state policy to improve its graduation rate, the university decided to look internally at what was not working. The problem came down to too many choices and too little information. "As a result," Selingo tells us, "students often make bad decisions based on convenience or ease that leads them to classes that are a bad fit—either they do not need the class for their major or they end up failing." After implementation of a new program, Degree Compass, which recommends courses to students based on past performance and degree trajectory, course completion rates are on the rise, which benefits students and the university. Success took a well–thought–out change in institutional policy, propelled by a state-level call for improved performance outcomes.

For State Policymakers

States are in a unique position to incentivize improvement at their public universities. First, state policymakers can support the scaling of effective institutional policies into better state-level policy. Or, new policies might nudge a change in behavior, such as state initiatives that build databases of student outcomes by institution and program. Sometimes, new policy will mean a clear break from old policy, perhaps through a new funding model for higher education. Finally, states can encourage innovation by reforming the state authorization model.

On the first count, we return again to Austin Peay State University's Degree Compass. In February 2014, Tennessee Governor Bill Haslam unveiled his administration's new higher education initiative, Tennessee Promise. Within this initiative is a budgetary allocation to help make Degree Compass available to students across the state (Haslam, 2014). "The model combines hundreds of thousands of grades with current student transcripts to make an informed recommendation," said Governor Haslam. "That's exactly what we should do; help our students find the subjects and skills that allow them to graduate and pursue their dreams" (Osborne, 2014).

States also can implement policies that incentivize a behavioral change at the institutional level. Take the recent efforts to track labor market outcomes across states' public institutions. States like Florida, Texas, and Virginia now make publicly available average salaries for recent graduates based on college, study area, or program. Nationally, 34 states have entered into a data-sharing partnership under the Wage Record Interchange System 2 (WRIS2). While the work to improve labor market outcomes must happen at the institutional level, states can nudge public institutions to improve by equipping students with better information about expected program outcomes.

A number of states prefer a more direct approach to policy incentives, turning to performance-based funding to elicit a response from their public colleges and universities. Performance-based funding dates back to 1979, but only recently have states begun to incorporate performance metrics into the allocation of higher education appropriations. This funding model is not without its problems. For one, it could incentivize institutions to artificially inflate performance outcomes, whether by preferentially admitting academically prepared students or by shrinking the total number of students admitted. Either behavior would improve outcomes, but at a cost: the erosion of access, a trait that historically has defined so many comprehensive universities. Moreover, research on the effectiveness of performance-based funding is mixed; in many cases, it seems to have a minimal, if any, impact.

Even so, there is little reason to believe that state policymakers will abandon their efforts. With that in mind, Michelle Lu Yin reminds policymakers to proceed cautiously. By using observed rates to measure a school's performance and improvement, policymakers fail to account for differences across universities, whether they relate to the composition of the student body or an institution's geographic location. For instance, the percentage of Pell-eligible students at a given institution is associated with a lower graduation rate, and performance-based funding systems reward higher graduation rates. Therefore, schools that need to improve graduation rates have an incentive to enroll fewer Pell grant recipients. By accounting for these differences using adjusted metrics, state policymakers can better understand institutions' relative performance before making decisions on policy changes.

Finally, if the state authorization model is especially burdensome, otherwise effective delivery models might not have a chance to operate. As authors Michael B. Horn, Michelle R. Weise, and Lloyd Armstrong point out, many of the new delivery options threaten to disrupt the existing model of higher education, and comprehensive universities are most vulnerable. But the flip side is that many of these programs provide tangible skills that students can use to build their careers. The end goal of education policy should not be to force success through the existing model, but to consider new ways to improve student outcomes. If students at comprehensive universities would be better served by more-targeted programs, then they should have that opportunity. And if comprehensive universities can partner with new knowledge delivery models—while passing the savings along to students—then everyone wins.

For Federal Policymakers

In K–12 education, there is a precedent in federal law for holding school districts accountable for the federal dollars they receive. The same is not true in higher education. For one, institutions of higher education have a strong incentive to keep federal accountability at bay. Take the initial decision to treat the Pell grant as a voucher, rather than something more like direct aid provided to K–12 schools. Institutions fought vigorously in favor of the voucher because doing so limited the degree to which the federal government could hold colleges and universities accountable for federal student aid dollars. Instead, the primary requirement for Title IV eligibility is that an institution be accredited by an accrediting agency recognized by the U.S. Department of Education. This keeps accountability among institutions, and out of the hands of the federal government.

The powerful higher education lobby acts as an impediment to many changes that could increase accountability. Although institutions are required to report basic information to the National Center for Education Statistics' Institutional Postsecondary Education Data System, the submissions are often incomplete and inaccurate. Combine mediocre self-reported data with performance metrics that fail to accurately capture institutional differences, and the outcome is not promising—yet it is supported by many institutions and trade organizations.

President Obama has made it clear that the past 40 years' focus on improving college access is no longer enough, but the policy that supports a shift toward completion and post-graduation student success may be dead on arrival. The administration's proposed ratings system intends to incorporate three crucial measures of institutional quality—access, affordability, and completion. What about job placement and earnings data? Without the appropriate adjustments, the ratings system could cater to institutions that offer generous aid packages and use their small cohort sizes to maintain impressive graduation rates. Comprehensive universities, with their low tuitions and open access, might get punished for their low completion rates. As this volume has highlighted, many of these institutions will not survive unless they improve their student outcomes. But there are institutions that have already improved student outcomes. These efforts should not be masked by an accountability system that fails to distinguish between the profiles of institutions.

OUT OF THE SHADOWS, INTO THE LIGHT

When American pop culture depicts higher education, it is never a comprehensive university. It is the flagship public university and its active social life, or the small private liberal arts college with a generous endowment, or the ivy-gilded universities that symbolize prestige. Higher education is defined by these examples. Comprehensive universities have always struggled to find their place within higher education, constantly changing to meet a new set of needs. "With the research university and elite liberal arts college models as the only well-developed models for four-year institutions, the [comprehensive universities] are left without a model that fits their situation," writes Bruce Henderson (2009), himself a professor at a comprehensive university. Instead, they cobble together pieces from all over higher education and tweak them when necessary.

But what has worked in the past will no longer suffice. Federal calls for accountability, state-level policies that allocate funding based on performance (at a time when appropriations are already down), and new initiatives that attract students by offering a more targeted and more affordable education all threaten the future existence of the state comprehensive university. Now, however, is not the time to give up or ignore these institutions. They represent the colleges and universities with the most potential for growth. If they can rise to the challenge, if they can once again adapt—moving to the front of the conversation, rather than remaining relegated to their former position as the undistinguished middle child—they can help America meet its goals of increasing access, graduation, and labor market success for all students. Endangered though they seem, there is still the opportunity for these institutions to thrive.

REFERENCES

Breneman, D. (1994). *Liberal arts colleges: Thriving, surviving, or endangered?* Washington, DC: Brookings Institution Press.

Haslam, B. (2014, February 3). *Haslam unveils visionary Tennessee promise.* Office of Tennessee Governor Bill Haslam, The Newsroom and Media Center. Available at news.tn.gov/node/11955

Henderson, B. B. (2009). The work of the People's University. *Teacher-Scholar: The Journal of the State Comprehensive University, 1*(1). Available at www.fhsu.edu/teacher-scholar/resources/Previous-Issues/Volume-1/Introduction.pdf

McCann, C., & Laitinen, A. (2014). *College blackout: How the higher education lobby fought to keep students in the dark.* Education Policy Program, New America

Foundation. Available at education.newamerica.net/sites/newamerica.net/files/policydocs/CollegeBlackoutFINAL.pdf

Ogren, C. A. (2003). Rethinking the "nontraditional" student from a historical perspective: State normal schools in the late nineteenth and early twentieth centuries. *The Journal of Higher Education, 74*, 640–664.

Ogren, C. A. (2005). *The American state normal school: "An instrument of great good."* New York, NY: Palgrave Macmillan.

Olwell, R. (2011, March 25). Where the action is. *Inside Higher Ed.* Available at www.insidehighered.com/advice/2011/03/25/essay_on_working_at_regional_public_universities#ixzz2wWp0uVTn

Osborne, M. (2014). A closer look: Gov. Haslam touts degree compass. *Middle Tennessee Public Radio 89.5 FM, NPR Digital Network.* Available at wmot.org/post/closer-look-gov-haslam-touts-degree-compass

Selingo, J. (2000). Facing new missions and rivals, state colleges seek a makeover. *The Chronicle of Higher Education.* Available at chronicle.com/article/Facing-New-Missions-and/31282

About the Editors and the Contributors

Mark Schneider is a visiting scholar at the American Enterprise Institute and vice president at the American Institutes for Research, based in Washington, DC. Prior to joining AIR, he served as the U.S. Commissioner of Education Statistics from 2005–2008. He is also a Distinguished Professor Emeritus of Political Science at the State University of New York, Stony Brook. He is the author and editor of numerous articles and books on education policy, including *Getting to Graduation: The Completion Agenda in Higher Education* (2012), *Higher Education Accountability* (2010), *Charter Schools: Hope or Hype?* (2007), and *Choosing Schools* (2000), which won the Policy Study Organization's Aaron Wildavsky Best Book Award. Schneider has been working to increase accountability by making data on college productivity more publicly available. To that end, he is one of the creators of www.collegemeasures.org and serves as the president of College Measures LLC, a joint venture of AIR and Matrix Knowledge Group.

KC Deane is a program manager at The Aspen Institute's College Excellence Program. Previously, she was a research associate at the American Enterprise Institute's Center on Higher Education Reform. Her research focuses on workforce readiness and financial aid and admission practices in higher education. Previously, she worked for 2 years as an assistant dean of admission at Reed College. Deane graduated from Reed with a bachelor's degree in economics, and from the University of Pennsylvania with a master's degree in education policy. She wrote her undergraduate thesis on enrollment and financial decision-making processes at liberal arts colleges during periods of economic decline.

Lloyd Armstrong is a university professor and provost emeritus at the University of Southern California. He served as USC provost and senior vice president for academic affairs during the period 1993 to 2005, a time when the university increased greatly in quality and reputation. He led the planning that resulted in the 1994 Strategic Plan of the University, and the 1998 Four Year Update. Much of the improvement in the university can be attributed to the strategies and approaches articulated in those two documents. He also led the creation of the 2004 Plan for Increasing USC's Academic Excellence. Before coming to USC, Armstrong was a professor of physics at Johns Hopkins University. While at Hopkins, he served as chairman of the Department of Physics and Astronomy, and dean of the College of Arts and Sciences. Armstrong's current research interests are focused on the future of research universities, with special emphasis on the effects of globalization.

John Dorrer is a senior consultant at Georgetown University, Center on Education and the Workforce. He previously served as a senior advisor for labor market and workforce research at Jobs for the Future (JFF) where he advised JFF's emerging work in the development of labor market information and workforce research and its application to meeting the challenges of aligning postsecondary education and training with regional economies. Dorrer has 30 years of experience in workforce development as an economist and researcher. His work has focused on workforce development, human capital, and labor market policies at the state and local levels. Previously, Dorrer worked for the Maine Department of Labor, where he served as Acting Commissioner and Director of the Center for Workforce Research and Information. He also served as Deputy Director of Workforce Programs at the National Center on Education and the Economy in Washington, DC.

William Doyle is an associate professor of higher education and coordinator of the Higher Education Leadership Program in the Department of Leadership, Policy, and Organizations at Peabody College of Vanderbilt University. His research includes evaluating the impact of higher education policy, the antecedents and outcomes of higher education policy at the state level, and the study of political behavior as it affects higher education. Doyle's work has appeared in outlets such as *The Journal of Higher Education, Educational Evaluation and Policy Analysis,* and *Economics of Education Review.* Prior to joining the faculty at Vanderbilt, he was senior policy analyst at the National Center for Public Policy and Higher Education. Doyle holds a master's degree in political science and a PhD in higher education administration from Stanford University.

Alisa Hicklin Fryar is an associate professor of political science at the University of Oklahoma. Her research and teaching focus on higher education policy, issues of accountability for public universities, bureaucratic politics, and public management. Hicklin Fryar received her PhD in 2006 from Texas A&M University, and her work has appeared in various journals including *Journal of Public Administration Research and Theory, Public Administration Review, Journal of Politics,* and in the edited volume *Higher Education Handbook of Theory and Research.* She completed her undergraduate degree at Lamar University, a comprehensive university located in Beaumont, Texas.

Michael B. Horn is a cofounder of the Clayton Christensen Institute, a nonprofit, nonpartisan think tank, and serves as the executive director of its education program. He is the coauthor of *Disrupting Class: How Disruptive Innovation Will Change the Way the World Learns* (2008) with Harvard Business School professor and bestselling author Clayton M. Christensen and Curtis W. Johnson. *Businessweek* named the book one of the 10 Best Innovation & Design Books of 2008, *Newsweek* named it as the 14th book on its list of "Fifty Books for Our Times," and the National Chamber Foundation named it first among its 10 "Books That Drive the Debate 2009." He was selected as a 2014 Eisenhower Fellow to study innovation in education in Vietnam and Korea. Horn has written several white papers about blended learning. *Tech&Learning* magazine named him to its list of the 100 most important people in the creation and advancement of the use of technology in education. Horn holds a BA in history from Yale University and an MBA from Harvard Business School.

Alison Kadlec, senior vice president of Public Agenda, leads the design and implementation of its stakeholder engagement and research projects in the areas of higher education and workforce development. She is also active in the design and implementation of the public engagement work at Public Agenda. She is the author of a book on the democratic theory of John Dewey, *Dewey's Critical Pragmatism* (2008), and was also among the coauthors of *Toward Wiser Public Judgment* (2011), edited by Daniel Yankelovich and Will Friedman. Before joining Public Agenda, Kadlec was a visiting professor in the political science departments at the University of Minnesota, Macalester College, Baruch College, and Hunter College. She holds bachelor's degrees in political theory and constitutional democracy and English literature from Michigan State University, and a PhD in political science from the University of Minnesota. Her areas of expertise include democratic theory, history of ideas, and American political thought.

Mario Martinez is a professor of higher education in the department of educational psychology and higher education at the University of Nevada–Las Vegas. His work focuses on innovation and organizational strategy within higher education. Martinez consults with foundations and institutions of higher education on initiatives related to his research, and he also regularly provides training for professional staff on topics that encompass human dynamics and change.

Awilda Rodriguez is an assistant professor at the University of Michigan's School of Education. Previously she was a research fellow at the American Enterprise Institute's Center on Higher Education Reform. She completed her PhD in higher education at the University of Pennsylvania's Graduate School of Education. Her research interests include access issues for traditionally under-represented students in higher education, particularly college guidance and information. Before beginning her doctorate program at Penn, she worked as an analyst for the New York City Department of Education and in the education nonprofit sector. She has a master's degree in education administration, planning, and social policy from Harvard Graduate School of Education and a bachelor's degree in electrical engineering from Princeton University.

Jeffrey J. Selingo, a higher education author and columnist, has spent his journalism career covering colleges and universities worldwide. His first book, *College (Un)Bound: The Future of Higher Education and What It Means for Students* (2013), explores the college of the future—how families will pay, what campuses will look like, and how students will learn and prove their value in the job market. His second book, *MOOC U: Who Is Getting the Most Out of Online Education and Why*, is an inside look at the debate over massive open online courses. Selingo is a contributing editor to *The Chronicle of Higher Education* and a professor of practice at Arizona State University. He also blogs for LinkedIn. From 2007 until 2011, he was editor of *The Chronicle*, where he worked for 15 years in a variety of reporting and editing roles. His work has been honored with awards from the Education Writers Association, Society of Professional Journalists, and Associated Press, and he was a finalist for the Livingston Award for Young Journalists. Before coming to *The Chronicle*, he covered environmental issues as a reporter for the *Wilmington Star-News*, in North Carolina (1995–1997), and worked for *The Ithaca Journal*, in New York (1994–1995). As a recipient of a Pulliam Journalism Fellowship, he covered business technology for *The Arizona Republic*, in Phoenix.

Michelle R. Weise is a senior research fellow at the Clayton Christensen Institute specializing in disruptive innovation in higher education. Her commentaries and research on competency-based learning, student-learning outcomes, workforce solutions, and public–private partnerships have been featured in a number of publications and outlets such as *Inside Higher Education*, *New England Journal of Higher Education*, *USA Today*,

National Journal, KQED, SxSWedu, the Presidents' Forum, VentureBeat, and GigaOm. Prior to joining the Institute, Weise served as the Vice President of Academic Affairs for Fidelis Education. She also has held instructional positions, serving as a professor at Skidmore College as well as an instructor at Stanford University. Weise received her BA in literature from Harvard University and both her MA and PhD from Stanford University in English literature. In 2005, she was selected as a Fulbright Scholar to South Korea.

Michelle Lu Yin, PhD, is an economist and senior researcher in the Workforce program at AIR, where she focuses on labor economics. Yin has led a range of research studies using quasi-experimental designs in the areas of disability, higher education, and adult education. Yin has a strong background in policy evaluation design, survey design, and statistical analysis. She received her PhD training in economics from the University of Florida, and was a visiting scholar at Northwestern University prior to joining AIR. She is also a What Works Clearinghouse certified reviewer. Yin's training has equipped her with extensive methodological tools and knowledge on impact evaluation design. Yin's recent research interests include examining the impact of different research funding structures on the training of graduate students and postdoctoral fellows, teacher effectiveness evaluation in K–12 and adult education, design and consequences of accountability in adult education, and higher education finance and accountability. Yin has served as lead methodologist on impact evaluation projects at both state and national levels. In these projects, she designs and conducts impact analyses of program interventions and randomized control trials. Yin has extensive experience linking and analyzing large-scale, national-level databases in addition to several district- and state-level databases from Florida, New York, Ohio, and Texas.

Index

Page numbers with *t* denote tables.